"A beautiful and captivating story
to find meaning and purpose in ;
author's journey as she attempts
begins to realize they have been with her all along."

–Michelle Spaulding, MA, psychologist and author of
Bliss Is an Aisle of Organized Soup Cans

All Who Believed

All Who
Believed

A Memoir of Life in the Twelve Tribes

Tamara Mathieu

To Brian

Tamara Mathieu

Rootstock Publishing

Montpelier, VT

All Who Believed ©2023 Tamara Matthieu

Release Date: May 21, 2024

All Rights Reserved.

Printed in the USA.

Published by Rootstock Publishing,
an imprint of Ziggy Media LLC

info@rootstockpublishing.com
www.rootstockpublishing.com

Softcover ISBN: 978-1-57869-117-3
Hardcover ISBN: 978-1-57869-169-2
eBook ISBN: 978-1-57869-170-8

Library of Congress Control Number: 2024903210

Cover and book design by Eddie Vincent, ENC Graphics Services.
Cover photo credit: FangXiaNuo.

Author photo by Emmet Mathieu.

For permissions or to schedule a reading, contact the author at
tamara.mathieu@gmail.com.

This is a work of creative nonfiction. The author has strived to create a true story based on her memories, diaries, and letters. While all the stories in this book are true, some names and identifying details have been changed to protect the privacy of the people involved. In other cases, permission has been granted to use real names. The beliefs contained in this book do not reflect the opinions of the publisher.

I dedicate this book to my children: Emmet, Meyshar, Darakah, and Arek. I hope you all know the choices I made were always with your best interests in mind. I never wanted anything other than safe, meaningful, and happy lives for all of you. You all are resilient and amazing and I'm beyond proud of each of you.

"And all who believed were together and had all things in common. And they were selling their possessions and belongings and distributing the proceeds to all, as any had need. And day by day, attending the temple together and breaking bread in their homes, they received their food with glad and generous hearts, praising God and having favor with all the people. And the Lord added to their number day by day those who were being saved."

—Acts 2:44–47 New American Standard Bible
(biblehub.com)

Prologue

My dreams are always the same. We've decided to go back to the community. I'm in our new bedroom, unpacking and feeling a little excited to see everyone. At some point, someone comes in with a stack of teachings for me to "catch up on." They place them on my bed and tell me the women are waiting in the kitchen for me to come help with dinner. My heart sinks, and I'm overcome with a feeling of dread. How had I forgotten about the endless teachings and long, grueling hours in the kitchen? Why are we back here? How did this happen? Suddenly I panic. I remember our house and our dogs. Is anyone even caring for the dogs? I desperately need to get home. I run out of the room, frantically looking for my husband. He's walking away from the house, and I hurry to catch up. "I just want to go home," I plead.

He turns around. "We're not going anywhere. I have a meeting I need to get to," he replies and hurriedly continues on his way. I watch him go, filled with despair. This can't be happening again. What have we done?

I open my eyes and take in my surroundings. I'm home, in bed. My two dogs are sleeping at my feet. My husband is sound asleep next to me. Sweet relief calms my pounding heart. It was just a dream; I am not back in the Twelve Tribes. Many years after leaving, these dreams still occur regularly.

This is my personal testimony of my experience in the Twelve Tribes.

※

Joining a cult begins like a budding romance—everything is new and amazingly wonderful; you can hardly think of anything else. No one can talk you down from your excitement and euphoria. Concerns from loved ones are quickly dismissed as misunderstandings or uninformed prejudices.

We joined the Twelve Tribes in August 2000. There was no social media back then and very little on the internet to dissuade us. It wasn't easy to find ex-members to make a well-researched decision. There certainly weren't any memoirs published by former members. In hindsight, I realize I had no idea what we were getting into.

Since leaving, I've read reports that accuse the Twelve Tribes of drug-induced orgies, and gang rape as a form of punishment. I laugh to think how boring my book will be without such shocking tales! My purpose is to give an honest, behind-the-scenes look at the years my family was part of the Twelve Tribes (TT). There are many who went through far worse situations in the TT than I ever encountered. There was horrific abuse, including sexual, that was swept under the rug. There were deaths that could have been prevented with medical care. There were extramarital affairs. But those are their stories to tell if they ever choose to.

I realize there are much greater sufferings that go on around the planet—and that kind of thinking helped me endure years longer in the TT than I otherwise might have. I'd tell myself that millions of people around the world would be so thankful to have my life; how could I ever complain? We had food, clothing, and shelter, which not everyone is adequately privileged with. Above all else, we were God's chosen people, handpicked out of the billions of people on earth, chosen to represent His love and bring about the end of the age, thus putting an end to all evil. It could only be my selfish, ungrateful nature that would cause me to be discontented. But even thinking like that, there came a point fourteen years later where enough was enough.

Chapter 1

Laying the Foundation

 ho doesn't desire a simpler life in this complex, fast-paced, polarized world? Is there anyone who watched *Little House on the Prairie* as a child and didn't wonder what it was like to have lived back then? I watched that show obsessively, every day after school. There was something inexplicably appealing about the idea of getting into a horse-drawn wagon in your best, handmade, calico dress and heading into town for church, with Ma smiling prettily at Pa from under her lace-trimmed bonnet. Or walking two miles each way to school, coming home at the end of the day to Ma in her apron making fresh bread for dinner and Pa working out in the field. You'd rush to the barn to get your chores done and hope you had time for a quick dip at the swimming hole before being called in for supper. Then Pa would play his fiddle, while you and your siblings worked on your homework by candlelight and Ma rocked in her chair by the fireplace, busy with her mending.

Life seemed much more meaningful and satisfying back then. "Wholesome" is the word that comes to mind. Life was rustic and handmade. Children learned respect and how to work hard as soon as they could talk and walk. There was a sense of security in how the citizens of Walnut Grove were integrated into each other's lives. It was true community. Of course, we were seeing a glamorized, sanitary TV version of life and not experiencing firsthand a polio epidemic or someone we loved dying in childbirth, but it did impart in me a desire for an old-fashioned life.

Today, we have modern conveniences we love and couldn't live without. It's normal for everyone to be glued to their screens. For many, human interactions have become more virtual and less about connecting with an actual person. Children are rarely seen playing outside or doing yard chores anymore. When I first encountered the Twelve Tribes, I already hated the direction society was heading, with kids spending hours playing increasingly violent video games. It seemed we were rapidly losing sight of what it means to live a purposeful and dignified life. Old-fashioned values were being lost, the family unit growing weaker and weaker.

My parents were very young when I was born, and they divorced two years later. My childhood was spent being shuffled to my dad's on weekends, often passing on less-than-civil messages between the two of them. By the time I was ten, both my parents had remarried, and the transitions were awful. My mom and I didn't even have the same last name anymore. Were we still a family? I used to wonder. The addition of stepparents to my life was not welcome, and I had fantasies of the two of them meeting and falling in love. That was selfish of course, but I was just a child trying to hold on to what little stability I'd known in my broken family life. The upside was gaining a stepsister and five more half-siblings over the next few years, all of whom I adored.

I remember vowing to myself at some point that I would never raise my children in a split family. I would give my children what I never had— being raised in a home with both biological parents. No niggling over child support checks, arguments over pick-up times, switching weekend visits, or needing to figure out how both families could have adequate time with me for holidays or my birthday. I just wanted a "simple" family life.

I wasn't raised in a particular religion, yet around the age of nine I decided there must be a God who could hear me. My stepmother had had a baby girl, and she had a hole in her heart that required surgery. I began faithfully praying every night for her, as well as the rest of my family, to be kept safe. I also threw in a prayer for myself to stop getting in trouble at school for talking too much. I was a very social child and always desired to be interacting with my friends.

I always felt better after I prayed, like I had done something tangible to contribute to the welfare of my family. If I had a friend spend the night, or if I was sick and couldn't partake in my nightly ritual, I would silently mouth, "Please accept my regular prayers," before I would allow myself to doze off. I was a superstitious child and couldn't bear the thought of anything bad happening to any of the people I loved, and then realizing I had forgotten to pray for them the night before. I would have blamed myself and been tormented with guilt. This heavy weight of responsibility was completely self-imposed.

Even though I secretly desired to have been born in the 1800s, and prayed diligently every night, never in a million years would I, or anyone who knew me, have thought I'd join a cult one day. I grew up in a small Vermont town that bordered Canada. I was a good student and a hard worker, had lots of friends, and loved having fun. In high school, our fun often involved trips to Canada, where the drinking age was eighteen and dive bars just over the border couldn't resist the steady business that came every Friday and Saturday night, as mainly underage teenagers, pockets crammed with newly exchanged Canadian currency, filled their parking lots with cars with Vermont license plates. I remember feeling sorry for my Christian friends, who rarely joined in on our wild good times.

Yet the truth is, everyone goes through times when they may be more susceptible to a radical message of a "brand-new culture." It makes perfect sense that many people who joined the TT in its early days came in from places like the Grateful Dead scene, where they were seeking a lifestyle of love, belonging, and acceptance. For me, that time came at the age of twenty-two, when I was a new wife and mother.

After high school, I moved to Burlington to attend the University of Vermont (UVM). It was here that I met my future husband, André. We started dating, and everything was great until I found out he was from a born-again Christian family and was a strong believer. Growing up, I'd had relatives of the same faith, and I'd been influenced my whole life by my paternal grandmother, who couldn't stand "that religion." She said the people from it were pushy, judgmental, and "spoke in tongues." Nothing about that sounded appealing. Why anyone would choose to be a part of that was beyond me.

I had one experience in high school of attending an Assemblies of God youth group. A friend's parents made him attend, and one evening he begged me to go with him. I agreed, somewhat nervous but also a tiny bit curious. We entered the church and were shown to a room full of teens who all looked normal and seemed friendly, some of whom I recognized from school. There was a stage up front, and musicians were warming up their instruments. So far, so good; I was always up for live music. Soon the band began to play, and we took seats in the chairs that were arranged in rows in front of the stage. It wasn't typical "church" music but seemed hipper and more modern. People began singing along and clapping, and everyone seemed to be having a great time. I smiled at my friend and relaxed a little.

The first song ended, and the next, obviously a church favorite, began immediately. A couple people stood up on their chairs and started waving their arms above their heads. More followed suit, along with an occasional "Praise Jesus!" being shouted out. Suddenly I felt strange sitting amid all this. My friend, who did not stand on his chair, shot me an apologetic look as he sensed my discomfort. The next song brought even more people out of their seats to stand on their chairs. I'd had enough. "I'm going to go wait in the car," I said and quickly ducked through the towering, swaying crowd. That experience—feeling completely out of place and creeped out by what I considered bizarre behavior—stayed with me.

So, when I found out André had grown up in an Assemblies of God family and was a devout Christian, I was dismayed. I wanted nothing to do with that; it repelled me. We had many long, intense debates about religion over the next few months. During one such conversation, André became emotional, expressing through tears that I was going to Hell if I couldn't become a believer, and that tore him up because he loved me so much.

I couldn't relate to his gut-wrenching belief that the God I had gotten to know as a little girl, who I felt had been with me my whole life, was going to throw me into Hell when I died if I didn't believe in Jesus. Something was flawed with that theory, and I told him I could never believe that way. Sure, I wasn't perfect and had done "bad" things, but nothing so different from anyone else my age—even André! I wasn't a con artist, drug dealer, or some other vile person. I was pretty "good."

He asked if I would just be willing to attend church one time with his family. "Will anyone be speaking in tongues?" was my first question. He assured me that wasn't going to happen, so I agreed. It was the least I could do. I enjoyed his family—his mother, Annie, was so friendly toward me, and his younger brothers were fun to be with.

We picked a weekend to spend in Benson, Vermont, and accompany his family to Sunday service at Faith Chapel in White Hall, New York. It must have been a pretty benign service, as nothing good or bad sticks out in my memory of the experience. I didn't hear anything that drew me to want to know more or attend a future service. But I hadn't run out of the building in disgust at any point, so that alone must have satisfied something in André that all hope wasn't lost, and he backed off the religion subject.

Chapter 2

A Change of Plans

n the winter of 1998, we moved into an apartment with several friends, living the typical lives of twenty-one-year-old college students in Burlington. At one point, one of my best childhood friends, Michelle, moved in with us.

One day I saw an irresistible ad in the paper for miniature dachshund puppies. This was my dream dog, and I needed to have one. On a sunny day in July, André and I drove down to Middlebury and picked out Mollie from a litter of impossibly tiny puppies. She fit perfectly into our lives.

At this point, I was working the night shift as an LNA at Burlington Health & Rehab, and I tweaked my back one night as I assisted a patient getting into bed. I was sent to urgent care at the end of my shift, and André and Mollie came to take me to the appointment. I checked in and was soon brought into an exam room. A woman came in holding a clipboard, flipping through the papers on it. "Are you pregnant?" she inquired. "It says here your last period was June first." It was now the beginning of August.

"No," I told her. "I've taken two tests, and both were negative, and a nurse where I work told me it's normal to miss a period when you start working nights."

"OK," she replied, "we just need you to take a test here for our records." I accepted the small plastic cup and went to the bathroom.

After handing over the sample, I sat in a chair and leaned my head back against the wall, closing my eyes. I was so very tired and couldn't wait to be in bed snuggling my puppy. I was just dozing off when the door opened. I opened my eyes and sat up to see the smiling face of the woman who had taken my pee sample. "Well, . . ." she said expectantly, "our test came out positive!" I just stared at her. Finally, she asked, "Is that OK?"

I took a deep breath and nodded. "Yes, that's OK." I don't remember anything else about the appointment.

When it was over, I emerged into the beautiful, sunny morning and headed slowly toward the parking lot to find André and Mollie. What was I going to say? How would he take the news? I saw them near a stand of trees, Mollie sniffing all around. She saw me coming and excitedly strained against her tiny leash to pull André toward me. I bent down to pick her up as André nonchalantly asked, "How's your back?"

"Fine . . . but I'm pregnant," I blurted out.

"Oh wow!" he responded. "They're sure? What about the negative tests?"

"They told me it's more common to get a false negative than a false positive."

We were both in shock as we drove back to the apartment, where I immediately collapsed in exhaustion. I awoke later to discover that André had never gone to work but had called his mother as the full weight of the responsibility that was now ours hit him. His mom told me he was an emotional wreck on the phone, but an amazing sense of peace had come over her somehow. Despite their religious convictions that made us "sinners," living together and procreating out of wedlock, she was able to stay positive and calm, letting him know that everything was going to be fine.

And I'll never forget later that day, when Michelle walked in the door, laundry basket on her hip, and casually asked me, "Anything exciting happen today?"

My life changed irrevocably from that moment on. I was going to be a mother. Suddenly I felt a love and protectiveness I'd never known. It was fierce, and I didn't let a day go by that I didn't pray for the health of my baby. I didn't care that I was only twenty-one, that my education would have to take a back burner, that I was leaving behind the fun, carefree lifestyle of going to parties that my friends would be partaking in for years to come. Everything I did from that day forward was in preparation for our baby.

Thankfully, André would soon be graduating from UVM with a degree in business administration. He was already making enough of an income as a budding software engineer that we were able to move out of the apartment and, with a loan from his grandmother, buy a cute little house in Burlington's New North End. It was ideal for our soon-to-be small family. There was a fenced backyard, perfect for Mollie and, eventually, our child, to run around in. At our age, with all we had going for us, things seemed perfect.

We found out we were having a boy. I spent hours combing the babynames.com website and making lists of names. After one such session, André scanned my list and said, "I like Emmet." It was an Irish name that meant hardworking and industrious. Those were desirable qualities, so it was settled.

Around this time, I met my first Twelve Tribes people. André's aunt Sharon had joined them in 1981, so he had grown up knowing about the community and visiting Island Pond on many occasions. His two older cousins also lived in the TT, and the older of the two, Mason, had gotten married only a few months prior. He and his new wife, Joanna, were also expecting their first baby around the same time I was due. So, when we heard that they, along with Sharon, would be spending a couple days in Benson visiting family, we made plans to go to André's parent's house to see them.

I had no clue what to expect, and on the drive down I bombarded André with questions. He tried his best to explain that they were part of a religious community who all lived and worked together, but he didn't seem to know many other details.

I remember being mildly curious about them that weekend. Sharon (who went by Esther, as members of the TT are given Hebrew names) was sweet and friendly and wore long, floral cotton dresses. Joanna (Yahannah), who was also twenty-one, was very quiet and dressed peculiarly in baggy pants that were cuffed at the ankles and long, vest-style tunics over floral, short-sleeved T-shirts. It was the end of August and I wondered if she was hot. She wore her hair in a braid that reached past her waist. Neither she nor Sharon wore any jewelry, I noticed as I fidgeted with my diamond engagement ring.

I remember watching her make breakfast for Mason (Ephraim) and quietly serve him while he sat at the table. I wondered if that was required of her. I wondered if they thought we were terrible people because we were expecting a baby and weren't yet married. They seemed nice enough, a bit odd, but I didn't dwell on them much after that first encounter. (Years later, she would confess to me that she envied me during that visit.)

We spent the next few months getting everything ready for Emmet's arrival and planning our wedding, which would be three months later. I had quit my job as an LNA, feeling it was too strenuous and exhausting. André found me a temporary position at UVM as office manager of the Department of Mechanical Engineering. As I got closer to having my baby, my boss came into my office one day and wanted to know if I'd consider taking the position full time after maternity leave. They were offering to start me at $35,000, plus I'd get free tuition to finish my degree. UVM has its own daycare, and I could get Emmet on the waiting list right away. It was tempting, but the thought of handing my baby over to someone else at twelve weeks old, then sitting in that office worrying about him all day was unimaginable to me. I declined the offer.

Emmet arrived one week early during a big March snowstorm. My mom, Annie, and Michelle were all there to witness his birth. I loved him so much—he was so beautiful and perfect. I wanted to be such a good mother but was overwhelmed by day three. Annie had spent the first night home with us but then had to get back to her own home. After the third night, André pleaded with her to come back and, thankfully, she did for a few more days. I had no idea how taxing having a newborn was. He didn't sleep much, and I was fraught with fear and postpartum emotions. I was dreading being home alone with him every day and wished I had people around all the time.

On April 20, 1999, the Columbine school shooting happened. I remember watching the live coverage of the horrific events, clutching my five-week-old baby in my arms. Now that I was a mother, it had an overwhelming effect on me. I cried as I pictured all the parents who were out of their minds with terror at that moment, not knowing if they would ever see their child again. What kind of world had we brought this precious baby into? How could I feel comfortable sending him off to school in a few years? Would schools be even more dangerous by the time he went to high school? That event had a profound effect on me. Nothing was more important to me at that time than the safety of my child.

We made it through the first harried weeks, and I fell into a routine with Emmet. I'd made a group of local mom friends through prenatal water aerobics at the YMCA and La Leche League meetings. We soon had a rotation among us to host a weekly playgroup. I enrolled Emmet in baby swim lessons, and we were regular attendees for story time at the local public library. I tried to fill our days, going shopping and taking daily walks with Mollie. But I was bored, and the days were long. I didn't know how to be "domestic." I didn't cook or garden or craft. In just one year I'd had a radical transformation, from carefree, college student living with my friends to new mother living in my own house and about to get married.

I lived for the weekends and 5:00 p.m. on weekdays when André got home from work. Emmet and I would sit on our front stoop, watching for his car to turn down our street. I was envious that he had a life outside our house. I knew his days flew by as he was engaged in a job he loved, working with people he enjoyed being with.

It was in this void that I began to desire a faith to raise my child in, some purpose to give life meaning. I didn't know how to make myself believe in Christianity, and I thought back to the church service I had attended with André and his family. If God was calling me to be a believer, wouldn't I have heard something profound during the sermon that stirred my heart? I began to talk with Annie, and she recommended Josh McDowell's book, *Answers to Tough Questions Skeptics Ask about the Christian Faith*. I read it and found it informative, but I didn't feel any "pull" or "calling" or anything like that. There was no lightbulb moment. But I was trying, and I felt good about that.

Chapter 3

Sheeplike

hen Emmet was two months old, we were visiting André's parents and I noticed an interesting piece of literature on their coffee table. It said *Marriage Covenant*, and there was a picture of a smiling young couple. Annie told me they had attended a wedding at the TT community in Cambridge, New York, the previous weekend and they were considering taking a break from their church and instead going to "Friday Night Celebrations" at the nearby community in Rutland. That certainly caught my attention, as I knew how involved they were in their church. She must have found something truly better, and I was eager to know more.

I was highly intrigued as she described what the wedding had been like. I bombarded her with questions, fascinated by the whole thing. She told me the groom had even given the bride a new name! I poured over the pamphlet, which had a lot of Bible verses and things I didn't fully grasp, but my curiosity was irrevocably piqued. My own wedding was coming up in another month, after all!

Emmet and I stayed in Benson the week before our wedding, and a few days prior Annie and I went to Rutland to buy decorations for the reception. I couldn't stop thinking about that wedding pamphlet, and I was curious to see what the community was like. After our shopping was done, I asked her if we could drop by to see her friends there. She loved the idea, and we soon found ourselves being warmly welcomed at the Cottage Street house. The woman who answered the door seemed genuinely delighted by our spur-of-the-moment visit, as Annie explained what we had been doing that day and how my curiosity had prompted our drop-in.

We were brought through to the kitchen, where an apron-clad woman in a long skirt was busy washing dishes at a huge three-basin sink. An enormous pot of soup was simmering on the stove, and it smelled delicious. She lit up at the sight of Annie, quickly wiping her hands on her apron and coming over to give her a huge hug, like they were long-lost friends. She embraced me with the same fervor, and though I'd never met her in my life, it somehow felt perfectly normal.

We were shown to a living room where we were hosted by a woman with two teenage daughters aged fifteen and seventeen, all dressed modestly in long dresses or the baggy pants I recalled Joanna wearing the previous summer. I suddenly felt self-conscious in my fitted, short-sleeved top and jeans. They all had very long hair, worn in a ponytail, braid, or bun at the nape of their neck. No one wore any jewelry or had makeup on.

The large, old house was tidy and clean. The living room was simply decorated, with futon couches covered in pretty floral fabrics, and rustic end tables with unique wrought iron lamps that had intricately cut shades. Lush, well-cared-for plants were placed around the room and hung from windows trimmed with pretty, white-lace curtains. There was a piano in a corner of the room.

We were served cookies and maté—a Brazilian tea the community drinks instead of coffee—as the older of the two girls sat down at the piano and started playing beautifully. The younger girl sat next to me, her attention focused on baby Emmet. "That's funny you had a baby first and are just getting married now," she said innocently, smiling sweetly at me. I cringed inwardly, not knowing how to respond, feeling like a horrible example to these virtuous, chaste girls. I'd never met girls this age who were so mature, yet at the same time so unabashedly innocent and pure.

At one point, a young woman named Rivkah who had a baby the same age as Emmet came and sat on the couch opposite me. I couldn't help but stare curiously at her baby, who was naked except for what looked like an ACE bandage wrapped tightly around his upper body, pinning his arms to his sides. "He's swaddled," she explained to me. "It helps bring him peace." And he was indeed peaceful, content in his mother's arms, just looking around, in contrast to my squirmy Emmet. That must be so nice, I thought, for her to live here with other, seasoned mothers who can give her advice on caring for her baby.

After an hour or so of pleasant conversation, a woman came in and announced that her "training" group had an "offering" for the guests. A small group of children probably aged eight to eleven were brought into the room. I noticed all the boys wore their hair just long enough to keep in a short ponytail. On cue, the older girl played a few opening notes on the piano, and the children sang us a song about being obedient to your parents and living a long, happy life. They were all smiling, seeming happy indeed! Was this for real? Kids singing about wanting to obey their parents? They apparently had their own home school, so no worrying about safety at public school for these lucky families! I was absolutely enthralled.

As we pulled out of the driveway a short time later, Annie remarked, "It's like entering another world, isn't it?" That summed it up perfectly. Another world existed discreetly, yet smack-dab in the middle of Rutland, Vermont!

⚶

Our wedding was only a couple days away. We'd be married in his family's church, built by André's great-grandfather, where his own parents were married. Our reception would follow at the Benson Town Hall, which Annie and I decorated ourselves with blue-and-white crepe paper and those tacky bells. For food, we ordered cold cuts, cheese, and veggie platters from Price Chopper. André's brother Chris would be our DJ playing CDs in one corner of the room. No one had money to help make things more extravagant, and we didn't see the point of going into debt. We also were not having a honeymoon. It seemed too stressful with a three-month-old, and André didn't want to take too much time off work.

Our wedding day dawned beautifully sunny—and oppressively hot and humid. Our service was nice, and the pastor even did a family blessing, having someone bring Emmet up to the altar after we took our vows. At the reception, we did the traditional things—cutting the cake, a champagne toast, throwing the bouquet, and father-daughter dance. It was swelteringly hot, and people were sweating at their tables, trying to move as little as possible. There was no AC in this quaint but very old town hall.

We had invited André's TT relatives, who hadn't been at the church but were all at the reception. At one point, one of my relatives asked me who our caterers were. The food was set out and people were helping themselves. I followed her gaze and noticed a young couple—a woman with a baby on her back and a man—who were busy clearing empty platters, setting out new ones, and making sure we weren't running out of napkins and plates. From the man's beard and ponytail and the way the woman was dressed, I knew immediately they had to be from the community. "I don't really know. They must be friends of André's cousins," I replied.

At one point I found myself in a back room nursing Emmet, and Joanna came in with her baby and we nursed together and chatted amiably for a few minutes.

The reception ended early, the sun still high in the sky when we returned to André's parents' house. Emmet was exhausted, and his mom offered to care for him so we could go for a drive. As I was upstairs nursing him to sleep, I cried. My wedding day had not been at all what I had always dreamed of. It was anticlimactic. I had wanted it to be a blast, with everyone dancing and lasting into the night. Our ceremony hadn't even started until 3:00 p.m. All the months of planning and anticipation and the whole thing had been over in less than three hours. No one had fun. It seemed everyone had simply tolerated the oven-like reception hall until it was acceptable to leave in their air-conditioned cars. We'd go home the next day, André would soon be back at work, and I'd be home alone with Emmet again. At least having the wedding coming up had given me something to look forward to during the previous months. Now what would there be?

We ended up driving back over to the town hall to assess the cleanup that we needed to do the next day. As we entered the building, to our surprise, the community people were still there working away, with the cleanup nearly finished. The young woman I noticed earlier helping with the food now had a broom in hand and was sweeping the large room. Her husband, who was pulling a full bag out of a trash can, now had their baby on his back—who was still contently watching the action. They were all shocked to see us back there! We thanked them for all their help, and were introduced to the couple, Benyamin and Talitha, who had driven André's aunt Sharon up from their community in Hyannis. I was struck by this couple who didn't even know us and had been laboring for hours in the heat on our behalf.

We left and drove around until I had that mother's intuition that Emmet was probably awake and needing to nurse. That evening, after Emmet was asleep, we opened our gifts in André's parents' living room. Afterward, his mom exclaimed, "You guys should get upstairs to bed. It's your wedding night, after all!" Again, extremely anticlimactic.

The next day, several people from the community in Rutland came over to see André's TT relatives before they headed home. There were probably about a dozen or so community members who congregated at André's parents' house that afternoon. I spent the day sitting on blankets on the lawn or taking walks up and down the long driveway with various community women, most of them around my age or a few years older. I asked questions about their life nonstop, becoming more and more captivated by these peculiar people. Everything they told me about their life sounded amazing, but they did not give off an air of pushy religious people. They were so nice and normal, obviously having a strong bond with each other. I was a little envious, being an "outsider." Suddenly, my bad feelings about the day before were gone, replaced with excitement over having made new friends and a growing eagerness to know more about this group. We even got invited to a wedding that would be in Cambridge, New York, in a couple months!

Before we left to go home, Annie gave me a bunch of community literature called "free papers," which were an assortment of articles and personal testimonies. She told me that in a couple weeks she and André's dad, Scottie, were planning to visit the community in Hyannis for a few days and thought maybe we would like to go too. André had just gotten a promotion at work and didn't feel he could take several days off, but he didn't mind if Emmet and I went with his parents. I was so excited! Between that trip, and the wedding, I now had so much to look forward to during the long, lonely days. I'd often think of the women I'd gotten to know and fantasize about what it would be like to live in the community, surrounded by my friends all day long, working together and helping each other. It all made my little house seem even more lonely.

I devoured free papers every time I sat down to nurse Emmet. The articles were all so well written and relatable, giving me what I considered a solid understanding of their beliefs. The personal testimonies had the most effect on me—people from all walks of life who found themselves in various difficult circumstances had cried out to the universe for help and miraculously met the Twelve Tribes shortly after. Now they were experiencing wonderful, abundant lives made possible by giving up their old, selfish, purposeless lives and submitting to Yahshua the Messiah. Yahshua is the Hebrew name for Jesus—what His parents would have actually named him. Maybe this was why "Jesus" never appealed to me—it wasn't even His name!

At one point before the Hyannis trip, I wrote a letter to the Twelve Tribes website, just to have another avenue to connect with community folk. This is that letter, dated Friday, July 16, 1999, 8:01 p.m.

> *Hi, my name is Tamara. I'm 22, married, and have a 4 month old baby boy. Lately I've learned a lot about your communities, met several people and even have family members on my husband's side who live in a couple communities. I enjoy so much being around community members. I visited the Rutland community and was very touched by everyone. I couldn't stop thinking about that visit, and still think of it often. I am going to spend the next week at the Hyannis community with my in-laws and baby next week and cannot wait.*
>
> *My mother-in-law has given me several free papers to read. I read them any chance I get. Everything makes so much sense to me, and is making me see how truly meaningless my current life is. I want better for my children. I want them to grow up with a purpose, never feeling as though they don't belong, never wondering why they are here. Basically never feeling like I've felt many times.*
>
> *I have been feeling so lonely lately. I stay home to care for my son, and long for others to be around me. I wait for my husband to come home from work and wonder what I can do to make each day go by faster. I don't want to live my whole life this way. I am realizing how shallow many people are.*
>
> *I love my husband. He has a wonderful, caring heart and is a great father. He also has workaholic tendencies, loves TV too much, and is preoccupied with making tons of money and having nice "stuff." Money and things used to be important to me too, but not anymore. My husband wants to be millionaires and retire at age 35. I want to enjoy the life we have now, not keep thinking about how much better the future will be if we have more money. It won't be better, it will be just as empty. No matter what fancy car is sitting in the driveway, I'll still be lonely and wondering how to make the days go by faster.*

I hate what the world has become and am scared to raise my children in it. I can't stop thinking about your communities. I have always believed in God and have always prayed for Him to show me what is right to believe in. What you have to say in your free papers finally feels right.

I'm nervous to tell my husband these things. I know I'll have to, he knows something is bothering me lately. I know I'm not going to want to come home after staying next week in Hyannis! We are going to the wedding in Cambridge next month. I'm sure he'll enjoy himself and will hopefully begin to feel as I do.

I feel better now having wrote this. Feel free to contact me, I'd love to correspond with you all.

Love, Tamara

The next two weeks passed by, and soon it was time for the big trip down to Hyannis. My in-laws came up to Burlington to get us, and we headed out on a sunny Friday morning. After several hours we were pulling into the Camp Street house in Hyannis, Massachusetts. We were given such a warm and lavish welcome like nothing I'd experienced before. A huge banner was hung above the fireplace in the large living room that read, "Welcome Scottie, Annie, Tami, and Emmet! We love you!"

I was shown to the room Emmet and I would be staying in. It was simple but neat and clean, and on the bed was a beautiful basket filled with fruit and baked goodies. Someone had drawn a lovely card as well. I felt so loved and at home, even though I barely knew anyone!

Over the next few days, we spent time with Esther and Mason's little family, as well as getting to know other families. I really enjoyed my time with Joanna. We were the same age, and our two little boys were only a couple weeks apart. We went for long walks and on a couple excursions to local beaches with other families. I grew fond of so many people in that short time; they all seemed so genuine and caring. The lifestyle was full of purpose. No one was sacked out watching TV or playing video games all day. Girls were sewing, doing laundry, or helping their mothers make meals. Boys were helping their fathers work on vehicles or projects around the property. It was the perfect mix of a modern-day old-fashioned life! Many of the children became friendly toward Emmet, and he would light up whenever he saw them. There was always something to do, or someone to have a conversation with. No one was bored or lonely.

They had gatherings twice a day, morning and evening, that lasted anywhere from thirty to sixty minutes. Someone would give three loud blasts on a huge conch shell called a "shofar" to signify it was time to gather. They started with singing and dancing, and then anyone (men and women) who had something "on their hearts" to share, including the children, could do so. They didn't have a pastor who did most of the talking. Sharing often began with simple thank offerings—how someone was grateful that Our Father saw their hearts and called them out from their meaningless life in the world. Then an older member would often read a passage from the Bible and expound on it, and then others would follow suit.

The baptized women all wore head coverings to the gatherings. This represented their unity with their husbands and each other, I was told. For the men to demonstrate their unity, they would all lift their hands over their heads at the end of the gathering to pray and dismiss. Everything they did seemed full of meaning. Annie, Scottie, and I took turns with Emmet at the gatherings, so we all had a chance to hear at least part of it. I was impressed with how well-behaved the community children were in the gatherings, even when the meetings were quite long.

It was hard leaving at the end of the week. I could never offer Emmet the fullness of a life like that, even with our playgroups and story times. It all seemed so pointless. I went home full of stories to tell André about our trip and couldn't wait to visit a community with him.

We didn't have to wait long, as a few days after we got home Annie called to ask if we would like to go with them to a Friday Night Celebration in Rutland the following week. On Saturday they observed the Sabbath, which began at sundown Friday night and was a festive event each week. André agreed, and my mood markedly increased as I now had another community-related event to look forward to.

The Rutland community held their Friday Night Celebrations at their soap shop, and I can still remember the soothing scent of lavender and peppermint as we walked in. We arrived early, so people were just wrapping up their work in the shop and someone offered to give us a tour. I remember being shown the lab where they formulated the natural, handmade products labeled Common Sense Soap and Bodycare. There was an older man working at the counter mixing something in a beaker, and next to him on a stool stood a little boy carefully holding an open bottle. It was his son, and that sweet little scene made such an impression on me. It was straight out of a Norman Rockwell painting. That's the kind of life I wanted for Emmet. André was a software engineer; he wouldn't be able to include Emmet in his work for years. But here was this little boy, who couldn't have been more than five, helping his Abba measure ingredients into a beaker and looking so happy to be doing it. We were introduced to the boy's father, Elad, who said, "Your son's name is Emmet? Did you know that means 'truth' in Hebrew?" I certainly did not but thought that was pretty cool, maybe even a sign.

We continued the tour, being introduced to more and more community members. I recognized some from the day after our wedding and felt like I was seeing old friends. Soon we heard the blast of the shofar—a ram's horn in this community—and knew it was time to gather. We were served a delicious, iced maté as everyone arrived and greeted one another with a hug, saying "Shalom!" or "peace" in Hebrew. I loved the music and dancing, especially watching the little children participate and having the time of their lives. Families seemed so loving and tight. Just sitting there, sipping my tea and taking it all in, I felt a sense of awe. They did this every Friday night! These children were so lucky to have this as part of their normal lives. Again, I noticed how well-behaved and respectful the children were, sitting quietly with their parents when the music stopped and people began sharing. Emmet would get fussy during this part, and André and I and his parents all took turns walking him around the back of the room.

The night passed in a blur of festive music, smiling faces, delicious food, and much thought-provoking conversation. At one point I needed to nurse Emmet and was offered an office that had a futon couch. As I sat there looking around, I noticed a thin, flexible stick next to me. I wondered if it was used for spanking. Annie had told me they spanked their children, which up until this point I had been adamantly against. I was going to raise my child without such a barbaric and abusive act. But now I wasn't so sure. Obviously, these people were doing something right. The children were absolutely delightful and their love for their parents was obvious. I had to resign myself to considering that maybe spanking wasn't so bad, and whatever the community's secret was for raising children, I wanted in on it.

Leaving that night wasn't difficult, because we had the wedding in Cambridge just around the corner! I was beyond excited to experience firsthand what sounded like a phenomenal event. I remember telling my mom about the group I was getting to know, our trips to Hyannis and Rutland, and now the wedding we were going to. "You're going to someone's wedding that you don't even know?" was her skeptical response. I tried to explain that community weddings were basically public events and they loved having outside guests attend. She didn't understand but has always been a "to each their own" type of person.

I counted down the days and was filled with anticipation when we finally arrived in Cambridge for the wedding. I was struck by the sheer number of people we could see bustling about as we walked down the long drive after being directed to a makeshift parking lot across the road in a field. The atmosphere was charged with excitement and anticipation. It felt like going to a concert or something! There were beautiful, tie-dyed banners hung all over the sprawling property, and we were escorted into a large tent under the largest one that formed an arch and proclaimed in beautiful calligraphy, WELCOME TO THE MARRIAGE SUPPER OF THE LAMB. Under the tent we were served lavish hors d'oeuvres, as a group of musicians played festive music in one corner.

As guests, we were constantly attended to by various community members. We were becoming well-known, having visited several places over the past month and being relatives of Esther and her sons. Happily, I spotted Mason and Joanna, and she and I immediately stuck together, having become fast friends during our stay in Hyannis and bonding over our baby "cousins."

The action of it all riveted Emmet, who loved the constant music and hustle and bustle around us. Often at home he was so fussy, and I struggled to know how to keep him entertained. Soon, the music stopped, and someone made the announcement that the "King" had come! Excitedly, en masse, we headed to another section of the property where the groom, wearing all white, except for a crimson jacket, sat regally upon a beautiful green throne. Different people began to speak passionately about the state the world was in, the problems facing humanity and how the only hope lay in the King receiving His Bride. The groom was representing Yahshua (Jesus), on His "Emerald Throne" in Heaven, waiting for His "Bride,"—His faithful people—to make herself ready so they could wage war on all the enemies that have plagued mankind for centuries. It was all very relatable and captivating, especially when I recalled the school shooting only a few months prior.

Suddenly, a group of people ran into the scene, shaking tambourines and exclaiming, "Oh King, your Bride has made herself ready!" With a great shout of joy, he leaped up and proclaimed, "Let's go get her!" The crowd exploded in clapping and cheering, and on cue, the band struck up a lively tune and everyone followed the exuberant King across the property, where he took his spot atop a long ramp that was decorated with a backdrop of clouds. This represented midheaven. Nearby was a wooded area marked by a banner that had a verse about the bride being prepared in the wilderness. Another man spoke for a few minutes, explaining the significance of the scene.

Then, there was a moment of quiet. The anticipation in the air was palpable, and the groom shouted at the top of his voice, "Basmat, my bride, come to me!" I can't even describe the emotions that coursed through my body as I watched a woman, all dressed in white, come running out of the woods toward the ramp. Practically leaping, she reached her betrothed and they grasped each other's hands, jumping up and down so exuberantly that the whole platform was shaking. With everyone screaming and cheering it was impossible not to get swept up in the moment, and I was having a hard time holding back tears for these people I'd never even met!

"Behold, this is Yahshua, who will take away the sins of the world!" the bride breathlessly exclaimed. "Let's wage war on our enemies!" commanded the beaming groom, and off we were led to the next scene.

The atmosphere visibly changed and became more somber, as the music now only consisted of a single drum, pounding out a rhythmic, consistent beat. We made our way toward a big bonfire, and once we were all assembled on the outskirts, several black-hooded figures suddenly appeared, moving closer to the fire. It looked rather frightening, and I was glad Emmet was asleep in his stroller. The figures formed a circle around the bonfire, and I noticed they all had words written in large, white letters on their backs—

words like *selfishness, greed, lust, lover of money,* and *idolater.* A man holding a large Bible stepped out of the crowd and began reading the verse from 2 Timothy 3:2 about what people will be like at the end times. It was a powerful speech, as those "enemies" were things we could all identify with, and it was clear how those vices divide and destroy human relationships. So now, Yahshua and His Bride were going to put an end to all that stood in opposition to God's love.

Slowly, a single-file line of community people emerged from the crowd, all holding hands. The King and Bride led the procession as they made a bigger circle around the imposing, black-cloaked horde. The tempo of the drumbeat increased, and the rest of the band joined in as everyone began to sing, "*See the Son of Man, coming on the clouds . . .*" It was the war dance. At each chorus, the outer circle of dancers would lunge toward the enemies, who seemed to grow weaker with each verse. "*Every knee will bow, HEY!! and every tongue confess, Yahshua Messiah, has won the victory . . .*"

By the end of the song, the enemies were lying defeated around the fire and the victorious dancers on the outside stood still in their circle, hands linked and raised above their heads. All was quiet. Then the King stepped forward and took off his red jacket, revealing his gleaming white shirt underneath. With a great flourish accompanied by a drum roll, he shouted, "It is finished!" and threw his coat on top of one of the slain bodies. The crowd roared and the band began a joyous tune. "Let's go to Jerusalem!" he announced, and everyone followed him and his bride toward an elaborate throne, where they took their seats amidst feverish cheers and clapping.

We were served a delicious meal, and the rest of the wedding was a series of "offerings" to the bride and groom. There were women's and men's dances, couples' dances, and the sweetest children's song and dance. The couple even had written songs they sang to each other!

I grew more overwhelmed as the day went on, being on the verge of tears constantly. Never had I witnessed such an incredible and fascinating outpouring of love for a couple on their wedding day! I thought back to my own wedding, and it seemed all the more pitiful now that I'd seen this. These people must have been preparing for months, learning all those dances and songs. They must have spent days setting up the property with the various scenes and decorations. I thought back to my mother-in-law and I hanging cheesy crepe paper bells around our reception hall. Imagine having hundreds of friends put on a wedding like this for you! I cringed thinking of what my reception must have looked like through the eyes of the TT people. But, I reminded myself, I could offer this to my child. Emmet could grow up and have a wedding like this! And he didn't have to go to public school but could be educated in the safety of the community. There was another option in life, and I was so grateful to have found it.

The last part of the wedding was the vows. The couple took their places under a traditional huppah, the man vowing to lay down his life for his wife, and the woman promising to submit to her husband one hundred percent. They were then pronounced husband and wife, and she gave him the "kiss of submission," which was their first kiss ever. After much cheering, the crowd formed two long lines facing each other and holding hands above their heads to create a long human tunnel for the newly wed couple to run through, ending in their vehicle that was all set for them to drive to their "first night" destination. Once they were in the car, everyone gathered around and sang the iconic TT wedding song, "*If I could have all the riches of this world . . .,*" and then finally waved them off. It was only sheer willpower that kept me from bawling my eyes out. Then dessert was served and a festive celebration of Israeli dancing ensued.

The thought of heading back to my desolate little abode was almost unbearable the next day. I had exchanged email addresses with a few people and promised to stay in touch. I needed something to ground myself, so on Monday I contacted my college advisor and registered for a couple classes that would start in just a few weeks.

Michelle offered to babysit during my classes, and I found them interesting, but between being preoccupied with how Emmet was doing and constantly daydreaming about the community, it was hard to stay focused. Finishing college seemed like such a waste of time since I'd discovered a purpose worth so much more. I did well in my classes but decided to not take any more the following semester so I'd be completely free to spend time with the community whenever possible.

Once or twice a month, we visited Rutland on Friday nights with André's parents—something I lived for. I even managed to get André to Hyannis for a few days that fall, along with my father-in-law, Scottie. A hurricane happened to be blowing up the coast, and they jumped right in, helping the men board up windows and clean up the property of all possible projectiles.

Scottie bought a much-needed toilet for the downstairs bathroom, which he and André installed together. That action alone granted them hero status in a household of thirty with only one working toilet. A couple women went thrift store shopping one day and came back with several cute things for Emmet. I was just a guest and felt so cared for already!

Over the next few months, I acquired any community literature I could get my hands on and pored over it continually. Annie was privy to their private Intertribal News or ITN, which was a monthly publication of what was going on in their communities all over the world. She would send them to me when she was done reading them, and soon every end table in my living room was piled with community reading materials. I emailed Annie one time after I'd finished my latest ITN, asking her to please send me more—"I feel like I am a community junkie and need my daily dose!" I was completely enthralled and felt so special when I would see our family written about in one of the entries. People from all over the world were reading about us! I even got a letter one day from a young woman in Brazil, wanting to reach out to me. I was being "drawn" and "sheeplike," as the community would say.

One day I read an article called "The Three Eternal Destinies of Man." It was about how a righteous God would not send someone to the Lake of Fire simply for not believing the right doctrine. It talked about the good people of the world who worked by the sweat of their brow and obeyed their conscience but never became "Christians" during their lives. Those people were going to have eternal life in the next age as part of the nations being ruled over by the Holy. And not only that but they hadn't made this up—it was in the Bible (Rev. 22:11)! I could believe in this; something finally made sense. Even the way they lived was backed up by the Bible—"All who believed were together and shared all things in common" (Acts 2:44). They were obeying that verse literally and living an abundant, wonderful life as a result.

It was all starting to make sense. Especially what they said about God needing a people on the earth who truly represented Him. The world was certainly getting scarier, and if there was a solution being offered, I didn't want to miss out. I was always asking André to read some article or another, and we constantly had conversations about the TT. He'd say things like, "I was really looking forward to Emmet playing baseball when he's older." To which I'd reply, "It seems like we are being shown a greater purpose for his life than sports." I knew there was much we'd be giving up, but it seemed worth it. In exchange we would be living the simple, wholesome life I'd always wanted away from the distractions of modern life and able to focus on what was really important: God, family, and friends. In the long run, those things trumped any "worldly" pleasures.

I lived for emails from Esther, who always had something poignant to help me get through my day and not lose hope that we weren't destined for a life of futility. She would send me lyrics to their songs, which I would memorize as I sang Emmet to sleep. I emailed Annie daily too, always expressing my longing to be in the community. One time I wrote, "This is ridiculous, here I am sitting in my house, bored and lonely, when there is a whole group of people who love me and want me to be with them."

André was happy to go to Rutland, and he enjoyed the people but was not as determined as I was to live there. During one conversation, he told me if he thought for a second the community was the best place to raise Emmet, we'd be there in a heartbeat. So, I made him a list of forty reasons we should raise Emmet in the community. I could envision us a few years down the road, fairly wealthy and raising spoiled, rich kids. André was always talking about all the nice "things" we'd be able to afford someday. That didn't excite me at all. I desired the rich fellowship and family-oriented lifestyle of the community. I already found myself putting Emmet in front of cartoons to get a little break and I'd feel so guilty. I wanted more for him.

I'd spend the whole day waiting for André to get home and would be irritated when he'd soon be at the computer responding to work emails, playing video games, or watching TV. We'd go on an evening walk with Mollie and Emmet, which was nice, but then we normally passed the rest of the night in front of the TV. Life already seemed humdrum and meaningless. I remembered my vow to raise my children with two married parents. Was this going to work? We hadn't been married very long and I was already discontented. I didn't know what I was doing; I was so young. Wouldn't centering our lives on God and having the encouragement and support of other married couples at all times in an old-fashioned, tight-knit community be a guaranteed no-fail?

Chapter 4

How to Join a Cult

n the early spring of 2000, I was invited to spend time at the community in Rutland. It was during the week, so André would be working, but I accepted the offer and Emmet and I headed down for a couple days. I felt so accepted there, like I really was becoming part of a family. Everyone, including all the children, were genuinely delighted when we arrived. We spent a relaxed and pleasant day with our friends, being invited to different women's rooms for tea and conversation. One single woman showed me a green clay powder that she was experimenting with using as deodorant. She explained how toxic store-bought deodorants were and that she wanted to use only natural and pure substances on her body. I thought that was so cool.

I noticed no one had photographs displayed in their bedrooms, unlike my home with framed photos of Emmet all over the living room walls. I asked about this and was told that the reason people take so many photos is that they get stuck in the past, in a place of nostalgia and fearful of the future. But babies grow up no matter how many pictures we take, and in the community, their focus is on the amazing future that is in store for them. Most families did have some photographs they kept in small albums, but I recall one woman saying, "I like to just use my memory." (Thankfully my mother is a photographer, so every time she visited over the years, she took beautiful photographs of my family.)

We walked to a playground in the afternoon with a couple women and several children, and on the way we played, "What do I have in my pocket?" We simply had to ask yes/no questions to guess what object was in one of the women's pockets. All the children were excitedly asking questions, and I was struck by how entertained and enthusiastic they were. It ended up being an acorn! The next person took a turn and had a clothespin in her pocket. Such good, clean fun. No TV really did have a good effect on children!

That night, we settled into a tiny room that barely fit a single bed, end table, and dresser and a playpen for Emmet. Of course, there was the customary welcome basket. As I nursed Emmet to sleep, I could hear other families getting their children to bed. I liked the comfort of having people around. André had begun traveling for his job, and I detested being home alone at night. I would sleep on the couch in the living room, with all the lights on and the cordless phone right beside me. I would be on pins and needles all night, waking at every little noise. At the community, I felt the opposite of that, and the safety in numbers concept was reassuring to me.

Suddenly, the comforting domestic sounds changed to the obvious sounds of a child being spanked. I could clearly hear "whacks," each followed by a cry of pain, and it went on and on and on. The crying grew more intense, as did the strikes. What was going on? It was clear that a child was being beaten within a few feet of where I sat.

Once, in our apartment in Burlington, Michelle and I had heard what sounded like abuse—screaming and crashing—next door, and we had called the police. That wasn't even an option for me, having no cell phone. I looked at my precious baby and wondered if joining this group would mean I would have to do that to him. Then, thankfully, it stopped. For several minutes I could hear muffled voices in the hall and doors opening and closing. Then it was eerily silent.

I had to go to the bathroom. I waited a few more minutes, then laid Emmet down and slowly opened my door and peeked out into the hallway. There was a teenage girl sitting on a chair outside the door to the adjoining bedroom, where the brutal sounds had emanated from. She glanced up at me, looking somber, but didn't say anything. I quickly used the bathroom and slipped back into my room, avoiding further eye contact with the girl.

Suddenly, I wanted to scoop Emmet up and get out of there. I could have been at André's parents' house in twenty minutes. Instead, I sat down on the bed. I didn't want to create more of a stir by fleeing without a word. I decided to just go to sleep and find an excuse to leave early the next day.

Several hours later, I was awoken by a soft knock on my door. I opened it to see Miriam—a nice, young mother I'd been getting to know—holding a tray with two cups of steaming hot maté and a flickering candle. She asked if she could come in, so I opened the door, and she followed me into the dark, cramped room. Emmet was still sound asleep. She set the tray down on the end table, and sat on the floor, her back up against the playpen and I sat on the bed still half asleep and thankful for the maté. She told me she assumed I had heard the commotion of the night before, to which I nodded. I can still picture half her face illuminated by the candlelight as she apologetically let me know that what happened was unacceptable and being taken very seriously.

Basically, the couple in the adjoining bedroom had six children ranging in age from a baby to thirteen years old. The husband had been working a double shift at the café, and the mother, Qavah, had been having a hard day, particularly with her ten-year-old son. What I heard was her losing her temper on him as she was trying to get her younger children to bed. The sounds were so loud because she had been using a yardstick to spank him with, which, Miriam assured me, was not condoned at all. She had totally forgotten about the young guest spending the night in the neighboring room. Others in the house had heard the incident and intervened as quickly as possible, removing the woman from her children and bringing her to her husband at the café. The teenager I saw in the hall had been enlisted to listen out for the other children until the parents got home.

I didn't say much, just listened as she finished up and assured me that, "Our Father's heart" had not been represented through this situation. Emmet began to stir, and she got up, gave me a hug, and said she hoped she would see me at the morning gathering. I got Emmet ready, and when the shofar blew, we headed downstairs. I didn't see Qavah, but her husband and a few of their children were there.

When the gathering was over, we ate breakfast with everyone, then I planned to leave. As I was getting our things together, there was another knock on the door. I opened it and saw the puffy-eyed, tear-streaked face of Qavah. She looked completely disheveled, like she'd been up all night, crying. In her arms, she held a swaddled baby of about six months who gave me a big smile, oblivious to his mother's distress. In that moment, instinct took over, and I stepped out in the hall and gave her a big hug. She began sobbing and apologizing to me over and over for reacting in anger to her child. "It's OK," I said. "I don't know what it's like to have six children, but I'm sure it's not easy." She tried to smile and thanked me for being understanding and said she hoped I would come back again. I assured her I would.

It was a cloudy, chilly day as I drove to Annie's house. I thought about how children were abused all the time, but how often were friends there to step in and stop it? How often was there a sincere apology to anyone who may have been affected by the incident? I thought of what I said to her, about not knowing what it was like to have six children. It was true, I couldn't even fathom what that was like. I knew how exasperated I felt when Emmet had been up most of the night and I was exhausted. And I only had him to care for. Imagine having several more? How could I judge her? She was a human who messed up. She was obviously torn up by her lack of restraint, and luckily she had the support of a whole community of friends to help her be different. Who had that out in the real world? I guess only those "lucky" enough to have neighbors like Michelle and I who would call the police when the screaming and crashing became unbearable. But had we really helped? Had we shown any love and compassion for them and their children, any kind words of encouragement the next day? Of course not; we had branded them child abusers and avoided them at all costs.

When all was said and done, this incident at the community had the effect of strengthening my resolve. It made me see how much we need friends who will love us and help us no matter what. I also respected the courage it must have taken Qavah to come and talk to me afterward. I had nothing but compassion in my heart for her.

It did not occur to me at the time to wonder whether, had I not been there, would there have been the same intervention. Looking back now, I can say probably not.

I went back to my life in Burlington, and one day I came across the diary I'd kept since junior high. I hadn't written in it recently, and I flipped to the last entry. It was from when André and I were at odds about Christianity and he was wanting me to be a believer. The last lines I'd written in my journal were, "*I am struggling with religion. I am open-minded to anything. I just need a push toward what's right.*" I was floored.

I remembered how Emmet meant "Truth." It was like all the pieces of a puzzle were coming together. This is what we needed to do. I was convinced beyond a shadow of a doubt. I just had to convince André. I knew if he spent more time there, things would become clear to him also. I mean, I wanted to join a Bible-believing group! The reality was it was more than he bargained for. He liked our life and would have been happy to have just gone to church on Sundays. I excitedly showed him the entry in my journal, and to my delight he said, "I guess you got your push!" My mind and heart were set, and he agreed that for our one-year wedding anniversary we could go to Hyannis for two weeks to truly experience community life, and then make a decision.

We arranged for Mollie to stay with his parents for our trip, and we packed out his '95 Saab 900 and headed down. We had even given up going to a Sting concert that weekend with friends, a decision I'd come to regret years down the road. We had let the community know that we were seriously considering "giving up our lives," and we wanted to experience the real deal during our stay. We had no way of knowing how impossible that is. We were twenty-three and very naive.

On our anniversary, Esther offered to watch Emmet, and we were treated to a nice meal at their café. We returned to our room that night to find it cleaned and decorated with fresh flowers, with candles lit and a beautiful handmade card on our bed. We were so affected by the level of love and care. People didn't normally do that kind of thing!

Needless to say, we had an enjoyable two weeks. I spent time with all the women, went on so many walks, helped a little in the kitchen, and even learned how to sew a tunic with fabric I bought at their sewing shop in Plymouth. We would end our trip with another wedding, this time at the community in Boston, and I had an authentic community garment to wear!

André stayed busy during our visit, helping with various projects around the property and accompanying the men to local jobs. He naturally sees needs and loves to help, so by the end of the two weeks it was clear how much he had to offer these wonderful people. Believing in the Bible was second nature to him, and even though I still didn't understand everything, this was the closest I'd ever been. I believed God would reward my willingness to join this new, radical life with the unshakeable faith I desired. No one was pushy or shoving their beliefs down our throats, but the very nature of their life caused me to ask questions constantly. At the two gatherings each day, we heard enough that we felt we were making an informed choice. And to top everything off, I found out I was pregnant while we were there!

We took a walk down to the harbor the day before leaving. The visit had its desired effect, and André told me he planned to give his notice when he returned to work the following Monday. We would put our house on the market and move down there in six weeks or so. I couldn't believe it. I was so relieved that he had come to see what I had—the amazing, meaningful life we were being given the chance to be a part of. Another clincher for him was that since he was a little boy, he'd had an intense fear of eternity, which also explained his fear of Hell. He suffered regular nightmares growing up, waking up terrified in a cold sweat. He didn't feel this way anymore, even when eternity was mentioned in gatherings, which was frequently. This was monumental for him.

We had a wonderful time at the wedding in Boston, and I couldn't believe we were about to be a part of something so big and significant. We were confident to return home and tell all our family and friends about the wonderful purpose we had been called to and that we were expecting baby number two!

I remember getting to André's parents' house and being greeted by the most excited little Mollie. And it broke my heart. I knew that in choosing to move into the community, we were also choosing to give her up. There were no dogs in the community. I didn't know about their extreme dislike and intolerance of them at that point, I just looked at it from a logistical point of view. Of course, it made sense that there weren't a bunch of dogs running around and needing to be fed. I knew we'd have to begin looking for a new home for her, but I was still convinced we were doing the right thing. Of course I was going to choose the best life for my child over my pet.

We had so much to do when we got home. We had to put our home on the market for starters. We contacted the realtor who helped us buy the house, and, less than two years later, she went to work helping us sell it. In great angst (he loved his job), André put in his notice at work, and their response was to offer him a twenty-five thousand dollar raise! He turned it down of course, as we had been prepared for something like this. We were told anyone who chooses to do Our Father's will is going to be opposed by the Evil One, so not to be surprised if suddenly we were presented with situations that would tempt us to change our minds. It was comparable to Jesus being shown the kingdoms of the world by the Evil One during His forty-day fast and being told "... *all this could be yours.*" It excited us that we were causing such tumult in the spiritual realm.

Most of our friends were receptive, supportive, and even intrigued when we told them of our decision. This excited me—maybe some of them would join someday! My family was a different story. André had it easy as his entire family was already familiar with the group. My family, while we had filled them in here and there on our activities of the past year, were completely taken aback and alarmed by the news.

One of my aunts contacted Bob Pardon, a well-known deprogrammer who works for the New England Institute of Religious Research. He has studied TT extensively throughout his career and has been involved in exit counseling for ex-members of a variety of cults. The fees associated with his services were steep, so my family backed off that route.

I enlisted the help of Annie, whom my family liked and respected, to call various relatives and assure them that we were not joining a "bizarre cult," but a group she had known for years and that we would be safe and well cared for. This helped, but I'll always remember my father's mother telling me I would get "stagnant" in such a group. At the time, I couldn't see how that would ever be possible.

So, our house was on the market, André was preparing to leave his job, and all our family and friends were informed of our monumental decision. Now, Mollie. I knew I'd only be able to leave her in full confidence that she was happy and in a loving home. I put an ad in the Burlington Free Press, stating that her owners were moving to a place that did not allow dogs.

I began to receive calls almost immediately. I asked potential owners to come to our house so we could see how they took to Mollie and, more importantly how she took to them. The first couple people were an immediate no. Mollie literally hid when they came in, and I didn't get good vibes either. I began to get discouraged, as I was convinced she knew what was going on. I started praying to God that if we were making the right decision, to please find a good home for our little dog.

Then, one day, a man named Brian called, and we set up a time for him to come over. This time, I held Mollie in my arms when I opened the door to let him in. I'd barely started to introduce myself when she literally leapt out of my arms toward this stranger, licking his face excitedly as if he were a beloved friend. She had never done that before! He came in and sat in our living room, and André and I began the normal small talk about where he lived, what he did for work, and so on. The topic came around to where he was from originally, and, come to find out, he was the son of the pastor of a church that André's family had gone to many years ago. They had always loved this man's father and spoke highly of him. What confirmation!

We were feeling good about him and planned a day to bring Mollie to his house to meet his wife and teenage son. We were equally satisfied upon visiting their home. They lived on a nice, quiet cul-de-sac only twenty minutes away. Mollie immediately made herself at home, running around, tail wagging excitedly, sniffing everything curiously. She had been excited to see Brian and also had a favorable response to his wife and son. It sealed the deal when she jumped up onto the back of their couch and perched there to look out the window, exactly the way she did at our home. I was comforted and completely believed that God had sent us this family to help us overcome the opposition of moving into the community.

By another miracle, within four weeks of putting our house on the market, we had a buyer—at seventeen thousand dollars above asking price! It was a nice, young couple who were expecting their first baby, just like we had been. The husband was a teacher and would be working at the school right next door, which is why they really wanted our house. We were so happy it was going to be them moving in. Everything was going so well.

We began offering our furniture to friends at bargain prices, and someone André worked with was willing to take over the lease on my '99 Ford Escort. I brought all our books to a used bookstore, as I learned they didn't read novels in the community, and I gave my clothes that I knew weren't community-worthy to Annie or my friends. I gave all my jewelry, except my wedding rings, to my mother and Annie. André and I sat together in excitement one evening and cut up all our credit cards. We wouldn't be needing those anymore!

Life felt surreal during these weeks. A teenage girl had given me a bag of community clothes before I left Hyannis, and I was like a little girl playing dress-up, putting on the baggy pants and modeling in the full-length mirror before changing back into my jeans, knowing that soon I would never wear them again. Everything I did was always with the thought, "This might be the last time I ever do this." I remember my "last" TV show—the season one finale of *Survivor*—and the last movie I watched—*The River Wild*—with my mom the day before we moved. I savored every cup of coffee, knowing soon I would only be drinking maté. I took Mollie for extra walks and made sure Emmet had one last playdate with all his friends. It wasn't like we were just moving to the Cape, as families often relocate. We were switching worlds and we knew it.

Even though I knew I wouldn't have an ob-gyn in Hyannis, I made my first prenatal appointment with my doctor in Burlington. I wanted to confirm that all was well, and then I'd put my trust in the community midwives for the rest of my prenatal care. The many children in the community were testimony that birth was a normal household occurrence. They obviously knew what they were doing and how to care for women. The appointment was on a Friday, three weeks before our big move. It just so happened that Benyamin and Talitha were coming up later that day to spend the weekend with us.

I went through the first-appointment routine: I was weighed, had my blood pressure taken, and did a urine test to confirm pregnancy. All seemed well. They would do an ultrasound and I would be done. The doctor ran the cool Doppler over my lubricated belly for a couple minutes, not saying anything. I kept waiting for her to point out the tiny, beating heart.

Finally, she looked at me, and I could tell right away something was wrong. "I'm so sorry," she began, "it looks like you have a molar pregnancy." She showed me a small mass of tissue that potentially started out as an embryo but, due to a probable chromosomal abnormality, stopped developing. She told me I would more than likely miscarry within the next few days, but if a week went by and I still hadn't started bleeding, I would need to have the mass surgically removed. I was devastated.

I left the office and went straight to a friend's house, where I cried on her shoulder for a few minutes before heading home and breaking the news to André. He was supportive and comforting and we distracted ourselves by getting things ready for our community friends who were due to arrive soon. I was glad they were coming. I knew they would be consoling and encouraging, and I was right. Over the weekend they did their best to answer any remaining questions we had and pass "Our Father's Heart" on to us. I ended up miscarrying naturally a few days later, having come to terms with the fact that I was not pregnant but feeling hopeful that I would be again within a few months.

The next few weeks passed quickly as we finished tying up all loose ends. I only remember one moment of panic ten days before our big move. Emmet was asleep and I was in bed with Mollie in her customary spot under the covers at my feet. I suddenly scooped her up and was overcome with emotion. André was at the computer, and I came over to him, clutching Mollie, with tears streaming down my face. He was able to calm me down and reassure me that everything was going to be fine, I was just having cold feet.

My mom came over the day before we moved. She played with Emmet and took a nap on our couch, and we watched a movie together. She hadn't expressed any negativity about what we were about to do; as a matter of fact, she had said very little. My sister and brother were young, only eight and eleven years old, so she was understandably busy with them. I assured her we would see her whenever we could and said that I hoped she would come visit us. At this point, my mother had never even been to a community. As she was leaving and saying goodbye, I could tell she was fighting back tears, and I was taken aback. I'd had no idea how much what we were doing was affecting her.

The community often quotes Matthew 10:37: "*Whoever who loves father or mother more than me is not worthy of me, and whoever who loves son or daughter more than me is not worthy of me.*" It was explained to me this doesn't mean we don't love our relatives in the world, but we don't love them "more" than our calling to be disciples. We would never allow their influence to cause us to betray Yahshua. We clung to the hope that the example of our "poured-out lives" would lead them to the Kingdom as well.

Brian came to get Mollie early the next morning. We all stood on the sidewalk as he took her from my arms and got in his car with her. I had to fight back my emotions and just keep going. Michelle would be there soon, as she was coming with us to Hyannis to see the place we were moving into. By midafternoon we were all set to go. With Michelle in the back with Emmet, and a U-Haul hitched to the back of the Saab, I drove away from 71 Cayuga Court for the last time.

Chapter 5

Year One

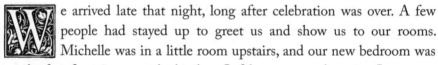e arrived late that night, long after celebration was over. A few people had stayed up to greet us and show us to our rooms. Michelle was in a little room upstairs, and our new bedroom was on the first floor, just past the kitchen. It felt so strange, knowing I was now "home," not just on another visit for a few days. I was so excited—and even more so to have Michelle see the community for the first time. I was certain she would fall in love with it, just like I had. We had always been so alike growing up, bonded since we were little girls.

That was not to be the case. She absolutely hated it there. At the time, she smoked cigarettes and later told me she was so glad of that because it gave her an excuse to leave the gatherings and take a short walk. This first occurred Saturday evening, during the weekly children's story when someone was talking about the "evil" people of the world in their flashy, red sports cars. Then, the Sunday morning teaching was given by a Black man called Abraham. Michelle remembers him as "arrogant and opinionated" and recalls him waving his hand around in imitation of gay mannerisms and speaking of the evils of homosexuality. Another smoke break for her. Chances are I missed much of what was said at gatherings that weekend, due to Emmet not being accustomed to having to sit still.

Despite the bad taste in her mouth, she didn't want to burst my bubble and end our last time together for who knew how long on a negative note. But she made it clear to André on the long drive back to Burlington (he had a few more things to wrap up at our house) that she hadn't been impressed by our new life and still hoped we could be talked out of it. She wrote to me a few weeks later, expressing how she felt but telling me she respected our decision, and it wouldn't affect our friendship. I was sad but felt with more time and, hopefully, more visits, her opinion would change.

I began to settle into community life. At that time, the Hyannis community consisted of a large house on Camp Street that had several former motel units out back that were used as living quarters. There was another house about half a mile down the road on Main Street called the Carriage House. It was a three-story, traditional clapboard-style house that only had bedrooms and bathrooms with no kitchen or common area. All meals were prepared and eaten at the Camp Street house, where we lived. The community was in the process of renovating and adding onto a big house on the same lot as the Carriage House, and the Camp Street house was to be sold. There was a Common Ground Café, also on Main Street. About fifty people lived there. People with several children had two bedrooms, and families like us with just one small child had one room. One sad thing for me was that Mason and Joanna had moved to Rutland.

The only furniture we hauled down were bedroom necessities—beds, nightstands, dressers, my rocking chair that had been my mother's, and a tall wrought iron and wicker decorative shelf. This was a special shelf that had earned the name "wicker from Hell." We got it at Pier 1, and it was so tall that the iron feet ended up scratching the radio panel of my husband's Saab 900S. I brought my houseplants and a few other decorative items I felt attached to in some way.

As I was busy setting up our new room with the meager remnants of our once full house, people stopped by to see how I was settling in. A fourteen-year-old girl came in and sat in my rocking chair. She looked around and said wistfully, "I've always dreamed of having nice things like this one day." I didn't see anything extraordinary about our belongings at the time but would understand her comment more as the years went by.

A couple women helped me go through my clothes. The dress code for women was extreme modesty. I was told we did not want to cause our men to stumble; we wanted them to remain pure in their thoughts. A stretch knit shirt was never worn without a tunic over it. Sometimes we even asked guests to wear a tunic (that we provided) over a tight-fitting, revealing shirt. Tops had to be loose and long enough to cover your bottom (the length of shirts should be to the fingertips when your arms were resting at your sides.) Undershirts were standard. Fabrics couldn't be too thin or clingy and had to be of all-natural fibers such as cotton, wool, rayon, or linen. Polyester was not allowed. Necklines had to be above the collarbone. Knickers (women's shorts) and swimsuit bottoms had to be below the knee, and women's pants had to be extremely "blousy" and cuffed at the ankle. Typically, between three and four yards of fabric were needed for one pair of pants. Skirts had to be ankle length, and we always wore bloomers under a skirt or dress.

I was provided with a couple pairs of hand-me-down community pants, known as "sus" pants. They were named after Sus, France, where they were approved of for the TT women, but they are otherwise known as genie, harem, or "hammer" pants. I cried over the first pair that were made for me. I had picked out olive-green, wide-wale corduroy, since winter was coming. Someone took my measurements, and the fabric was handed over to one of the household seamstresses. I was so excited as I came into my room one day and saw the finished garment folded neatly at the end of my bed. But when I put them on, I was horrified. They were massive. Two of me could have fit in each leg. I thought, surely they didn't need to be so wide, so I used what few sewing skills I had to sew a couple inches in from the inseam. I still didn't wear them until later that winter when I was bigger with my second pregnancy and felt a little more justified in them.

There were even standards for undergarments. Women were encouraged to only wear brief-style underwear. I was told that wearing attractive undergarments affects how you carry yourself and could cause you to give off a sexual spirit. I had mainly bikini underwear, which went right in the trash, and I found two new packs of briefs on my bed a couple days later. Of course, I'd later find out that many women secretly bought underwear they liked better. As far as bras were concerned, black or red bras were discouraged, as were lacy, "sexy" types of bras. Underwires or any type of padding was not allowed.

There were standards for men too, just not as extreme. Men had to wear shirts when swimming. Shorts had to be below the knee, so we usually just shortened men's pants a few inches. Their shirts were to be long enough that when they raised their hands to pray, no belly would be exposed. Men's shirts were never tucked into their pants. Their clothing also had to be made of natural fibers, and no logo or writing was allowed on T-shirts, sweatshirts, or hats. This included anything from the Nike symbol to a hoodie that said Gap, to a business logo on a baseball cap. Even our own community logos, like those on café T-shirts, weren't supposed to be worn around commonly, but only while working. We wanted to avoid "label spirits;" that is, coveting and esteeming certain brands of clothes. There was a teaching about this. We would painstakingly use seam rippers to remove embroidered logos or sewn-on labels from a nice piece of clothing. There were to be no unnecessary decorations either, such as beads or sequins.

I received help to go through Emmet's things. Any toys and books that were "foolish" were set aside to be donated at a church down the road. This included books that had animals that talked or looked cartoonish. Luckily, he was young enough to forget quickly and didn't seem to miss anything, and André's childhood set of wooden blocks and Lincoln Logs thankfully passed the test.

I was totally compliant as I watched the pile of our unacceptable worldly possessions grow. The women were mindful of us, and a few days later, I discovered a pile of "appropriate" children's books, mostly nature books, left on my bed.

The first challenge for me was that, contrary to my belief that our life was going to be more family oriented, André was gone more. After a few days of washing dishes at the café, he was put on a work crew that left right after breakfast and got home right before the evening gathering at 6:00 p.m. They also worked every night after supper and all day Sunday on the new house that we hoped to be moving into by summer. At least in Burlington he was home every evening and the whole weekend. Emmet and I not only saw him less, but I also had many more responsibilities as a "community woman."

Boredom was no longer an issue, but I'd gone from one extreme to another. I was put on the meals schedule and kept busy in the kitchen nearly every day, unless I was doing laundry. My household chore was the full first-floor bathroom, which I was told needed a thorough cleaning each day. I wasn't allotted much free time.

It was an incredibly hard transition for my active seventeen-month-old to suddenly adapt to being confined in a high chair for several hours a day and not being allowed to run around and "play." Many women carried their babies and toddlers in backpack carriers for hours while they worked in the kitchen. I had a really nice Kelty frame backpack carrier, but as I'd rarely ever used it, it was impossible for me to have him on my back for more than a half hour without being in pain. Plus, he would thrash around and rip my hair out when he'd had enough.

Being relatively unskilled in the kitchen, I'd usually be given the task of "just" making the salad for supper, which any of the other women could have knocked out in a couple hours or less. This consisted of six to eight large heads of romaine that needed to be soaked in vinegar water for 15 minutes, washed under cold, running water, then chopped into bite-sized pieces; several carrots to be peeled and grated; and usually a couple other vegetables like bell peppers or tomatoes to be washed and chopped. If I was lucky, the café would have an out-of-date salad dressing they would send home. Otherwise, I would need to make a gallon of homemade dressing.

Sometimes there would be another woman in the kitchen with me, but it was usually another mother and I soon learned that it was not approved of for children to "distract" each other while doing their "Imma's will." If Emmet saw any child, it was impossible for me to keep him from trying to engage with them, so it was easier for me to take what peeling and chopping I had and do it alone in the dining room or out on the front porch where a table was set up and Emmet could be somewhat entertained watching the traffic go by.

It would usually take me the entire day, from the time breakfast was cleaned up until 4:00 p.m. or so, to accomplish my supper task as well as care for Emmet, as he had to be at my side and given a will the whole time. I longed for his nap, during which I frantically tried to knock out whatever was left before he woke up. I would get to the end of my afternoon and be worn out and then have to face the evening gathering, where Emmet needed a lot of training to learn to be peaceful and quiet.

The women tried to teach me how to keep him occupied in the kitchen. One woman took a spoon and a fork and taped them onto his high-chair tray with several strips of masking tape. "This keeps my son busy for hours, trying to take them off," she told me. Well, within two minutes Emmet had ripped the utensils off the tray and thrown them across the room. Someone else showed me how to take a kitchen trash bag and cut head and arm holes in it so he could stand on a chair at the sink and "help" wash dishes and vegetables. Emmet was the kind of child who put everything in his mouth, and we soon were battling pinworms, undoubtedly from him eating unwashed organic vegetables and drinking the water we soaked them in.

Not surprisingly, pinworms were a common ailment in the community.

It was horrible, checking your child's bottom with a flashlight while they were asleep (the worms only come out at night to lay their eggs) and seeing the tiny, white, threadlike worms crawling around. Great care was taken in preparing veggies, but outbreaks were common because of the number of people using shared bathrooms and how highly contagious they are. They cause itching, so little children spread them easily to each other. We were encouraged to use natural remedies, such as thyme tea, pumpkin seeds, and garlic suppositories. This is how I treated Emmet in Hyannis, and it takes weeks of faithful treatment. Years later, when I had four children, we would discreetly opt for the over-the-counter, one-time remedy.

Laundry day was blessedly more low-key. I could keep Emmet under control much more easily, having him follow me up and down the basement stairs to the laundry room countless times, and then out to the clothesline, where he could run around in the yard. It was his most active day when he was only confined to the high chair for meals. I was assigned a single brother to do laundry for. He was an older man and extremely picky about how his shirts and pants were folded. He was sure to let me know if I had buttoned a shirt wrong or folded his pants in a manner that did not produce a neat crease down the front.

I was put on a weekend team for the four-week rotation of different meal responsibilities: Friday Night Meal, Sabbath (Saturday) breakfast, Sabbath lunch, and Breaking of Bread.

Friday Night Meal preps began Thursday night and continued throughout the day Friday, which was dubbed "Preparation Day," as we were preparing for the Sabbath. The "day" began the night before with "Preparation Night." A list was made of all common household areas, and families were each assigned a chore, so that the cleaning on Friday would be lighter on the women. There would be a snack, which was served only after an adequate interval of time for cleaning had passed to ensure no one would skip out on their chore. When our little family was cleaning or doing preps together, this was often a pleasant evening. Years down the road, when André was away or pulled into a "circumstance" and we had several children, this night was awfully stressful.

Friday began with an early morning child training teaching. All the parents would gather, children were allowed to sleep in, and one of the leading men would go over a teaching from the child training manuals. Sometimes there were specific situations going on in the household that would be addressed. We were supposed to be open and honest with our struggles with child training. That lasted about an hour or so until a few pajama-clad children stumbled into our midst. Then we prayed for grace for the day and were dismissed.

The children went to training Monday through Thursday, so on Fridays, the most busy and hectic day of the week, the children were all home with their mothers, who either had renewed zeal in consistent discipline because of the morning teaching or were feeling completely condemned, having had all their lacks as parents made painfully obvious. Either way, it could be a rough day for the children.

Much of what we did was symbolic. The Bible teaches that the end of the age is going to be brought about through much fasting and prayer, so, since the Sabbath represented the thousand-year reign of peace and the end of this evil age, we fasted for the first part of the day on Fridays. Children were expected to help with the cooking and cleaning all morning and, if they were aged three and over, fast until noon without complaint. It was deemed OK to make an "overcomers' tea," which was typically a milky carob tea to help the children fast until "Fruit Break" at noon. This started out as simply yogurt and fruit being set out and morphed over the years into a fruit salad with a crunchy granola topping. This is all we would eat until light hors d'oeuvres were served at 6:00 p.m. that evening. I remember Annie sending me a large box of Goldfish crackers from Costco, and I would ravenously consume a couple handfuls with Emmet when he woke up from his nap.

At one point, I questioned whether it was a good thing to make young children fast until noon while expecting them to "serve willingly" by our sides all morning, being disciplined for every infraction. All they would have had since dinner the night before was a sweet snack during Preparation Night. I was told it was "very good" that the children learn to suffer and overcome from the youngest age possible, and to give in to their "appetite" would ruin them.

We were expected to do a deep cleaning of our rooms on Friday as well. Catch-up laundry was going all day long, and the worst nightmare was having wet beds on a Friday morning. (There were women who got up in the middle of the night to do laundry, as there were only two or three washers and dryers for forty to fifty people.)

There never seemed to be enough time or enough showers, and, by 5:45 on Friday, most people were scrambling to finish up their last-minute cleaning and have all their children showered, dressed, and ready for Celebration at six. This was symbolic also, as the years leading up to the end of the age, called the Race, are predicted to be intense and full of opposition. Our Fridays were to mirror this, and they certainly did.

Friday Night Celebration was the highlight of the week. People's spirits were high as tea and hors d'oeuvres were served, and everyone was dressed in their nicest clothes. Most of us even had a special pair of Celebration shoes that we only wore to the weekend gatherings. Oftentimes there would be guests, which always made the atmosphere more festive, as we wanted to showcase the "fruit" of our long week with all its "trials and tribulations." We had endured and made it in peace and unity to the Sabbath, one week closer to Our Master returning, and we could now enter our well-deserved rest.

After some singing, dancing, and sharing we would have Friday Night Meal, which was the nicest meal of the week, including dessert to be served later. Families sat together, with the old-fashioned standard of children remaining peacefully at the table until the adults were ready to move out into the gathering room for Celebration (easier said than done). The actual "Celebration" began at this time and consisted of traditional Israeli folk dances. We'd begin with easier ones for the children and work our way up to more complicated, faster "adult" dances. Then we'd sing a slower song, pray, and dismiss, usually by 10:30 p.m. or so.

During the festive feeling of Celebration, while eating a delicious dessert and watching my children having fun dancing, I'd really feel thankful. Especially in the years to come, I'd think to myself how lucky I was to have all my children home every Friday night enjoying this good, clean fun as a family, instead of worrying about where they were and what they were up to, as I remembered the shenanigans my friends and I pulled when I was younger.

※◊※

I was definitely struggling to adjust to my new life. To say I was in culture shock was an understatement. I talked often to different women, being honest about the things that were hard for me, and everyone was kind and understanding. One woman likened what I was going through to someone who had just escaped a burning building. A crowd was standing around watching and tried to persuade the person to remain outside, in safety, saying, "Stay with us, people are dying in there.'" Unbelievingly, the person said they needed to go back in and see for themselves one more time, and they headed into the flames. I was the one who had just escaped the burning building—"the world," where people were being destroyed daily. Now I was tempted to go back, but I needed to trust my new brothers and sisters that it really was death out there and I'd been rescued and found true life.

I still saw the good that I wanted for Emmet, and I knew I was just in the adjustment period. I watched the other women function, most with several children in tow, and figured I'd get the hang of things eventually. All I had to do was look at the respectful and helpful older children to remind myself why I had wanted to be there. People talked to me often about how it was only due to having the Holy Spirit and being able to cry out for grace daily that anyone could make it as a disciple. No one could live that life "in their own strength." It was even in the Bible, in 1 Peter 4:12: "Dear friends, don't be surprised when the fiery ordeal comes among you to test you as if something unusual were happening to you." That was the proof you were in God's will— that He tested you and gave you strength and grace to overcome when you asked. Of course, things were even harder for me. I couldn't even call upon the Holy Spirit to help me when I was suffering. All I had to go on was my own strength, which I was discovering sold me short most of the time. I was raising a child too; one surely needed the wisdom and grace only Our Father could provide for this monumental task. I was sure that once I had faith and got baptized, that would be the key to making life more manageable.

After a few weeks, we were sent to a job with our Forest Keepers tree crew up in Booth Bay Harbor, Maine, for five days. Emmet was now nineteen months old, and I breathed a sigh of relief when I heard we would be going on this trip, as the long days in the kitchen with him were becoming increasingly stressful. We were going with a nice family who had two teenage daughters, aged seventeen and fifteen, and a thirteen-year-old son whom Emmet adored. We would be staying at the home of a man who had hired the Forest Keepers to clear some of his land. I was excited; it felt like an adventure.

We left early, before the morning gathering. It was such a treat to stop at a store and get cereal and milk for breakfast! André also got me a coffee, and I savored every drop. We arrived in the early afternoon. It was beautiful, right on the ocean, and the weather was still mild in late September. After a preliminary period to settle into our rooms and take a quick tour of the property, everyone set about business as usual. There were a few single men who came along for the job, so in total there were about twelve of us.

I came to realize that, for women, the routine of life was always the same. I was immediately needed in the kitchen with the two girls and their mother to prepare supper for that night. Once that was served and cleaned up, we began prep for breakfast the next morning. We were up early to prepare breakfast, and as soon as that was cleaned up, we would start on the men's midmorning snack and maté break, and then on lunch. As soon as lunch was served and cleaned up, we started on their afternoon snack and supper. As soon as supper was cleaned up, breakfast prep began once again. At one point, the younger of the two girls said to me in a cheerful voice, "Breakfast, lunch and supper—that's the life of a woman!" I cringed inwardly, but just smiled at her.

We returned from Maine, back to our new "normal." We had lived there around seven weeks, and André was growing more in faith every day, even sharing at gatherings. So far, I had only shared once—just a small thank offering. Public speaking had never been easy for me. But the encouragement and appreciation people expressed toward me afterward were inspiring, and I wanted to gain the confidence to speak more.

One morning, Wednesday October 11 to be exact, before we left our room, André let me know it was "the day." He was going to "express his heart" to be baptized at the minchah. I knew it was inevitable, and I was happy for him. He was the first to share and expressed how he wanted to give his life to this purpose and surrender to Yahshua. He wanted to learn to be a good husband and father. Those kinds of things were usually the gist of an immersion speech. At this point, people had a chance to ask any questions they may have had—like a "speak now or forever hold your peace"—for immersion into the Body is seen as a marriage of sorts. No one questioned André's sincerity or understanding. It was tradition for everyone to yell "AMEN" to confirm unanimous faith for a baptism, so after a thunderous confirmation, we all grabbed our coats and headed to the harbor.

It was a brisk, sunny fall morning as all fifty of us stood on the shore, the rest of society going on with their day around us, casting curious looks at what must have been quite the spectacle. We all gathered at the water's edge, as one of the elders spoke for a few minutes of the significance of what was about to happen- André was about to die to his old, futile life and emerge as a new creation, equipped with the Holy Spirit and counted among the chosen. The angels were looking down and rejoicing.

I stood there, holding on to Emmet's stroller, and watched as André walked out into the water, an elder on either side of him. They each placed a hand on his back and clasped one of his hands with the other. Looking up into the bright, sunny sky, André cried out for Yahshua to save him and give him a new life. He proclaimed his total surrender to the Body of Messiah. He was fully plunged under the water by the two brothers and brought back up to the sound of excited clapping and cheers from shore. "Abba swim?" asked little Emmet, somewhat confused. Happily, I lifted him from his stroller and joined the crowd, who were forming a huddle around my blanketed husband to pray for him.

The crowd parted to allow Emmet and I to get in the center with him. He engulfed us in a big, wet hug, and I could see his eyes were shiny with tears. We formed a human island, as everyone placed their hands on the person in front of them, with my family at the center. Several people at once began calling out thanks for André's salvation and imploring the Holy Spirit to reside in him. After another uproarious "AMEN!" someone said, "Is there anyone else who has a pounding heart and wants to surrender to Our Master?" It was customary to say this at every baptism, because even members who were struggling and wanted a new start would often get rebaptized, but I felt it was aimed at me. I suddenly couldn't speak even if I wanted to. I froze in fear. I just couldn't do it. I buried my face between André and Emmet and remained quiet. After a few moments, we dismissed and headed back to the house.

I remember calling Annie that day and telling her André had been baptized. I was truly happy for him, but also felt strange. He had entered another realm that day, his spirit connected to a source of life that I still wasn't a part of. I realized he would go to Breaking of Bread (the special, members-only gathering) without me that weekend, and I would still be at the guest meal. I couldn't bear that thought. We should be doing this together. The ironic thing was that I was the one who wanted to go there initially, and now he was a disciple, and I wasn't! I decided I just needed to do it—why put off the inevitable?

I spent the day building up the courage to express my heart at the evening gathering. I rehearsed what I would say over and over in my head, I didn't think I could just fly by the seat of my pants in front of everyone. It was still from my heart, it was all true, I just didn't want to draw a blank and look stupid.

When André got home, I told him I was ready to get baptized too. Of course, he was pleased and supportive. I was extremely nervous as we stood at the gathering, waiting for the singing and dancing to finish. I wanted to be the first to share, before I lost my courage. As the song ended and the dancers went back to their families in the circle, I handed Emmet over to André and took a deep breath. "I want to follow my husband," I began confidently, following with the typical mantra of wanting to learn to be a good Imma for Emmet and a good wife, and wanting a new start.

Whatever I said was met with an enthusiastic amen, and we once again began the procession down to the harbor, this time under the cover of darkness, which made me feel a little more comfortable. I did not want a crowd of curious onlookers. I couldn't believe I was doing this, but the affirmation I was receiving from everyone gave me the determination and fortitude I needed. Adrenaline was prompting me forward as I ventured into the chilly water, an elder on either side of me. I don't recall what I proclaimed out in the water, but I felt I was sincere in what I was doing, even though not everything made sense to me yet. I hoped my leap of faith would be rewarded by God and I'd emerge as a new creation, like everyone said, ready to prosper and be completely fulfilled by our new lives. It just had to work.

Since André had been baptized that morning, there was already a "Lost Coin Celebration" planned for after dinner. This was a traditional festivity to honor new disciples. An impromptu skit was performed about the parable of the lost coin, where a widow has saved for years to buy a field and then loses one of her coins. It's an analogy of Our Father finding one of His "lost sheep" and how precious each of us is to Him. I was feeling joyous and hopeful. Never in my life had so many people been celebrating anything to do with me!

All disciples were exhorted to take a prayer walk every morning, invoking the Holy Spirit to be at work in our lives as we went about the day, "doing the deeds prepared for us." I got up early the following morning and went for a walk to pray for the grace I could now receive for the first time ever.

I was given a pretty head covering and felt special to be able to wear it to the gatherings like the other women. More was spoken about the significance of the head covering. This is from a teaching called *Being in Salvation is Being in Order*:

> *A wife wears a head covering for her husband and Messiah. It is a wife's privilege to wear the head covering. For a wife to take off her head covering in the meeting was a sign of disgrace.*
>
> *". . . but every wife who prays or prophesies with her head uncovered dishonors her head, since it is the same as if her head were shaved. For if a wife will not cover her head, then she should cut her hair short. But since it is disgraceful for a wife to cut off her hair or shave her head, let her cover her head." (1 Corinthians 11:5–6)*
>
> *If you dishonor your head, you are not worthy of Messiah. She might as well have her hair cut off as a sign that she had been publicly disgraced or was flaunting her independence and refusal to submit to her husband. A wife wears her head covering for the angels. Angels are sensitive to our behavior and the proper order of things. They are interested in our order, behavior, character, decency, decorum, and propriety. The angels see every wife with a head covering and every wife who does not respect her head.*

The next few days did seem better. It may have been the residual endorphins from the excitement of it all and the continuous praise and encouragement I was receiving from everyone. Or it could have been a placebo effect—I believed I now had access to a powerful spiritual realm that could give me strength during my struggles.

I began making sure I read something from the Bible every day, and made an effort to share at least a couple times during the weekday gatherings. It's hard to be the quiet type, as we were encouraged not to let more than three gatherings go by without sharing. What you shared was supposed to go along with the conversation and not just be an out-of-place anecdote. We were told if we were in the gathering and our heart started pounding that it was the Holy Spirit trying to speak through us, and if we hesitated, the spirit would move to someone else.

(I came to realize a few years ago when I was back in college, that whenever I raised my hand to contribute or ask a question, my heart pounded. I don't believe it was the Holy Spirit trying to communicate to my Food Science class. I think it was just normal "nerves" that most people experience when speaking in public.)

I was also looking forward to our first Breaking of Bread! That gathering was still a mystery, reserved only for baptized members. Esther told me it was the high point of the week, the greatest form of fellowship. I was filled with anticipation.

We spent an enjoyable Sabbath taking walks with different families down to the boat docks, which Emmet loved, and around Hyannis's quaint Main Street. We had tea at the café and rested for a while in the afternoon. Then we excitedly got ready for the Resurrection Celebration, which is the Saturday night gathering preceding Breaking of Bread. It started out with lots of children's dances, then a few adult dances. Then the sharing began, focusing on the topic of Yahshuah's resurrection.

It was also the night for the Victory Cup. Each week, we were to judge ourselves and our children on whether we overcame and had victory in a specific area of our life. Parents were to set goals for the children to work on that week and talk to them at preparation time about whether they were going to drink from the cup (which was Manischewitz Concord grape wine). Common goals for children were being respectful to their parents, receiving their discipline, being kind to their siblings, or not striving for their own will. They were expected to proclaim before the household why they were drinking or not. A few adults would share about their victory or lack thereof as well.

After the Victory Cup, all the children and any youth who were not baptized congregated in the center of the room, facing out toward the circle of adults, and sang the traditional song asking for their weekly story. "*Mah nishtanah, ha-laylah ha-zeh, mi-kol ha-leylot. . . .*" This means, "Why is this night so different from any other night?" Then an adult who had prepared a story would sit at the front of the room with all the children gathered on a rug at their feet. Some of the stories were entertaining. Afterward, children were encouraged to share something they'd learned. Young children might say something like, *"I learned in the story I want to be like Reah and trust."* Older children were expected to share something with more substance. Then we prayed for them and dismissed to start the frenzy of feeding and getting them to bed so the adults could regather for Breaking of Bread about forty-five minutes later.

After the gathering that night, I nursed Emmet to sleep, eager to get back out to participate in setting up the room for Breaking of Bread. This was our first time not heading to the café for the guest meal. I emerged to the hustle and bustle of many people lighting candles around the room, putting tapestries over the many mattresses strewn around the floor, setting up a low table in the center of the room with a beautiful tablecloth and twelve small candles (only ten being lit at the time because the last two tribes weren't established), and hanging up a curtain to separate that room from the adjoining dining room. The mood, high-spirited and festive, was even more heightened since it was André's and my first Breaking of Bread. People kept spontaneously hugging me, saying how happy they were to be my "brother" or "sister," and how much our family was loved.

The Breaking of Bread is supposed to be the culmination of our week, the renewing of our covenant with Yahshuah. It is to represent the "Holy of Holies"—the curtained-off room in the Temple of old Israel that only the high priest was allowed to enter once a year. He had to have a clean conscience when he entered, lest he be struck dead inside.

Thus, we didn't just walk into this room casually and find a seat. We all waited expectantly outside of it, as two men stood as gatekeepers on either side of the curtained doorway. We'd sing a few songs, then begin to enter, older disciples first, followed by couples, and then single people, all being greeted with a hug and a "shalom" by the gatekeepers. We were supposed to enter this room totally "clean," having no unconfessed sin. This was someone's last chance to pull one of the gatekeepers aside if they had something they needed to confess. No one wanted to "defile" this holy assembly.

Once we were all in, whoever made the loaf would designate two couples, or a few single people, for the honor of lifting it. The loaf was the centerpiece of the table and represented Yahshua's body. They would kneel around the table while the rest of us kneeled on our mattresses or the floor. We had a traditional song we sang, and at a certain point the couples would lift the loaf into the air and the rest of us would bow down completely, faces to the floor. Some would prostrate themselves fully. The loaf lifters would each say a short prayer, blessing the loaf. Then we'd all say "Amen" and sit up, and the loaf would be broken into four pieces and begin to be passed around clockwise from four "corners" of the room, representing the corners of the earth that the gospel needs to reach. Bowls of soup would be passed around as well. Then everyone was expected to share, most often expounding upon their appreciation to be in salvation and for Yahshua's sacrifice. Some people were succinct, some would talk for ten to fifteen minutes. It was hard for others to talk at all.

Whenever there were new disciples, the significance of the loaf and what it represented were carefully explained. It was made of flour, oil, and salt. The flour represented the individual wheat berries being ground up together "in unity" and heated to form the loaf, much like our lives, as we died to "ourselves" and lost our individual identities to be in unity (one mind) with our brothers and sisters. The salt gave flavor and represented the correction that comes to us in love through each other to give our life the proper essence. The oil helped hold it all together and represented the grace Our Father gives us to love and endure daily.

The bread was considered consecrated and holy. It had to come out whole and perfectly cooked. If it was blemished in any way—slightly burned, too cracked, or crumbling apart—it was deemed an omen that our offering wasn't pure. The Breaking of Bread would be canceled and the loaf burned. It couldn't be consumed outside of the holy assembly. Introspection would then ensue, as each of us wondered if it was our sin that caused God to oppose the gathering.

Since everyone was expected to share, at the end of the gathering there would always be a long, awkward pause with everyone sneaking furtive glances at the few remaining people who hadn't spoken yet. I was often in that place, finding it hard to know what to say and not wanting to open my mouth in front of thirty or more people and end up not making any sense.

After it seemed most people had shared (two hours later in a large community), we'd be called to stand up. There was another song we'd sing and at the end we "cried out." Everyone screamed and shouted to be saved and whatnot for nearly two full minutes. We were told this was our chance to ensure we had received the Holy Spirit. Then a cup of wine was passed around representing the blood of Yahshua. More people who hadn't shared yet would continue during this time. After everyone had drunk, we'd all hold hands and put them in the air and pray. If you still hadn't shared by this time, you were definitely expected to pray. Then we would do one dance around the table and a sparkling juice would be served. This was the same, week after week.

I entered the Breaking of Bread room that first time filled with anticipation and delighted at my new status that permitted me to attend. I left feeling disappointed and unnerved. It had felt creepy. When we were all bowed down during the lifting of the loaf, I peeked up and it looked so bizarre—the dim, candlelit room, the people in the center holding the loaf above their heads, the rest of us face down on the floor. I had a déjà vu moment, being brought back to the uncomfortable feeling I'd had at the church youth group. This time I couldn't just go wait in my car—I would be doing this every Saturday night for the rest of my life.

From the beginning, I avoided going anytime I could, offering to do childcare or guest meal when it was our team's turn for such responsibilities. If Emmet or, eventually, any of my other three children were sick, it was a relief to know I'd be able to stay in my room and go to bed with them. I hated the awkwardness of being stared at after someone asked, "Is there anyone who hasn't shared yet who wants to give thanks?" I made a point of going to "check on my children" right after I drank from the cup and not coming back into the room until I heard them praying. Then I could quickly say something like, "Thank you for our children. Please give us grace to pass on your heart to them this week," and I would be off the hook.

When I was pregnant, it was often hard to stay awake, as it was usually after 11 p.m. by the time it ended. The oily loaf often made me feel sick, and we could not refuse at least a small piece. During the summer, the room would be swelteringly hot—there was no AC in those huge gathering rooms. One time, I brought a cup of ice chips into the room to suck on. I was enormously pregnant, and Breaking of Bread was in a stuffy, windowless room. I was pulled aside and told we don't bring anything else into the room that would take away from Our Master's Body. If we needed a drink of water, we were to leave the room.

Thus, our first Breaking of Bread came and went. After the heightened emotions and excitement of the past few days, the new week began as normal, and André was soon gone for the day on a job. I was doing my best to be faithful, to pray for grace, and trying to learn how to rule over Emmet. As a guest, I was only given kind and sporadic advice about parenting. Now that I was baptized, I was more accountable to the standards of discipline and subject to everyone's input. We were given more rods—the flexible, reed-like switches used for discipline. I had started spanking him lightly on his hand when we were still in Burlington so he would get used to it. It was amazing to me how fast he made the correlation, and I already saw success in areas such as teaching him not to touch my sewing machine or plants. We did not childproof in any way; we trained our children. We were to tell them "No" one time, and if they did it again, they got disciplined. We never were to repeat a command. This was called "discipline on the first command." It was supposed to teach them early on that our word was law and put a fear of disobedience in them. Discipline was supposed to restore the connection between parent and child, which was broken when the child willfully disobeyed or was disrespectful.

I often witnessed other women disciplining their children, and it was still shocking. Sometimes, right in the middle of the living room or kitchen, a woman would take her small child over her knee, pull down their pants or lift up their dress, and spank their bottom, sometimes over their underwear, but if they were wearing a thick, cloth diaper, it would often be on their bare bottom. With older children, discipline was done privately, and since one of our bedroom walls abutted a small bathroom, I could often overhear discipline sessions. I would hear phrases like, "Take your pants down," "Put your bottom in the air," "Close your lips," and "You need to receive your discipline." I would also inevitably hear cries of pain.

I learned children were supposed to bend over submissively and receive their discipline quietly, without screaming. If a child cried too loudly, they would quickly get their mouths covered and likely more whacks. If a child resisted the spanking by squirming or trying to get away, we were told it wouldn't reach their heart. We had to wait until we were sure the child was receiving it willingly. Then they could repent their wrongdoing and be forgiven. Through proper and consistent discipline, the child would know we loved them, and they would respect our word.

Train up a child in the way he should go, and when he is old he will not depart from it. (Proverbs 22:6)

Stripes that wound scour away evil, and strokes reach the innermost parts. (Proverbs 20:30)

Whoever spares the rod hates his son, but he who loves him is diligent to discipline him. (Proverbs 13:24)

These proverbs were drilled into us regularly at child training teachings.

The shock of witnessing daily public spankings and hearing them from behind closed doors soon wore off until it was just part of normal life—background noise. Emmet was a smart child and was receiving a lot of discipline, especially during gatherings and when I was working in the kitchen. I wanted his behavior to be on par with other kids his age, but he was coming from a deficit, and it showed. I was encouraged to start spanking him on the bottom. I wouldn't have been able to keep count of how many spankings he got in one day. He was around twenty months old at this time.

I soon was feeling overwhelmed, stressed, and homesick. We were seeing André less and less. I didn't feel like the Holy Spirit was helping me very much and feared perhaps I hadn't been sincere enough when I got baptized. I sought out a kind, older woman named Milkah. She was the wife of Abraham. She had beautiful dark, curly hair, and a dark complexion full of freckles. She listened compassionately and assured me in her thick, French accent that I had been completely sincere and that it was just the Evil One whispering doubts in my ear, which was completely normal for a new disciple. I took a little courage from her words and pressed on.

One day I noticed a woman cutting vegetables for lunch. Next to her, standing on a chair, was her two-year-old daughter, small paring knife in hand, cutting on her tiny cutting board. The scene was sweet, aside from the fact it was dangerous. If the little girl fell with that knife, she could stab her eye out.

"Is it safe, how she is standing on that chair with a knife?" I innocently inquired.

"I want my daughter to be doing what I'm doing," was the response. I wasn't satisfied with that and relayed the story to Milkah, who seemed to appreciate my concern.

One morning each week the single brothers made breakfast, and we had a women's meeting early before the gathering. There was hot tea, and we all sat in a circle on a big, braided rug. I had felt so special the first time I was invited. It was so cozy and felt like a real sisterhood. We would talk about our purpose as women, and there would be some Bible reading, nothing really heavy or controversial at that time, probably for my sake. I looked forward to this weekly time with the women. Emmet stayed sleeping with André, and I could relax in the company of adults. Household concerns could be brought up at these meetings too.

At the next meeting, Milkah brought up my concern about little children using knives and completely validated it. She exhorted the women to increase kitchen safety and even told stories from other tribes where children had needed stitches or suffered burns from not being careful in the kitchen. She said we should make sure children are sitting when using knives, and they should only be using butter knives and cutting soft things. I felt so good, like I had contributed something of value to the household and maybe even thwarted a potential injury. Maybe I was hearing from the Holy Spirit after all.

Chapter 6

Friends and Goats

round this time, I became pregnant again. I was excited and took it as a confirmation and reward of my faith. I thought about having prenatals with the women I lived with and bonding with them in such an intimate way. It seemed like a wonderful journey was starting, and I was so happy to find out Joanna was also pregnant and due just a few weeks before I was!

My euphoria was short-lived, as morning sickness (which I never experienced with my first pregnancy) and the bone-weary feeling of early pregnancy set in. I was still getting used to the diet, and much of what we ate made me feel horrible. I'd come out of my room in the morning to fragrant pots of hot maté and bowls of steaming, sauteed vegetables on the tables to top our millet or other grain, such as bulgur or rice. A couple dozen eggs would be scrambled or a few cakes of tofu diced up and baked and mixed into the grain.

Our lunches every day were some kind of sandwich "spread"—often the leftover breakfast grain, especially millet, mixed with grated cheese and homemade mayonnaise. The café would send home blocks of cream cheese that were past date, and we'd make cream cheese and olive spread. Egg salad spread consisted of a couple dozen hard-boiled eggs mixed with millet or rice and mayonnaise. Tuna spread was the same, always "stretched" with a grain.

Dinners consisted mainly of meals such as baked sweet potatoes with tofu cream, baked squash and Greek salad with a sprinkling of feta cheese and roasted sunflower seeds, or the famous rice and beans, served with unleavened bread, and always a tossed salad. Hyannis was a very poor community at the time, and fifty mouths were a lot to feed.

I was still nursing Emmet at this point and was worried I wasn't getting enough calcium and protein. I'd wake up at night ravenous and fantasize about the days not long before when I'd done all my own grocery shopping.

The food was markedly different for the men who went out on jobs. The women packed their lunches each day with two turkey sandwiches, veggie sticks, chips, a cookie bar, and plenty of juicy maté. The working men needed the extra protein more, I was told one day as I was helping pack their lunches and made a comment about how nice it would be if we all could eat like that. I bit my tongue on the knowledge that pregnant and breastfeeding women needed it just as much, if not more, realizing the inequality was likely a financial issue.

Thankfully, the men were working on a job only a few blocks away, so knowing I was suffering over food, André told me to stop by on my daily walk so he could give me one of his sandwiches. He also expressed my struggles to one of the men, and I soon experienced some much-welcomed "mercy" from the household. They got me cereal to eat in the morning instead of the grain and veggie bowls and even got me steak that someone cut into cubes and froze into portions so I could have red meat a couple times a week. I was feeling so sick most of the day, and one of the women told me the B vitamins in the red meat would help with that. I was also given permission to get a smoothie from the café every day, which I augmented with plenty of peanut butter and protein powder and shared with Emmet, who eagerly awaited his daily "smoovie."

I was grateful my dietary needs were being met, and I felt much better physically, but my emotions were another topic altogether. I began to desperately miss my home, my friends, my family, and Mollie. Getting through each day became grueling and made my lonely and boring life in Burlington seem like heaven. To cheer me up, we were sent to Rutland to visit Mason's family. It was Thanksgiving weekend, and I was feeling the void of the usual festivities of the season, as the Twelve Tribes don't celebrate "worldly" holidays. It did boost my spirits to think of going away for the weekend and seeing all our Rutland friends for the first time since we'd been baptized. We would also get to see André's family, and I invited my mother to come down for celebration, which she agreed to do.

It was just after dawn when we set out, and I remember putting Emmet in his car seat and getting into the passenger seat, feeling absolutely thrilled. It dawned on me that I hadn't been in a vehicle with my family since the Maine trip two months prior. My entire life consisted of the two community households and the walk down Main St. to the café. My world had become so small.

Benson was our first stop. André's mom offered me food, and I ravenously devoured two big hamburgers. They were the best hamburgers I'd ever had. We soon headed to Rutland, and I met my mom along with my little sister and brother in the parking lot of the soap shop. It was wonderful to see them, and she had all kinds of gifts for Emmet. We felt like royalty, entering the gathering as baptized members. People made such a to-do about us. I pulled my eight-year-old sister, Kalli, into the children's dances, my mom was taking pictures, and even my brother, Bradley, was clapping along to songs. They were really enjoying themselves, and I felt affirmed, like God was showing me we really had made a good decision. My spirits were high. It was great to see Mason and Joanna, she and I bonding over the shared difficulties of our pregnancies coupled with each having a two-year-old.

We had an enjoyable weekend, and on Sunday morning, as an afterthought, I suggested trying to see some of my relatives on the way home. My grandparents, father, and many aunts, uncles and cousins all lived in the White River Junction area, so we'd be passing right through. I hadn't seen any of them since we moved into the community. André agreed, so I called my grandmother and asked to meet later at my Aunt Kim's house. Unfortunately, the weather didn't cooperate. My dad and grandparents lived miles out in the middle of nowhere up a steep, windy dirt road.

We still went to my aunt's house and had a pleasant visit with her, and I talked to my dad and grandmother on the phone. Because it was Thanksgiving weekend, she had already put up some outdoor Christmas lawn ornaments. I remember looking at the lit-up reindeer in her yard as we pulled out. It really hit me that we were not going to be involved in the family festivities this year. The year before had been Emmet's first Christmas, which my grandmother had delighted in. The holidays had always been so special for me growing up, as I had many younger siblings and cousins, and we always had a big family gathering on Christmas Eve. Often, it was at this particular aunt's house, so I had years of fond memories there. I didn't know when I would see any of them again.

My mood got heavier and heavier as we headed back to Hyannis. I wished more than anything that André would suddenly turn around and go back to Vermont. I'd be back in the kitchen with Emmet the next day. And the day after that. I didn't have the excitement of the holidays with my family coming up. Christmas would be just another normal day there. I started missing my old life terribly. Regret was consuming me.

By the time we got home, Emmet was sound asleep. We had started weaning him at night, and I had taken to sleeping up in a little loft in our room so that he knew nursing wasn't an option when he woke up to only his father in our bed. André put Emmet in his bed, and I climbed up into the loft and curled up on my mattress, using pregnancy as a convenient excuse to go straight to bed. The rest of the household was preoccupied with a single brother's appreciation night. I had been involved for a couple weeks prior in learning a song that we were going to present to them as an "offering" along with a special dessert. I could hear the song being sung through the thin walls of our room. "*We appreciate you, from the depths of our hearts, our eyes behold your worth and dignity . . .*" I cried myself to sleep.

I woke up the next morning feeling depressed. André let me sleep in, and someone brought breakfast to my room. He was treading lightly, sensing I was suffering. He must have said something to the women, because soon Milkah knocked on my door. I poured everything out to her in a deluge of tears. I was homesick and missed my family, friends, and even my dog. I remember her grabbing my hands and looking imploringly into my eyes and saying, "Our Father has so much more for you than just dogs! He has given you a people to love for eternity! Your family and friends now have hope for their lives through you!"

(Years later I would have more understanding about dogs. There is a teaching called *We Do Not Touch Dogs*. Dogs were considered unclean in Israel. They were scavengers, and therefore disciples would never even touch them. If we did, we would be unclean and would need to shower. The close relationships that people in the world have with their dogs was trivialized and belittled. We were told it was the void of meaningful human relationships that caused people to turn to pets to make up for this lack. It was unnatural and base. Most TT children were petrified of dogs, and it was always awkward when we'd take a walk and meet someone with a dog. Often, they'd ask our children if they'd like to pet it, and we'd have to find some inoffensive way to explain the reason the children recoiled in horror.)

I tried to take courage from Milkah's words. I was now an important instrument in God's hands. Being chosen came at a great cost that was often painful—crucifying your flesh and dying to yourself. I needed to be a beacon of hope to all those I loved.

A few days later, I got a package in the mail from my dad's parents. It was an early Christmas gift for Emmet. In the privacy of our room, I let him open it. It was a toy train, complete with lights and sounds. Nothing like that was allowed. I quickly took out the batteries and let him push it around the floor, his pure delight bittersweet to me. I missed my grandparents so much and knew my grandmother would be suffering not having us there for Christmas. I crumpled up the festive Santa Claus wrapping paper and shoved it to the bottom of my trash can. I started to plummet again.

That evening, André was working through preparation time (the hour preceding the gatherings, meant as a time for families to read the Bible together and "prepare" for the minchah), so I was in our room alone with Emmet. I didn't know what to do with myself and ended up getting the household's cordless phone and calling Annie. I completely broke down on the phone with her. I told her I hated it there, missed everyone and everything about my old life, needed a break, and just wanted to relax and watch a movie. She did her best to remain calm and say things to help me "overcome," but in reality, this freaked her out because she blamed herself for our being there in the first place.

The next day, André arranged for Emmet to spend time with another woman and got Benyamin to come to our room for a meeting. His mother had emailed him and let him know about my phone call to her. He didn't know what to do, and asked wasn't that the reason we had joined a community? So there would be help when we needed it? I remember crying inconsolably and saying repeatedly, "I just want to go *home*." Benyamin looked at me with kind eyes and simply said "You *are* home." I looked pleadingly at André, who nodded in agreement and said, "We're not going anywhere."

This was the first time he had used his husbandly authority with me. I literally felt the walls of the room closing in on me and had an overwhelming sense of panic and entrapment. What had I done? I didn't want to be here. I'd made a big mistake. André didn't understand—his life hadn't changed as dramatically as mine. He didn't have to drastically change his entire wardrobe, and he left each day with the men to work on jobs in town, often getting coffee at Dunkin' and eating decent lunches. He loved working on the new house at night and had already been entrusted with a cell phone and, often, a vehicle. He had quickly become indispensable and much appreciated. Meanwhile, I was stuck at that dismal house in the kitchen all day, spanking Emmet constantly and missing my old life. The community calls this being "discontented with your portion."

At night in bed, I had started closing my eyes and remembering the sounds of our house in Burlington: the heat kicking on, the phone ringing, a hockey game on TV, the sound of Mollie's nails clicking on the hardwood floors, her whimpering at the back door to be let out. I didn't want to forget. I'd fantasize that I would open my eyes and be back there, and this all would have been an absurd dream. But it wasn't. This was my life now. I was "longing for Egypt," desiring to go back to the world after I'd been set free from its bondage. I had a toddler, and I was pregnant. André was resolute, and I didn't have the gall to leave him and be a single parent at the age of twenty-three. The irony was that it was my fault we were there in the first place. I'd been discontented in Burlington, longing to live in the community, and now I'd give anything to go back. What was wrong with me?

I am a firm believer that no matter where you are in the world or what you believe, there is a higher power—a God or creator—who can help us. So, two things happened at this dark time that served to increase my faith and help me get through the next few months. And not because I was in the TT and had access to the Holy Spirit but because I was desperate and pleading for help from the God I had believed in since I was a little girl.

The first thing that happened was Mason and Joanna's family moved back. I now had a friend and ally, someone in the same place in life who was kind and understanding and gave me the courage daily to keep going. This was huge.

Christmas Day arrived, a depressing, dreary, normal Monday. The household knew it would be hard for me, so during our boys' nap they sent Joanna and me to the café to have a nice lunch and take a walk together. It helped to do something special with her, and the hearty café food was delicious.

The second thing to happen was the Camp Street house was sold, and we moved to the Main Street property, most of us cramming into the already full Carriage House until the new house was complete. One small family even had to live in a shed inside which they put up a tent and made it as cozy and warm as they could with the help of a space heater. A few single men slept in a storage loft at the café. We were put in a tiny room right next to the laundry room on the first floor. This move happened in early January.

The greatest benefit of this situation was that there was no kitchen at this house. No more long days cooking with Emmet. All our meals had to be made at the café, where we couldn't work with little children for hours because disciplining them consistently would be a problem. We couldn't have whacking rods and crying children within earshot of patrons. So, all the women were given one day a week that our children were watched at home, and we went to the café to make supper for that night and lunch for the next day. There was even a single woman at the café set apart for a few hours to support. This was manageable—I could finally learn how to cook without the constant need of trying to give Emmet a "will" and spanking him when he wasn't obeying me. And I was able to spend a few hours with adults and have conversations! The other fabulous bonus was being able to order off the menu at lunchtime! I looked forward to my cooking day now!

Meals were sent home and set out in the laundry room, the only common area. We'd duck through the laundry hanging from the ceiling pipes to serve our families from the washers and dryers, which would be topped with steaming pots of soup and containers of salad. Since our bedroom was right next door, we'd often invite single brothers to eat with us. They'd perch on a corner of our or Emmet's bed or just sit on the floor of our tiny room. We started learning the importance of making the best of any situation.

The pace of our days slowed dramatically, and they weren't nearly as stressful as before. I'd be doing laundry, light cleaning, or spending time with another woman learning to sew or going for walks. I was invited on a few thrift store shopping excursions during this time and realized I loved helping look through people's needs lists and finding said items. It was like a treasure hunt. I also loved the fellowship of being out and about with another woman all day.

My twenty-fourth and Emmet's second birthdays occurred during this time. I had to adjust to no longer celebrating birthdays, as the community outlook was that it was the mother who does all the suffering on the day a child is born, therefore she is the one who deserves the honor. A child who is old enough to do so may make an announcement at the gathering, such as, "I'm thankful my Imma gave birth to me eight years ago." Occasionally a treat would be made for the mother, but there were no gifts or parties for the child or adult whose birthday it was.

André managed to obtain a couple Hershey's bars on my birthday, and I stashed them in a drawer, savoring one little section at a time over the next several weeks.

My morning sickness had ended as my pregnancy advanced, and I was enjoying my prenatals with the women. It was strange for me to not hear the baby's heartbeat until nearly twenty-six weeks. During prenatals, we would use a normal stethoscope or a wooden cone-shaped tool to listen for the baby's heartbeat. This made it common to not hear a heartbeat until the woman was at least twenty weeks or more, depending on the position of the baby. I asked why we didn't get a simple Doppler as all it did was magnify the sounds. It wasn't in any way intrusive. I was told that Old Israel didn't use them, so we didn't either. I pointed out that we use many things Old Israel didn't—phones, computers, cars, and more. I was corrected for "reasoning" and told pregnancy was about trusting Our Father, and we didn't need modern conveniences to do that. Those other things I mentioned were "tools" we used only to further our Father's purpose. A few years later, one of the head midwives was losing her hearing, and she got a Doppler. But it was clear it was only for her special situation, not an example for others to follow.

The baby was pretty active, and everything was progressing normally, so that helped me not worry too much. I was seven months along when my mother asked if we could stay with my sister and brother for a few days while she attended a dental convention. She was a lab technician for an orthodontics office. André and I had to "submit" our request to the council of the community "government"—the leading men. To my surprise, we were covered to go. I was feeling much more stable and secure, so there was confidence that I wouldn't have another setback. I was still nursing Emmet, as I had concern about him getting enough calcium through the community diet alone—there was a stigma against drinking cow's milk. It was used solely to make yogurt, which we ate only on Fridays and Saturday mornings.

People told me we ate things like sesame seeds, carob, and greens for calcium, but I was concerned about all the children who had serious dental needs that largely went unmet because we had no insurance for such things and couldn't afford to pay out of pocket.

The midwives were concerned about the drain on my body by continuing to nurse in my third trimester, and I was strongly encouraged to wean Emmet. I knew I needed to trust the direction that was coming from my sisters and decided I would wean him at my mom's. We were up there for four days with my sister and brother, who were nine and twelve, respectively, at the time. I nursed Emmet for the last time, sitting on my mom's bed the morning we were going back to Hyannis. This time, I wasn't dreading going back to the community. Life had been more bearable over the past few months. We had a wedding coming up in Plymouth that I was looking forward to, and work was almost completed on the Main House. We were being given a big, beautiful new room to have the baby in.

We pulled into the driveway in the early evening and were surprised to see most of the community outside at the back of the property. Excited children came running over to the vehicle to greet us and beckon us over to see what everyone was looking at. We pulled a sleepy Emmet from his car seat and walked over to see our new milking goats grazing happily in their new enclosure! While we had been gone, the community had obtained these two recently freshened goats from the community in Bellows Falls, Vermont. We would now have plenty of fresh milk available for the children to drink every day! I couldn't even believe it—the very day I weaned Emmet, still concerned about his nutrition, and goats arrived! That situation increased my faith that I could trust the Body to meet our needs and that God was looking after us and was pleased with us. Those goats served to restore my fortitude to press on.

Chapter 7

The Land of Plenty

ust a few months after we were baptized, we began hearing of a monumental event that would take place for two weeks during the coming summer on the Mall in Washington, D.C. It was called "Rekindling The Fire: The Birth of a Nation." This was to be an "extravaganza" to showcase our life to the thousands of people who frequented the Mall daily. Every tribe would be represented, with booths set up to display the various cottage industries or other areas of interest that made their location unique. There would be beautiful posters on display throughout the event and a huge gallery with pictures of the different communities and households. There would be a theater where plays would be presented on a rotating schedule. There would be a huge open-forum table for invoking passionate debates, and of course, the centerpiece would be the enormous Common Ground mobile café. There would be music and dancing all day, and the eye-catching Peacemaker buses and psychedelically painted "Hippie Bus" would be there. It would kick off with a big torch-lighting ceremony mimicking the Olympics, with everyone singing the emotional theme song written just for the event. This was to be the event of a lifetime.

Preparation would take months, and everyone would be called on to serve in some way to support the great endeavor. Just planning the meals for all the disciples was going to be a huge undertaking. There would be at least one hundred community people there who would need sleeping quarters and a kitchen. It was like setting up a refugee camp.

All disciples who were honored to be sent needed to represent the TT and the image we wanted to portray. It's hard to fathom how much was spent in money and time, between the various communities sewing new wardrobes for the women and finding quality button-up shirts and khakis for the men. No one could go with old, worn shoes—that wouldn't be a light to the nations. So new shoes were obtained for all who needed them. It seemed like money was not an issue all of a sudden, and no expense was spared for this event.

Of course, that meant those of us not chosen to attend had to be willing to "sacrifice" our needs for the greater good. Our children had to wait a bit longer for the new shoes they needed, or we had to cut back on the household food budget temporarily. But the excitement over this event spread like a virus through the communities, and we were all full of vision and anticipation, fully willing to make whatever sacrifices were necessary. We heard we were finally "fishing with nets," and the multitudes were going to come flooding in as a result. I felt so lucky that we had joined at this pivotal moment in history.

It was because of this event that our family ended up moving to Plymouth. The timing was difficult. I was eight months pregnant and finally feeling secure, even happy, in Hyannis. Joanna had had her baby—a boy—and I was looking forward to moving into the new house and spending the summer with her, our new babies, and our little boys.

It started out, as those things often do, with André and I being called to Plymouth for "three weeks." Not many in the tribes had his computer skills, and they greatly needed his expertise on all poster layout, printing, literature, and other technology-related endeavors. He went a day ahead of Emmet and I, and the next day, as Benyamin was driving us over, I asked, "We are definitely coming back, right?"

"Yes, of course," he confidently assured me.

Plymouth consisted of the enormous Warren Avenue house (which was under construction to be a showcase house for BOY—Builders of Yehudah—a construction crew that functioned mainly out of Plymouth), the Blue Blinds House in town, and a Common Sense Wholesome Food Market—and we would soon buy the Yellow House next door to Warren Ave. The community was full and consisted of a majority of "first-generation" couples and young adults. (First generation is how we referred to the children and young adults who had been born to "the stem," the group of people who first joined in the '70s and '80s or joined from the "world" and were grafted in, such as André and I. Our children would be second generation, and so on.) We were put in the bedroom of a young, childless couple, and they took up temporary residence in a small camper at the back of the property.

That began a long and exhausting three weeks. With the entire house under construction, it was common to leave my room and navigate a gauntlet of extension cords, sawhorses, and power tools to get my big, pregnant body to the kitchen or laundry room with two-year-old Emmet in tow. Naps were a challenge with a constant background noise of hammering, nail guns, skill saws, and the periodic shouting and conversation of at least a half dozen men. I ran a box fan on high to try to drown out some noise but was lucky if Emmet slept an hour before being startled awake by the cacophony.

Emmet and I rarely saw André unless we walked down to the print shop. He and three other men were taking shifts, printing enormous posters 24/7. They had a mat set up on the floor in a corner for a rotation of naps. Our two-year anniversary occurred during that time, and André was generously given a couple hours to come home and see us. We didn't get the same treatment as the year before when we'd been guests! I wasn't put on the women's schedule, because we were just there temporarily, but I helped out where I could in the kitchen and the household.

It soon became clear that my family was not going back to Hyannis. Plymouth was a hub for several community-run businesses, and André's business and computer skills were needed far more there than his construction skills were needed in Hyannis. He would still be invaluable once the DC whirlwind was over. So, we were moved to a permanent room in the house, and our things were packed up and sent from Hyannis.

There would be two more DC events over the next couple years, each demanding an unfathomable level of time, effort, and expenses. Each year we heard much prophesying about the multitudes coming in, bringing "the wealth of the nations." But it didn't happen. There was only one single brother who was "saved" throughout all the DC events, and he became jokingly referred to as "the million-dollar disciple."

But there was never an "oops, our bad" when prophecy was not fulfilled and thousands of new disciples did not come pouring in. Instead, prophecy just changed to fit the reality, and we were told that seeds sometimes take years to sprout. We may not see the actual fruit of these events for years, but we were not to lose faith. Many felt that these three extravagant events were a huge waste of time and resources, but we could never voice any skepticism or disapproval, or we would be rebuked for our lack of faith, trust, and respect.

I was so worried my baby would be born during the whirlwind DC event, which sometimes brought our household down to only five people. A birth would have been difficult to accommodate, although I was glad to be near my due date, knowing that was the only reason André hadn't been sent down to the event. Out of my four children, Meyshar was the only one who came late, six days after my due date and a few days after everyone had returned and recuperated from the DC extravaganza.

There were many responsibilities for a pregnant woman in the TT, so many in fact that a lot of women made themselves a "faithful chart" with all their daily duties to be checked off. If you weren't faithful to all the important things our Father had spoken about in order to have a safe birth and healthy baby, then those things were not guaranteed, and anything that went wrong could and would be blamed on your lack of diligence. Things did not just randomly go wrong during a pregnancy or birth. Any complications would result in a judgment meeting to find out what "sin" Our Father was trying to expose.

Hospital births were not outlawed but were looked upon with disfavor. Only those who lacked faith in Our Father would prefer the "worldly" doctors over the wisdom of the Body. There were emergency situations in which women were taken to the hospital, but there were many unfortunate stories of times when intervention could have saved a baby's life. But those aren't my stories to tell . . .

A pregnant woman was expected to drink two quarts of water and two quarts of red raspberry tea every day. We were to take a brisk twenty-minute walk and our prenatal vitamin daily. Floor exercises were assigned to strengthen our core. Sometime around thirty-two weeks, we were to start perineal massage—where our husbands literally stretched us to prevent tearing—and nipple preparation, where we roughly rubbed our nipples with a washcloth to prepare for nursing. Many women were anemic and had to take yellow dock tincture or some other iron supplement, such as "grape and egg." This was grape juice blended with raw eggs. Most of us also took chlorophyll or spirulina and squaw vine tincture.

Meyshar's birth was so fast and peaceful and happened during the day on a Sabbath, not causing anyone to miss a night of sleep! Her birth really increased my faith, as I'd been overwhelmed by the pain and taken a mild narcotic during Emmet's labor. I knew I wasn't going to have that option this time. But I had been faithful to all the responsibilities of a pregnant woman, and I felt proud when, after the birth, one of the head midwives said that I was made for having babies. Meyshar nursed and slept great from the get-go, and I felt so blessed.

Emmet absolutely adored her and didn't even go through a jealous phase. "Is that yours?" was his fascinated response when he was brought into the room to meet her.

Along with having a girl comes the eighty days. The community abided by Leviticus 12:1–5:

> *The Lord spoke to Moses, saying, "Speak to the people of Israel, saying, 'If a woman conceives and bears a male child, then she shall be unclean seven days. As at the time of her menstruation, she shall be unclean. And on the eighth day the flesh of his foreskin shall be circumcised. Then she shall continue for thirty-three days in the blood of her purifying. She shall not touch anything holy, nor come into the sanctuary, until the days of her purifying are completed. But if she bears a female child, then she shall be unclean two weeks, as in her menstruation. And she shall continue in the blood of her purifying for sixty-six days.'"*

During this time, a woman would not go to any gathering in which she wore a head covering and functioned as a priest, nor would she serve in the household on the regular schedule. It was also expected that a husband and wife would not "come together," the community's way to say "have sex," during this time. At the end of forty or eighty days came the baby's dedication, when its name would be revealed to the community and the parents would publicly dedicate the child to God and the Body. Then the parents would be sent away for a short time.

I was really looking forward to this break. It was summer, and for the first time since joining I'd have freedom with my children during the day. The first week I had lots of help, since postpartum women weren't to be going up and down stairs for at least seven days. Another woman in the house would offer to have Emmet for a few hours in the morning, then we would all nap together.

The hardest thing at that point was the heat. We were in a room that was blasted with sun nearly all day and would be over 90 degrees by evening. I couldn't swaddle my baby—something that was considered very important, as we were supposed to start the process of bringing our children under control in infancy through swaddling. So, the household got me a small AC, which was such a blessing.

Soon I was able to go up and down stairs, and the help dwindled away. It was a challenge to know how to fill the day. Emmet didn't have many toys, there was no TV (which I really didn't miss at all at this point; I hardly ever thought about it), and we weren't close enough to a park or the beach to walk there. Meyshar was a great sleeper, and I'd want to leave the room when she was napping so Emmet wouldn't wake her up. So even though this was my "break," I ended up in the kitchen nearly every day with Emmet, just helping with one small task such as peeling cucumbers. It was manageable because I was under no pressure to "complete my deeds." I was free to leave as soon as my baby woke up or Emmet started acting up, and there was no expectation for me to return.

Living in Plymouth came with the opportunity to live with Meshiah and Sheqer. Meshiah was our "apostle." They started the community when they opened their home to needy young people in Chattanooga in the '70s. They called themselves the Vine Christian Community, and after having their Bible study canceled for a Super Bowl party, they became their own church. They opened delis where they could all work together for the common good, more and more people joined their group, and the rest is history.

Sheqer was tall, with blond hair and a high-pitched, California Valley girl voice. Meshiah came across as the warm, grandfatherly type who enjoyed going to the Salvation Army on senior discount day and finding the men nice clothes for a dollar. They weren't at all intimidating, but it was obvious they weren't "normal" disciples. They had the most beautiful suite at the Warren

Avenue house, complete with a private bathroom and an office. I never saw Sheqer make a meal or clean any common areas. They had their own car, came and went as they pleased, and were pretty much left alone. I never spent much time one-on-one with either of them. We of course consulted them on the name of our daughter, Meyshar.

One day, Sheqer excitedly came to my room holding a handful of papers. "Well!" she exclaimed in her squeaky voice. "I found out the name Meyshar is actually a masculine name." I must have looked disappointed because she quickly said, "But that's OK, because so is Sheqer!" She absolutely loved the name and had printed out lots of information on its origin, where it was found in the Bible, and more. I felt honored she had taken such an interest in my daughter.

Living with Meshiah meant gatherings were sometimes as long as two hours. He would give a teaching, and then many people would share the revelations they gained. André would inevitably bring an exasperated Emmet to me at some point and return solo to the gathering, so I'd be twiddling my thumbs in our room, waiting for the gathering to end.

I started to wish I could go sometimes, simply for the social interaction and to hear something, anything, of interest. It's amazing that when you cut out all entertainment from your life—TV, radio, computers, newspapers, magazines, books, and music—you don't necessarily know you miss it, especially when you are kept busy all the time. But you start to crave any information or distraction that you can get, no matter how small, and even more so when you are with a toddler and infant all day and have limited adult interaction.

Sometimes they would gather outside on a patio near the house, and if André still had Emmet and Meyshar was asleep, I'd go into a room nearby and sit by an open window. Just listening to the singing and hearing part of Meshiah's teaching and a few people share seemed so nice. People told me it was because the Holy Spirit inside me was yearning to hear what Our Father was speaking. I know now it was just desperate boredom, and I think I would have been equally fascinated by watching a chess tournament on TV or listening to an infomercial.

One evening, after a particularly long gathering, André finally came into the room, where I'd been watching the clock, trying to calm a fussy baby and keep a tired and hungry Emmet entertained. I was starving, as dinner was after the gathering.

"That was ridiculous!" I exclaimed, referring to the length of the minchah. I was not expecting André's response.

"You want me to tell Meshiah to cut Our Father short next time?" he shot back at me, rebuking me for my disrespect. Meshiah was our Apostle, so I was basically complaining that God had spoken through him for too long. Stunned, I muttered an apology and said we were just hungry.

My eighty days were passing by. One day, I was looking through boxes of our things that had been sent from Hyannis and saw I still had a couple classical music CDs. I thought that would bring a welcome reprieve to our day, as Emmet loved music. I borrowed a CD player from a woman down the hall and put in my *Mozart for Babies* CD. He lit right up and began dancing happily around the room. It felt good to have music playing, and it gave me a little more energy to delve into cleaning.

A few minutes later there was a knock at my door. One of the women had overheard the music and had come to let me know that "we" didn't listen to classical music. She explained that it wasn't written by men of the Holy Spirit, so we didn't know what spirits were motivating and affecting the composers. It could therefore impart other, unclean spirits to us if we "gave ourselves up to it." We also didn't want to instill in our children a love for "worldly" music. I didn't fully understand the spiritual implications she spoke of but didn't want to be "in trouble," so I humbly received this new revelation and handed over my CDs. They ended up being sold in a yard sale the following week.

(Years later, we were told it was not even good to listen to community music in your bedroom during the day because it would dull you from lifting up your spirit to the music at the gatherings. I suffered under this rule since I loved and needed music so much. I wasn't obedient. I had found a small CD player at the local thrift shop and often had music playing quietly in my bedroom, as it seemed to help lighten the atmosphere. It was my oasis, my lifesaver amid difficult times. I'd close myself in my room, play music, and just breathe. I managed to obtain a pretty wide selection of acceptable music—mostly weddings, the DC event, music festivals, or the few "worldly" folk artists that had been sanctioned as OK and were played in our cafés. I knew which other women also discreetly listened to music, and we'd swap CDs.)

My eighty days came to an end, and Meshiah and Sheqer were at Meyshar's dedication, which was communicated to us as being an enormous honor. Meshiah gave André the name "Yeshurun" during the dedication. He saw how my husband judged fairly during volleyball games, even to his own team's hurt, so chose this name meaning "just judge" in Hebrew. I hated the name. I thought it sounded strange and could not get used to calling him that.

Months later, I was still calling him André. One day I called the Tribal Trading office where he worked, and a single brother, Zachariah, answered the phone. He was funny, and I always enjoyed being around him because he made everyone laugh. "Is André there?" I asked.

"No, sorry, there is no one who works here who goes by that name," came his sarcastic response. Then he hung up the phone! I was not laughing at this particular joke. I called back and asked through gritted teeth, "Is Yeshurun there?"

"Why, yes he is!" came his exaggerated response. I begrudgingly began to call André by his new name. He became a different person to me from that point on.

It's quite common when someone gets baptized that they are given a new, Hebrew name. Someone would have had a revelation about who they really were. It also was not uncommon for a man to rename his bride on their wedding day. But someone could have a revelation anytime about who someone else was and proclaim it at a gathering. The person being given the new name would be asked if they received it (except in the example of a husband renaming his wife; she was not asked in that situation). I never saw someone say no, so I don't know what would have happened if that had been the case. I was always so thankful no one ever gave me a new name. My mother named me Tamara—a Hebrew name meaning "palm tree"—but I went by Tami mostly, so it seemed to me that my true name had been preserved. I simply became Tamara "shel" Yeshurun. Shel is Hebrew for "wife of." That is how we referred to married women.

Unless you lived with someone when they first moved in, you might never know what a person's real name was. It's interesting now, being on Facebook and seeing a friend request from a name I never heard before but then realizing it's someone I lived with for years! The TT would be phenomenal for the witness protection program.

❧❧❧

After Meyshar's dedication, we were sent for our time away (six days) at a camp in Rhode Island that belonged to someone's parents. We had barely been gone three days when the community needed the vehicle back and asked if we minded coming home early. I was disappointed and relieved at the same time. It had been more than a year since we had been alone for that amount of time, and it was sort of awkward.

I was put on the household schedule and was mainly in the kitchen with my two-and-a-half-year-old and three-month-old. Luckily, Meyshar slept through the night at five weeks old, because breakfast mornings started at 4:30 a.m. We had to first cook and serve the men who were going out on jobs, then get their lunches ready, and then start on the household breakfast.

I was starting to learn more about the community's expectations for wives and mothers by this time. I recall a few married women's meetings in Plymouth, most of them around the time of a wedding. The main topic always centered on submission. As wives, we chose to submit every day, giving our husbands the dignity and respect they deserved as our "head." It was never our place to question them, usurping their authority, especially on matters of the family. Even though we were the mothers and were with the children all day, we should never conduct ourselves in a manner suggesting we knew more, or better, about "their" children. It's made very clear in the TT that children belong to the Abbas, not the Immas.

At this point, I was still outspoken and wanted a tangible example of what this would look like in everyday life. I asked what to do if my husband came home, saw the baby was fussy, and told me to go put her to bed, but I knew she'd just had a nap, was fussy because she was teething, and probably wouldn't sleep again for another few hours. Was it OK for me to tell him this, since it was simply information he wasn't aware of? One of the women spoke up and said if she were in that situation, she would humbly tell her husband about the nap and teething but say that she was willing to try to put the baby back to bed if that's what he wanted. We needed to respond with grace, never seeming strong in our thoughts or ideas and never interrupting, arguing, contradicting, or correcting our husbands.

Things like this made me squirm internally, but once the meeting was over, life would go on as normal. In the privacy of our bedroom, I knew my husband wasn't analyzing all our conversations or upholding me to the perfectly submissive "community speak" of women. But the fact that he could if he wanted to, and I could be in trouble or "cut off" for being disrespectful to him, remained always in the back of my mind. I really had to be on guard with how I spoke to him, especially around others.

❦

When Meyshar was four months old, I was invited to attend midwifery classes in preparation for the next birth, and I was asked to be on the team! I was beyond excited. Midwifery was one of the nicest things to be involved with for women in the community. I assisted in nine births during my fourteen years in the TT. We had monthly prenatals in which we checked fundal height, maternal weight gain, baby's heartbeat, and so on. As the due date drew nearer, the checkups became more frequent, and there were more responsibilities for the expectant mother and the birth team to attend to.

At my first midwifery class, I respectfully sat and listened as a twenty-one-year-old girl explained the components of the cell. Did they realize I had aced college-level anatomy and physiology just a few years prior? I should have been teaching her! But no, we didn't discuss the merits of our lives before being saved. All our worldly knowledge was rubbish compared to the teachings. I was just happy to have something to be involved with, and I knew I'd have to start somewhere. Being a midwife would be a dream.

We grew close to the women on our birth team, as everyone took turns palpating and measuring during prenatals, and at week thirty-eight, we began internal exams to check for dilation and effacement. Ideally, a woman was taken off the schedule a couple weeks before her due date, to give her some "nesting" time. There was a lot to prepare, for both the birth team and the mother. Someone on the team would be in charge of "packs." There was a cord pack, a suture pack, etc. The instruments were packaged into clean white cloths, tied, and then baked in the oven to guarantee sterility.

The mother had a list of needs and usually was given money for a nice shopping trip with her husband to buy all the typical things—disposable diapers (these were permitted for the first few weeks), baby wipes, bulb syringe, baby nail clippers, and whatever else hadn't been supplied through hand-me-downs. Newborn clothing made its rounds from community to community, and usually each community had totes we could go through and then return the clothes after our baby outgrew them for the next woman who needed them. Sometimes the mother would sew new baby bedding.

A couple weeks before I had Meyshar, I found some cotton fabric in the free store. (Every community had a free store, which was basically a household clothing drop-off. Ideally, it was organized like a little thrift store.) It was white-and-peach checkered, and on the white checks were little blue rocking horses. I enlisted the help of another woman to make bumper pads for my cradle and a matching blanket. I never finished the blanket, but another woman gave me a handmade, patchwork baby quilt that was the perfect size. It clashed horribly with my rocking horse bumper pads, being mostly dark green and purple hues, but it was in good shape, and my baby wouldn't care that its cradle wasn't perfectly coordinated.

Not long after Meyshar was born, a few of the first-generation women who had been married that spring were pregnant. When they all got nearer their due dates and began preparing for their babies, I noticed a stark contrast to me finding fabric in the free store. The sewing shop in Plymouth was run by a woman named Mary Martha, and she supplied fabric to all the communities in the region to make clothing or other household necessities, such as curtains or tablecloths. She would make runs to New York City to find good deals, bring back loads of new fabrics, and make sets of swatches that she mailed to each community. The arrival of new swatches was always such an exciting day!

So, all these young women were obtaining beautiful velvets and richly colored upholstery fabrics from the sewing shop and making elaborate bed sets for their newborns. The bumper pads were trimmed with gold cording, and there would even be several little accent pillows, complete with gold tassels and lace trim. These sets were so beautiful and professional looking, nicer than anything I'd ever had on my own bed.

Suddenly I felt bad about the shoddy, mismatched bedding that my daughter had. She had graduated to a normal crib by this time, and I'd made do once again with whatever I could find in the free store or whatever hand-me-downs had come my way. She didn't have a single decorative throw pillow in her crib, not to mention ones with gold tassels to boot. It was as though these young women were trying to outdo each other, as one woman even managed velvet curtains that matched her baby's bedding. I mentioned this to an older woman one day, who shook her head and said, "It looks like those sets are made for royalty. Why can't we just let babies be babies?" In other words, mirroring how I had felt about my clashing cradle ensemble—the babies don't care.

I was also noticing these women were shopping at Baby Gap and Old Navy Baby. I'd see tags in the trash in the laundry room, and those babies' receiving blankets and pajamas were definitely not from the hand-me-downs I'd folded back up and returned to the baby totes. Hadn't I left all that behind? I used to have the freedom to shop for Emmet at those stores. Hadn't I chosen a simple life where there weren't "haves and have-nots," where we were all thankful for our hand-me-down baby clothes instead of desiring new ones from Old Navy? I remembered feeling "less" than my friends in junior high who could afford Guess jeans and Benetton sweaters. I was always jealous and preoccupied with figuring out how to obtain these prestigious articles of clothing. I had wanted something different for my son, but the same thing seemed to be happening even here, with God's people.

I asked someone about this and was told that every spirit had to be conquered in the Body, so it was to be expected that we would see all the same "sins," and it was our job to see how we could be saved through such circumstances. Maybe jealousy was an iniquity in me, and God perfectly coordinated that I would live there at that time and see what I considered to be gross inequality and be able to judge myself and overcome my jealousy. Everything could always be turned back on you. We were told every situation was carefully thought out by God to reveal our wrong ways, to "save" us. These materialistic women were part of God's plan to save me! That's how I had to think of it, instead of casting judgment upon them.

I took this seriously and developed a reputation in the community of being thankful for whatever I was provided with, which unfortunately leads to being given "whatever" and watching others who had higher standards get nicer things. There was by no means an equal distribution of wealth in the TT. "No rich or poor among them" is absolutely untrue. In fact, it was very well-known which regions were better off and which places had bad reputations for being poor. Plymouth, or, more accurately, the entire Massachusetts region, was dubbed "The Land of Plenty."

(In the years to come, after we'd moved, it was always glaringly obvious whenever a family from that region would visit for a weekend or when we would visit our relatives down there, that they were living an entirely different lifestyle from the Vermont and New York regions. This was because of their construction crew that had several contracts doing doors, windows, and trim for upscale nursing homes. They were raking in the money, as was obvious by their expensive vehicles, nice shoes and clothing, and the fact that a good many children and adults were a little on the "heavier" side—a testimony of their much richer diet.

Visiting their household free stores felt like shopping at a posh boutique. I would always bring back a couple bags for my community, and the women would shake their heads in disbelief that such nice, quality items had been discarded. The bedrooms we stayed in would be pristine, carefully decorated with beautiful area rugs, fancy candle sets, pretty baskets, tasteful paintings or tapestries on the walls, and, of course, gorgeous bedding. My older daughter would take careful note of the celebration shoes the girls had and who had a super-pretty jumper. We would be in awe that they had *two* kinds of fruit set out on Sabbath morning. It was like going to visit our rich relatives.)

One day the following spring, I was outside with Emmet and Meyshar. Emmet loved running around outdoors, but it was nap time, which he hated. As soon as I said it was time to go in, he screamed "NO" and threw himself on the ground in a full-on temper tantrum. Hefting Meyshar in one arm, I pulled Emmet up off the ground and began awkwardly making my way toward the house, with him screaming and trying to get out of my grip the whole way. I felt my frustration building and was using every ounce of self-control I had to keep calm. I wasn't yelling at him or saying much at all, I simply had my eyes on the goal of the back door, where of course I would bring him to our room and discipline him for resisting me and "pitching a fit."

I made it to the house and to our rooms, where I spanked Emmet, then spent the next harried hour getting both children down for a nap. Feeling worn out from the battle I had finally won, I emerged from my room, planning on making a restorative cup of maté and having a few moments of peace. As I was waiting for the water to boil, a mother in her thirties named Yaqara came into the kitchen and asked if she could talk to me. That was never good to hear. She had six children, all of whom were more of the "in-line" variety.

While it was recognized there were in- and out-of-line children, there was also the commonly heard phrase, "There are no bad children, only bad parents." So, it never failed that the lucky families who produced mellow and easygoing children were hard on those of us who had children with lots of energy and a "strong will." It was always our fault when our children acted up. Somehow it was the "fruit" of our bad parenting and never just a normal stage of childhood.

I followed her around the corner to the empty dining room. She was a tall woman and looked down to tell me that she had watched the scene with Emmet from her bedroom window and was shocked that I hadn't been commanding him but seemed passive as I was trying to get him in the house. She said I wasn't using my authority and it was obvious he wasn't respecting me as a result. I tried to explain how I didn't want to react to him and that I had disciplined him as soon as we got inside. (I hadn't yet come to the realization that you do not defend yourself at all when someone comes to you like this.) She said it was alarming how rebellious he already was and that I needed to do better putting a fear in him of acting that way, especially since I had a baby. He was barely three years old!

It wasn't until later, as I was still stewing, that I wondered, if she had been watching me struggling out there from her window, why didn't she come out to help me instead of coming to me with her judgments afterwards? This goes to show how there were scrutinizing eyes everywhere, and I always felt under the microscope. We lived in a state of constantly having to be worried about what others were thinking of us, never knowing when someone would come to us with their concerns.

A couple weeks later, I was coming down the hall holding Meyshar, when Emmet started having a fit about something and threw himself on the floor. I was trying to pull him up when Sheqer came around the corner. My heart dropped. I didn't want to look like a bad mother in front of *her*! She took in the scene and came over, squatting down next to the thrashing, crying Emmet. I didn't know what to expect and just stood there nervously. "Hi Emmet!" she said cheerfully. He immediately stopped as she took his

81

hands in hers and helped him stand up. "Why are you giving your Imma such a hard time?" she asked, sounding completely bewildered. Gesturing up at me she exclaimed, "Look at her! She loves you and your sister so much, and she needs your help! Are you ready to help your Imma?" He just stared at her, nodding his head. "Wonderful!" she exclaimed, patting him on the back, "That's a good boy!" Then she continued down the hall. I was so relieved as I called out, "Thank you!" She never mentioned the situation to me again. What a different response from the situation with Yaqara!

Chapter 8

The Needy among Us

s summer of 2002 was coming to an end, we were informed that the Tribal Trading office would be moving to the empty soap shop in Rutland, Vermont, to begin packaging and distributing the Maté Factor products (an assortment of maté-based products that were becoming popular at health food markets). The soap shop had moved to nearby Cambridge, New York, so we would bring this industry to Rutland to help the community there build a thriving industry to support them. We were happy to help because they had been struggling financially for several years.

I was excited to be returning to Vermont. We would be able to see Annie and Scottie and, hopefully, my relatives more often. Just the familiarity of my home state was comforting.

Rutland ended up being the community that I have the fondest memories from, though it wasn't nice physically or materially. Compared to Plymouth, the houses were run-down, furnishings and decor were basic and sparse, and food was simple and limited, and there were people who hadn't gotten new underwear for over five years. They were dirt poor. The only consistent personal-needs money came from the change in the tip jar at the café. A couple women crocheted hats to sell at the café to try and meet needs.

There were no fancy bed sets in anyone's room. I vividly remember being invited to a couple's room for preparation time our first day there, noting their old, worn bedspread and faded corduroy bedrest pillow, and breathing a sigh of relief. Everyone was in the same boat here; everyone was poor and grateful for anything they received. I felt I fit in better here, as most of the women had joined as adults like me, rather than being born there. I had gotten to know many of the families when we were visiting as guests and immediately felt accepted and at home, like I was living with old friends.

We first lived in the Lincoln Avenue house. It was an old house, in need of repairs, a stark contrast to the pristine, "showcase" house we had come from. It was hard to keep clean, such was the state of disrepair. Within a couple weeks, my daughter, who had barely been sick a day in her fourteen months of life, was spiking fevers so high that she had a seizure. I screamed in horror as I watched her collapse, her eyes rolling back in her head. Miriam lived in the room next door and came running into my room to find me holding her limp body. We immediately called for a brother who had EMT training to come to the house. She was revived by the time he got there, and he said it was simply a febrile seizure, as her temperature had spiked quickly up to 103. We didn't rush to the hospital for things like this.

Soon after, massive amounts of black mold were found in the basement and kitchen, and it was suggested we move to another house. We then lived at the Green House.

By now it was nearly winter, and we were so poor that we could only afford to keep the heat at fifty degrees, except for an hour in the morning and an hour in the evening when we could turn it up to sixty. It was forced hot air, so we always heard the telltale noise of it kicking on a few minutes before the precious heat began to blow into the room. One of the vents was on a wall of our bedroom, and I'll never forget how Emmet and Meyshar would run over to that vent and huddle in front of it as soon as they heard the heat kick on, waiting with great anticipation for the heat to start blowing on them. Then they would blissfully sit there, basking in the temporary warmth.

I kept them in hats 24/7, and Meyshar only came out of her snowsuit during the day for diaper changes. We all slept in one bed together, as it would get so cold at night that a glass of water on our bedside table would show signs of freezing by morning. We had no storm windows, and many of the panes were badly cracked. All windows had a thick layer of ice on them most of the time, which the children loved scratching designs in with their fingernails.

There was no hot water at this house either, so we all had to shower and bathe next door. That was burdensome with a one- and three-year-old, in the middle of an incredibly cold and snowy winter. We used cloth diapers, so one of the women at the house next door would send her twelve-year-old son back and forth on my laundry day with buckets of hot water for me to wash my diapers in. There was a "one dryer load per week" rule, and I always saved that for my diapers. Everything else was hung on a makeshift clothesline in a huge drying room in the basement, and on multiple drying racks.

There was also no functioning kitchen at the Green House. We had a portable hot plate to heat water on, a coffee maker, and a toaster. Meals were cooked next door, at the White House, and were never overwhelming, as lunch every day was some sort of beans and rice dish and dinners were an easy sandwich spread on bread or a simple soup. We could only afford olive oil for the tables for Friday night, something that had been a staple for every meal in Hyannis and Plymouth. We also could only afford fruit for Sabbath morning. The one provision we had was free milk from the community in Bellows Falls. Women would make five-gallon buckets of yogurt, and every night after the gathering all the children would flock to the bucket with a mug, eagerly awaiting their scoop and a small drizzle of molasses. No one went hungry, but we were all skinny as rails.

Luckily, the café baker's family lived at the Green House with us, and he would bring home bread ends from the café, which we would gladly toast, brush with a little cooking oil, and sprinkle with salt. His wife was a fun and determined sort and was always scrounging up spare change to procure a half pint of milk, like the kind you get in a cafeteria. There was a Beer King beverage mart just a few doors down from our house, and on her way back from a "brisk walk," she'd quickly duck in there and get the milk. Then, in the afternoon when our children were napping, we would make a pot of maté in the Mr. Coffee and indulge in hot, milky maté. You start to appreciate the tiniest things when you live like that, and it's amazing how adaptable humans are.

I had to get creative to care for my children's needs. When Emmet needed pajama pants, I found a couple men's turtlenecks in the free store that were ripped and stained on the front, but the sleeves were still in decent shape. I used the cuffs of the sleeves as cuffs for the little pants and successfully fashioned him a couple new pairs of sleeve leggings. We would find pretty, oversized women's dresses for free at the women's shelter, and cut them down to make clothes for the girls. I loved learning how to do this kind of thing, and effectively cut down a woman's dress for a six-year-old girl, who was thrilled about her "new" dress.

Chapter 9

Being Social

ll this may sound dreadful, and it definitely wasn't easy, but I look back on this time with fondness because of the camaraderie. I loved that we were all living like this together, and I felt like I had true friendships with the women. We worked together and looked out for one another, which is what I thought the community was all about. My husband and I were quickly integrated into the center of life and treated more like "equals" than new disciples. I began helping with personal needs, and when the women found out I had attended two births in Plymouth, they included me on the birth team of the only pregnant women at the time. We even began going regularly to the much-desired "Social Meeting."

There was a hierarchy when it came to meetings. The first level was the "Cooks' Meeting." This consisted of the wives of men who were in government. Before I ever went to a Cooks' Meeting, I remember seeing the group of ladies outside, sitting on a blanket in the sun. There was always a nice maté and usually a snack prepared for them. I'd feel a bit envious as I watched them out the window, talking and laughing together. I couldn't wait to be involved in that special fellowship one day. The women wore their head coverings to the Cooks' Meeting because they were in an official gathering, hearing from the Holy Spirit and talking about important matters that would be brought to the Social Meeting. Common topics of discussion included household and weekend schedules, food and budget issues, personal needs, and clothing standards.

The women were not supposed to make any decisions of importance in the meeting but were to come to an agreement on whatever was on the agenda for the day, and then present the information for further discussion at the

Social Meeting, which was made up of couples—the husbands and wives who were leaders in that community. It was like attaining some small level of elitism to regularly attend this meeting. The Social Meeting was all over the place as far as topics went. Sometimes it felt like a gossip session or like attending a reality show that you were living. We talked about couples who were struggling, children who were out of control, training groups, upcoming event planning, household moves—basically, any "social" issues that could come up in a community of fifty-plus people. It was the most entertaining evening of the week.

One of the most common topics was the continual rearrangement of households and bedrooms. Due to the frequency of families moving from one community to another and the unavoidable social conflicts of so many people living together, we were often changing up the households. We could be told one evening that our family was switching rooms or houses the following day, and we had to be surrendered and willing, expressing no resistance or bad attitude. We might even be called to leave behind furniture. We weren't supposed to be attached in any way to "our" possessions but were supposed to be willing to give them up at any time.

We also had to be willing to live in unusual situations. I saw people live in sheds, tents, closets, crawl spaces, attics, porches, basements, offices, campers, storage units, tepees, and even an old silo. We had our first two children sleeping in our bedroom with us until my third child was born. Often, siblings of the opposite sex had to share a bedroom even into the teen years when we were really full.

We could also be told we were moving to another community at any time. The motto was, "We come when we're called and go where we're sent."

The last in the order of meetings was the "Government Meeting," which was for the leading men only. This was the most important meeting of the week and could last for hours, starting early in the evening and going until 1:00 or 2:00 a.m. Here, final decisions would be made about the various topics discussed at the prior two meetings.

I felt needed and respected in Rutland, and I became more confident and outspoken, having ideas and bringing them up at the Social Meetings. I wasn't intimidated by any of the leaders or their wives.

Sometimes we were so busy with the meals and household needs that it was hard to get our children outside. A family had moved to Rutland from the community in Spain who had three-year-old twins with developmental disabilities stemming from being born prematurely. One day the mother asked me, "When do you take your children outside? It's so important they go out every day for fresh air, sunshine, and exercise." I knew she was right, and soon most of the other women and I started making a point to take them out every day, at least for a little while. We'd invite each other's children to join us, especially if we saw a woman trying to get supper done with several children. It really felt like a big family.

⁂

When Meyshar was around eighteen months old, I started having severe complications nursing her. I was cracked and bleeding and in extreme pain. I was put on many home remedies, mostly special diets, tinctures, and salves, and at one point even tried some kind of electrode therapy. Three times a day, I would plug this strange contraption of wires into a Tupperware container that was connected to two pieces of copper pipe. I was to hold on to these pipes for seven minutes. I did this faithfully for a while, with no change, and was getting desperate. At the Social Meeting, I had to explain my embarrassing problem in detail in front of the men. We were given permission for me to go see a doctor.

The doctor (an urgent care doctor) was no help. He put me on antibiotics in case I had an underlying infection, and I was just finishing up the prescription when, after a short six months, the winds of change blew on my family again. It was decided the community in Cambridge—the Common Sense Farm—needed André for the ever-growing soap shop. On April 6, 2003 we were packed up and heading to our fourth community.

I soon went to a woman named Atarah, a leader's wife who was involved in midwifery, and explained what was going on with my nursing situation. She asked me to write down everything that had been tried in Rutland, and eyebrows were raised at the extensive and bizarre list I produced. It was decided I had systemic yeast and was put on a diet of zero sugars and had to do cabbage and clay poultices for forty-five minutes every day. I was also told to wean my daughter, which I did, and healed right up.

Chapter 10

Salvation Station

oving to Cambridge was a culture shock. Aesthetically, it was amazing—a beautiful 114-acre farm tucked into the rolling hills of Washington County, New York. We had an animal barn with cows and goats and arrived in time for "kidding." It was such a treat to bring the children to visit the baby goats. The Main House was a sprawling mansion that could house forty-plus people in the fourteen rooms that served as bedrooms. There was also Nahara's House downtown—a large Victorian that could house another thirty.

My involvement in Rutland had caused me to feel respected and needed and had given me the confidence to speak up about things. For whatever reason, as soon as we set foot in Cambridge I was knocked back down the ladder. My salvation had surely come.

The dynamics of the household were completely foreign to me. In Rutland, there was a nice sense of camaraderie among the women. We spent time together as friends. We would have tea during nap time or sew together or sit outside and talk. In Cambridge, it was not like this. The only time most people talked to me was to direct, correct, or instruct me.

The exception was a particularly quirky woman who constantly was trying to talk while our kids became increasingly boisterous around our feet, and she wouldn't stop. I had the thought that she was starved for fellowship and wondered if there were ways to increase in this area in the household. I was still my normal, outspoken self, and I told Atarah of the way it had been in Rutland. Her response was, "Well, their houses are always dirty, and when I had several small children, sometimes I'd go the whole week and barely talk to anyone who came above my knee." My concern went nowhere.

I continued to take my children outside every day as I'd been in the habit of doing, usually for a half hour after lunch and before nap to let them get some energy out. Sometimes this meant I was a little late getting out to finish lunch cleanup, especially if my children didn't go to sleep easily. But I always showed up.

After a few weeks, Atarah pulled me aside one day after she heard me tell the children to get their coats on to go outside. She rebuked me for the time I spent outdoors with them. She said it was unproductive and that we should be teaching our children to serve (most days I was making lunch, so my four- and two-year-old had been "serving" in the kitchen for three or four hours before nap time). She had a four-year-old son too and said it was totally normal that an entire week would go by without him going outside, and that was good because he was learning to serve. I felt I was being given conflicting advice and told her what the Spanish woman had said to me in Rutland. Her response was that those twins had "special needs," and those needs didn't apply to all children. I still made a point to get my children outside, I just learned to be more discreet about it.

Much to my dismay, we had moved to Cambridge only a month before the woman whose birth team I was on was due. One of the midwives in Rutland acknowledged my disappointment and assured me there were pregnant women in Cambridge and I'd be involved there. There were indeed a couple pregnant ladies, but weeks went by, and no one approached me or even asked if I'd been involved in midwifery before. So, one day I decided to let Atarah know that I'd been involved in Plymouth and Rutland and was wondering about being included in one of the upcoming births.

I was not expecting the response I got. She told me she was surprised at my audacity to assume that just because I'd functioned in a certain capacity in one place, Our Father was going to use me the same way someplace else. We did not strive for positions but waited to be raised up by Him. I felt terrible I had asked instead of trusting, and I walked away so discouraged, feeling like I had probably ruined any chance of ever being involved again.

We also were not included in the Social Meeting anymore, with one exception. There was a wedding coming up, and my husband was needed for some of the planning, as certain areas of the soap shop were going to be used. He was asked to come to the Social Meeting, so naturally he let me know we were going. I was so happy and eager to be involved, and I went to find out if there was anyone who could put our children to bed that night. I still hadn't heard who was going to help us by the time the evening gathering was over, so André and I began getting the children into their pajamas, figuring one of the youth girls would be showing up any moment to take over.

The awaited knock came to our door, and I opened it to see one of the elders instead. He asked if he could have a moment with my husband, and they stepped out of the room. André returned a few minutes later, looking rather uncomfortable. "What's going on?" I asked.

"Ummm," he faltered, "I guess they only need me to go to the Social Meeting, so you can just relax and get to bed early." He was trying to make it sound like I was off the hook for some tedious task, but he knew full well how much I was looking forward to going to the meeting with him. It was the couples meeting after all! I'd never seen just one spouse go to the Social Meeting unless someone was sick or had just had a baby or something like that. I felt so humiliated. André would be sitting there with the other couples, planning the wedding while I went to bed with my children.

He could see the discouragement on my face, but there wasn't anything he could do to make me feel better, so he kissed the children goodnight, kissed the top of my head, muttered, "Sorry," and left the room.

Chapter 11

We Don't Eat Popsicles or
Look at Balloons

hen we moved to Cambridge, the community was poor but nowhere near as poor as Rutland. One of the men did repacking jobs for a bulk discount store called Steals and Deals, and he'd often be given free food. One time he was given a couple pallets of organic fruit popsicles. We would see "certain" children eating the popsicles quite often, but since we were never offered any, and it was never announced that they were up for grabs, I had to tell my children to think the best as I was getting them a snack of toast or goat milk with molasses.

One Friday night, the meal team decided to use up the popsicles for dessert. They melted the popsicles, poured them over a graham cracker crust on sheet pans, and refroze them. Samuel, a leading elder and husband of Atarah, caught wind of this, and late Friday afternoon he commanded that the entire dessert be thrown away, meaning there would be no dessert that night. He said they contained organic cane sugar, which was just a fancy way to say processed sugar, and it wasn't good for us, so we weren't going to eat it. For weeks, a blind eye had been turned at the families who were snacking on these regularly, but when the whole community was going to eat them, suddenly there was a problem.

It was only those high enough up the chain of command who had authority to call for obedience on something such as this and have no one dare contradict their judgment. A single brother who had a strong opinion about cane sugar could have brought up the same concern and been rebuked for not being thankful for what Our Father had provided or not thinking the best of his sisters who labored to make his meals. Many rules and standards were not based on "Our Father's Mind" as we were told, but simply on the whims and opinions of who had the greatest authority at the time.

There is an elite class in the TT. My husband called them dynasties. Someone else called them empires. These (often) extended families always seemed to lead different lifestyles than the average TT members. They were privileged, traveled a lot, had access to money, and got their needs met easily. Most importantly, their words held more weight than others'. Their words were to be received as law, and most of them were spared from the daily scrutiny that the rest of us were subject to. If you did have the courage (or stupidity) to bring up a concern about these people, you would be deemed disrespectful, or "not thinking the best," or listening "to accusations from the Evil One." They were untouchable.

❦

Every summer, there was a hot-air balloon festival in Cambridge. It was a big deal for the town, and even though we didn't participate, our children always looked forward to it, even if only to see some cool balloons floating by. The balloon fest is always in June, so we had only lived there a couple months when the time came.

I remember waking up one Sabbath morning to a strange noise, as if great bursts of air were being released right outside my bedroom. In fact, that's exactly what it was—a balloon had landed in the field right across from our house. I woke my children, who were eager to go outside to see it. It was exciting being so close, and many people in the house began making their way curiously across the road. A few minutes later, another landed in the field near the soap shop, and more people headed over in that direction. Being on the breakfast team, I sadly had to leave this unusual and thrilling circumstance and head to the kitchen, but André kept the children outdoors so they could continue to watch the spectacle. It wasn't long before the gathering, and the balloons were still parked in the fields.

The shofar blew right on time, and everyone who was still outside hurried to the gathering room. Once seated, most of the children and many adults were still craning their necks to see the balloons, and since there was one behind the house and one in front of it, trying to focus on the Sabbath morning minchah was nearly impossible. At one point, a couple men got up and came back with several tapestries. A few other adults got up to help hang them over all the windows in that huge room, two walls of which were floor-to-ceiling French doors.

When all the windows were covered and everyone settled back down, the community received a scathing rebuke from Samuel. How shameful it was that so many of us were more interested in those balloons than in Our Father's Word. Those balloons were just the result of man's pride and had nothing to do with the Kingdom of God. Our children shouldn't care about looking at worthless, worldly objects such as those.

One by one, people stood up to repent for giving in to their "flesh" and being impressed with such foolishness. That became the theme of the gathering, and, thank God, by the time it was over the balloons were gone.

That event set the tone for the next few years, but by the time we left the tide had changed. Balloons continued to land in our fields, but the summer we left, we allowed our children to take turns climbing in the basket. Families were going to "Moon Glow—an evening event where they lit up the balloons at night. We had been strictly prohibited from this before. Now, a few years later, I saw a recent ITN and they went so far as to allow families to actually go up in the air a little bit! Did "Our Father" have a change of heart? Did He personally reveal to someone that hot-air balloons are not evil and it's OK to get excited and be in awe of something other than the Bible or a TT teaching? Of course not! It's the whims of the leaders that have changed.

Chapter 12

Love Not Your Possessions

hough women in the TT do not wear any type of jewelry, I had kept our wedding rings stashed in the back of a drawer in my nightstand. I had a diamond engagement ring and our wedding bands. I figured the day would come when there would be a need to sell them, and I'd be ready to part with them.

That day came a few months after being in Cambridge, when I became aware that many people had unmet dental needs. I simply could not have a good conscience knowing I had a way to help these people tucked away in a drawer. I conferred with André, and we decided to sell the rings and offer to put the money toward our friends' teeth. A man, Asah, had a connection with a jeweler whom he felt would give us a fair price. I took one last peek at our rings, sealed them in an envelope, and handed it over, feeling like I was overcoming and making the right choice.

I went through my day, looking forward to finding out how much money we got for the rings. I really hoped it would cover a lot of dental expenses, since not having any insurance at least meant the local places we went to would give us a sliding scale for paying bills up front.

We had just finished supper and were heading to our room when a vehicle pulled up. "I think Asah is home," I said expectantly.

A couple minutes later there was a knock on the door. Smiling, I opened it up, but Asah did not return my smile. "Can I come in?" he asked quietly. I backed up as he entered and nodded a greeting to my husband. We looked at him, waiting for him to say something. With a sigh, he dejectedly told us that he'd lost the rings! He said he had put them in the driver's side door pocket when he left that morning, and when he got to the jewelers they were gone. He said he went back and searched every parking lot he had been in up until that point and had no idea what could have happened to them.

I was extremely disappointed and upset but kept my composure. You chalk those up to "testing" in the community. *"The circumstances today will work in every way . . ."* were the lyrics to a minchah song. We never did find out what happened.

When we moved to Cambridge, the Main House was incredibly full with eight families, most with four or more children. Over forty people under one roof. Our first room had a walk-in closet that was large enough to fit the children's bunk bed and even had a window and tiny sink, so it sort of felt like another room. Aside from it being on the first floor, right next to the noisy kitchen and dining room, we were set up comfortably.

One day, a woman pulled me aside. She told me she noticed that our family always smelled "musty." Our clothes hung in our "children's room," so I took her in to have a look. One wall of the closet bordered the butler's pantry—a small walk-through room between the kitchen and dining room that held an ancient nickel sink in which all dishes were prewashed. Another wall bordered the large, three-basin stainless steel sinks in the kitchen where the final wash and rinse took place.

To my horror, we moved clothes and shoes aside and found areas of fuzzy green mold all over the walls. I was instructed to take all our clothes outside to air out on the clotheslines. Then, we pulled everything away from the walls and retrieved a five percent hydrogen peroxide solution from the soap shop. We began spraying the walls, and I was so disgusted to see them wildly foaming up. I was told to do this once a week to keep the mold under control and also keep the window cracked and a fan running constantly. I felt terrible, like my children had been poisoned in their sleep all those weeks.

I had my antimold routine down pretty well when, weeks later, we were informed we were moving out of the room. I was relieved—someone finally had the wisdom to realize no one should live in a mold-infested room. But no, that wasn't the reason we were being evicted. A family from "Gad" (Canada) was moving to Cambridge, and since they had three children and we only had two, they were going to move into our room, and we were being put in the library. We were told to leave all our furniture, as they were not bringing any. Since we were not supposed to be attached to any possessions, and we wanted this family, our brother and sister from another tribe, to feel the warm hospitality and love of our clan, we willingly stripped the beds, emptied the dressers and nightstands, and made the short move to the library on the other side of the dining room.

The household sprang into action to help me get set up. The many glass-doored bookshelves became our dressers. A bed frame was found in the attic, and someone found an extra mattress at the downtown house. A trundle bed I could push under our bed during the day was found for Meyshar, and Emmet would sleep on a futon chair that we set up as a bed every night and folded back into a chair every day. The only perk was that there was a functioning fireplace, and it was nice to start a fire at bedtime to warm up the room, since we didn't keep the enormous house extremely warm due to the heating costs. Thankfully, Rutland had toughened us up to such things.

Chapter 13

Warfare

o say the Main House was busy does not convey reality. Mealtimes were nothing short of chaos, with everyone packing into the dining room for three meals a day, except in warmer months when we could utilize porches. There were at least twenty-five children living in this house, and children as a rule were not supposed to interact with one another, unless they were "covered" by adults. Sending our children just to the next room was a gamble as they were drawn to each other like magnets, and you often heard mothers telling their children as they were being sent somewhere, "Don't talk to any children, and if any of them try to talk to you, you tell them you are doing your Imma's will and keep going." Then, their child's faithfulness would be questioned when they returned. "Did you talk to anybody?" was a standard question to ask your child when they came back from the bathroom or something. This was for a couple reasons: 1) to test your child's honesty and 2) to be prepared if someone came to let you know your child had been "distracting" their children when they walked by a few minutes ago.

Sometimes it felt like warfare to attempt to go from one end of the house to the other, your children gripped firmly by their hands, walking as fast as you could past other families and hoping your children didn't call out to any others and have to be disciplined when you reached your destination. The Main House had two floors and a full basement, providing several ways to get from point A to point B. Sometimes, if I was trying to get to the kitchen and saw certain children in the dining room, I would duck down the basement stairs in the entryway and cross the house that way to avoid the possible interaction between children. Our life was supposed to be about love and care, but a lot of times it was about carefully avoiding one another.

To attempt to bring order to the chaos, a new household rule was announced one day at the child training teaching. No children under ten years old were allowed to be sent anywhere in the house by themselves. Now this rule worked out well for the women who had an older child or two who could run down to the laundry room and grab a basket, or go fill her water bottle up, or make some toast for a snack while she stayed in her room with the younger children. It was frowned upon to leave your children unattended in your room. More than likely, they would emerge after a few minutes to find you and soon be brought to you by another adult in the house who would let you know that they were "wandering around uncovered," and you would feel like a complete failure as a parent. If something like that became a pattern for a mother, it wouldn't be long before she was called into a meeting to be corrected for not ruling properly over her children.

For those of us who only had children under ten—some women having three or four—this rule was a nightmare. It meant toting our children "by our side" every time we had to leave our room or the kitchen for anything. It literally could be overwhelming if I'd made it out to the kitchen unscathed, only to realize I left my recipe in my room. I could no longer say to Emmet, "Go back to the room and get Imma's recipe book." You had to either gear up to face the gauntlet of going to your room and back with your children in tow, or risk sitting them at the table, telling them not to move or talk to anyone, then sprinting to your room praying you didn't hear screaming and crying by the time you got back to the kitchen. It made an already intense and stressful situation even worse. It felt more like living in an institution than in a "home" where God's love was supposed to be "fleshed out." It certainly was not the life of camaraderie and close friendships I'd envisioned years before.

Chapter 14

Our Family Increases

iving in Rutland had afforded us the opportunity to spend more time with André's parents, and this continued after we moved to Cambridge. Even though Annie had been watching the community for more than twenty years, and harboring a desire to be there, it took them three years to follow us in. They still had a son in high school and did not feel they could make the move until he had graduated and could feasibly take care of himself. She always maintained her hope of living there someday, and they visited us regularly, often spending days at a time. My children were very attached to them, and Emmet would chase their car down the driveway, crying when they left to go home.

I would look at the people who had extended families in the community and think how nice it would be for my children to have a Sabba and Savtah in the Body, as relationships with "worldly" grandparents were very guarded. It was frowned upon for children to have close relationships with any relatives outside the community. We were cautioned against taking them to worldly relatives' houses because of the defiling influences they would encounter. We were to encourage our relatives to visit us in the community, where we could uphold our standards and possibly "draw" them to our life as well. It would never have been allowed to send your child to their worldly grandparents' house unattended.

So, from the time we joined, we spoke often with them on the phone and wrote many letters, encouraging them in making the decision to join. I remember her suffering over the children she helped teach at the elementary school, feeling like she would be abandoning them. I'd remind her of all the children in the community who badly needed a high-quality teacher like her.

My desire to have them join soon grew tremendously. I was lonely and desperate for an ally and some support with my children. I pictured them living there and going to their room for a respite from the exhausting household dynamics. It would be like an oasis of comfort and familiarity. I envisioned going for walks and spending quality time together as a family. How much more bonded we all would be! If I was frantically trying to get dinner made and Annie walked through the kitchen, she'd probably invite my children up to her room for a story to help me out. Life would be so much better once they were there.

We visited them in Benson whenever we could, and during the summer of 2003 it seemed they were close to making the big decision. We were sent to talk with them about how to proceed. As we walked in, the family dog, Max, began excitedly jumping on us. I tentatively patted his head, as I was keener on community views toward dogs at this point. "Hey, Max, still barking?" was André's greeting to his former dog.

"That's another thing!" exclaimed Annie, motioning toward Max. "What are we going to do about him?" He was so loyal to her, and she feared he would run away from anyone who might take him in. He had lived his entire life at their property in Benson. André assured her we would help figure that out.

Not two weeks later, we received a call from a devastated Annie. Scottie had accidentally backed over and killed Max in the driveway. Annie hadn't been home at the time, so in a frantic moment of panic, Scottie threw the dog in a garbage bag and took him to the dump. When Annie got home and was told of her poor dog's fate, she couldn't handle the thought that she hadn't even given him a proper burial. She went to the store in utter distress to get a bottle of wine and ran into one of her more adventurous friends. She explained to her friend what had happened, and her friend said, "Want to go get him?"

"Um, *yes!*"

They both went home to change and met up shortly after. They gloved up and broke into the dump, which had since closed for the day, in search of the bag containing Max. Scottie had told her the general area he threw the bag, and after a short time feeling around, they found him. Annie brought him back and gave him a proper grave at his beloved home.

Of course, we were all thinking that the problem had solved itself—

although it was disturbing to think that the same God who had found my dog a loving home had worked it out for Max to get killed taking a nap in the driveway.

In the end, Scottie and Annie moved to Cambridge with very little fanfare on a dreary November day in 2003. They went from their beautiful property and bright, spacious home to a small, dark bedroom in the Caretaker's House—a little house on the main property. The only perk was they had their own sink and toilet. Annie said she felt like they were "indoor camping."

Having them there was nothing like my fantasies. Annie was going through Hell. She badly missed her home and her other sons and was an emotional wreck most of the time. Since they weren't baptized yet and therefore didn't have the Holy Spirit, they couldn't help very much with the children. We were only supposed to have our children covered by a surrendered disciple who could discipline them when they needed it. I still had to be on guard that my children did not become "overfamiliar" with them, which was even harder now that they were around all the time. I also had to be guarded in what I said to them about my own sufferings. If they were to remain and become disciples, I had to help them grow in faith and vision about our life and purpose. I needed to do the same, and I prayed constantly.

I often wondered if they'd make it and was surprised they didn't simply flee back to their house. It was only an hour away, and their youngest son was still living there. I know I surely would have during those first few months if that had been an option.

Somehow, they pressed on, and after seven months they were baptized. First her, then him one week later. They received new names right away— Scottie became Shama (to listen) and Annie would be Amtsah (determined). They were still Sabba and Savtah to us though.

I did start to reap some fringe benefits from having grandparents living with us—more so from Scottie at first. He always had a basket of food next to his side of the bed, and during lean times it was nice to be able to go to their room and make my children a snack. Sometimes it was just peanut butter or cheese and mayonnaise on bread, but it really helped. He was called upon often to run errands for one reason or another and would invite one of my children to go along. He was always available at nap time to have a child crash on his bed with him while I tried to get lunch cleanup done.

Annie was quickly integrated into training and given a household schedule of her own, so she was much busier, making it harder to spend time together. We would go to their room now and then for preparation time, especially if André wasn't home.

For the first couple of years I was still nervous that they would leave any day. So many things bothered Scottie, and on the occasions that he would bring me to an appointment or shopping, I would get an earful of all his gripes. But he'd always buy me coffee and lunch, so it was a good deal for both of us. I still didn't divulge many of my troubles to them, not wanting to add insult to injury.

Understandably, instead of having an even closer relationship than before, Annie and I drifted apart. We hardly ever interacted socially, as she was overwhelmed with what was on her plate between training and her household schedule. She often felt more was expected of her than the other women her age, of which there were several. In many ways she was right, but, being a "new" disciple and someone who is a go-getter with a lot of energy to boot, she was at a disadvantage when it came to advocating for herself.

I missed the days when we emailed daily and talked nonstop when we got together. Years went by, and they became no different to us than other families we lived with. They even moved away a couple times for several months but always returned to Cambridge. All the children in the house called them Sabba and Savtah, and they were much loved.

Chapter 15

The Unattended Wedding

n May of 2004 I received an invitation to a wedding! One of my best childhood friends, Tiffany, was getting married to another of our high school friends, Craig. I hadn't seen her in years, and I was ecstatic. This was the first wedding invitation from any of my friends from "the world." The wedding was in August.

André spoke to one of the men in government, submitting our request to go to the wedding, stay at my mother's house, and come home the next day. I waited anxiously for the verdict of whether we would be "sent." Just because we had been invited and desired to go was no guarantee. There had to be counsel to see whether there was faith to send us.

The next night was the weekly Government Meeting, and André was asked to attend, presumably about the wedding. As usual, the meeting lasted until the wee hours of the morning, but I was awake when André quietly came into the room. "Are we going?" I asked eagerly. "Yes, we are," was all he said. I fell asleep happily, so thankful we were being sent.

Our Family Night (date night in the TT) was the following day, and as it was a beautiful spring evening we went for a walk around the property. "We need to talk about this wedding," André began.

"Do we need to work out the children?" I asked. Emmet and Meyshar were five and three at the time.

"No," he replied, "They can be with my parents." He was acting oddly uncomfortable.

"So, what else?" I prompted.

"We just need to make sure we are going for the right reasons, and we will only be going to the reception." He suddenly seemed more confident in what he was saying.

"*What?*" I asked unbelievingly. "Why? What am I supposed to tell Tiffany? I mailed back the RSVP card today saying we are coming!"

"We are going, just not to the ceremony." He went on to explain to me what the brothers had said to him at the meeting. For one thing, disciples don't enter churches. It would grieve the Holy Spirit because of the demons that rule Christianity. This is why André's relatives only appeared at our reception when we got married.

Two, we don't go to social events in the world to "hang out," reveling in a carnal party, but to seek and save the lost. Our focus had to remain on evangelism, on finding a potential lost sheep.

Three, only our Father can sanctify a true marriage, therefore only in the TT do we have the confidence to witness and support something as significant as a wedding. Were we to witness such an event, we would need to be true to our consciences and speak the truth during the ceremony, that the one true God was not necessarily approving of this union. The other option was to skip the ceremony and only attend the reception.

I was glad André wasn't preparing to give some odious speech in the middle of my best friend's wedding about how we weren't confident that God was putting them together, but I was mortified that we couldn't go to the ceremony. This was going to be my first encounter with a lot of my friends since joining the TT, and I didn't want to look like a freak. He could tell I was upset but didn't want to ruin our only child-free evening, so he told me not to worry, assuring me we would "figure it out." He told me not to say anything to Tiffany. It was still a few months away, so I put it in the back of my mind and went on with life.

When the wedding was just a few days away, I asked André what we were going to do about the ceremony. I have another good friend who lived in the area, and I was hoping to see her before we went home. André had an idea. "Can we go see Renée Saturday instead of Sunday?" His plan was to go to the church as though we were attending the ceremony, but we would hang around toward the back. Then, when all attention was on Tiffany walking down the aisle, we would discreetly duck out and leave. Surely no one would be thinking of us during the ceremony. Then we would go to Renée's house for a short visit and hopefully show up at the reception and blend in with other stragglers. If anyone asked, we would say that due to the shortness of our visit, I wanted to quickly see another friend, so we left the church a bit early to squeeze it in. Everyone's attention would be on Craig and Tiffany, so we were certain no one was going to notice we weren't there. I worked out the visit with Renée and prayed it was all going to pan out as planned.

One may wonder why I didn't just plead with André to go to the ceremony. No one from the community would ever find out unless one of us told someone. But fear of being disobedient and losing God's protection was already deep at work in me. If we attended the ceremony lawlessly and then received news of something bad happening to one of our children or we got in a car accident on the way home, I would have *known* we were being disciplined for our bad consciences about going against "Our Father's Will." Direction from the brothers was to be taken as coming from the Holy Spirit. I just couldn't take that risk. I don't know if the same kind of superstitious fear was at work in André. I would guess his willingness to be obedient came more from wanting to please the brothers, as he was in a place of being "raised up" and was already benefiting from some of the perks of having authority. The last thing he wanted was to be "pruned" for giving in to the carnal desires of his wife. So, a lot was at stake here.

We arrived at the church well before the ceremony was due to start, parking along the side of the road in line with all the other vehicles. We quickly found my friends gathered outside near the entrance. Tiffany looked so beautiful, and I could hardly hold back the tears when I hugged her. I'd missed her so much. Michelle was there too, and several other high school friends. We visited until it was time to go in, then we followed the crowd, lingering in the back. As expected, all attention went to the stunning bride about to walk down the aisle. So far so good. "OK," said André when he felt the timing was good, "let's go." We turned and quickly stepped out the back door of the church.

That's when we realized our grave mistake. The church was right on the side of the road where everyone had parked. We hadn't thought it through when we'd arrived, but we had inadvertently parked where we would have to walk all along the side of the church facing the road to get back to our car. We were going to be obvious to anyone who happened to look out the many windows along that side of the church.

"We should have parked at the store." André remarked tensely. There was a tiny general store just past the church, and, if our car had been there at that moment, we could have made a run for it and escaped unnoticed. I was horrified. He grabbed my hand.

"Just come," he ordered. I felt like we were fugitives. We tried as best we could to duck behind each car we passed on the way to ours. We literally had parked near the window closest to the front of the church, where everyone's attention was now. I could see curious heads turning in our direction from inside the building, and I desperately wished the ground would swallow me up. We got in the car and quickly pulled out. My heart was racing, and I was sweating.

"It's OK." André tried to console me. "I don't think anyone saw us."

"Are you kidding?" I shot back, "I think that whole side of the church saw us!"

"Well, it's over now. Let's just have a nice visit with Renée."

We rode the twenty minutes to Renée's house in silence. Did I, a married twenty-seven-year-old with two children, actually just flee my dear friend's wedding because we weren't allowed to attend? I felt like I was in the Twilight Zone. I had to get myself together, as I wanted to appear as normal as possible when we got to Renée's. She had a little boy the same age as Meyshar and was expecting another one soon.

We had a pleasant visit with her, although much shorter than I would have liked. We didn't want to get to the reception too late.

Thankfully, other cars were still arriving when we got to the reception, which was taking place under a huge tent at Tiffany's parents' beautiful lakefront property. We were directed to park and headed toward the tent, blending in with many others. I relaxed; maybe it would be OK after all. My hopes were dashed as soon as we entered the tent. Michelle spotted us right away and came rushing over.

"Where did you guys go?" she exclaimed. My heart sank, and I must have visibly withered from embarrassment and shame because André came to the rescue and took the lead in explaining our disappearance. Michelle was obviously confused by our choice of plans but brushed it off and showed us to our table, which was with her mother and stepfather.

Any awkwardness from that point on was smoothed over by the envelope of photos I had brought of my children. We saw many of my high school friends, whom I'm sure felt a little awkward around the "new" me. True to our calling, one woman took an interest in the group we had joined and mentioned she had been doing a lot of reading recently on religious movements. So, before we left, we made sure to give her one of the many free papers we had brought. There, we had evangelized someone. Our conscience was good.

Chapter 16

Milestones

ot long after the wedding, it was time to start the new training (school) year. This was one of many "milestones" for our children to reach as they grew up, and each was a celebrated occasion. The first milestone was dedication when they were forty or eighty days old.

The second was being able to stand in the minchah as a priest at three years old and receive their diadem—a special woven headband worn to gatherings. By now, they should be trained to stand quietly and pay attention.

At age four came the third milestone, being inaugurated into pitch class—formal singing lessons. The children loved pitch class, as they learned to sing on key, and they often performed "offerings" on Friday nights or other special occasions.

Around age six was their training inauguration. They would be starting Alef or first grade. The TT uses the Hebrew alphabet for the grade levels. Beth is second grade, Gimel is third, Dalet is fourth, and so on. The highest level most children completed was Zayin, about seventh grade. There was some curriculum for Chet and Tet, but materials and teachers for the higher levels were often hard to come by. By the age of fourteen or so, most children weren't having much training, but up until then their education was actually quite good. When my younger children started in public school after we left, they were ahead of most of their classmates academically. Socially, it was a different story . . .

The training milestone was especially significant. The parents would be passing on their authority to the teacher, which was represented by the parents handing over a rod to the child's teacher, who was usually still a child themselves—often a fifteen- to seventeen-year-old girl! There often were several children going into Alef each year, so this celebration included a few sets of parents and multiple rod handovers. The teacher had full consent from the parents to use the rod to discipline the child as they saw fit during the hours they were in training. The parents vowed to uphold the teacher's authority.

When Emmet was five and a half, he potentially could have started Alef. Up until that point, he'd been with me every day, mainly cooking in the kitchen. He could make a pot of chili or a six-gallon bowl of salad with minimal help for forty-plus people. There was a list of guidelines in the child training teachings that indicated when a child was ready for Alef. One criterion was: "The child can peacefully work at their Imma's side all day in the kitchen." Emmet had his issues and was not perfectly in line, but he was bright and already teaching himself to read, so I felt he needed the additional challenge.

At the time Meyshar was three, and I had just found out I was pregnant and due for baby number three in May. It would be nice if I had a few months of one-on-one time with her before the baby came.

The leaders had their annual training meeting to judge which children would be starting Alef. We were not included in this discussion, and it was judged that Emmet was not ready to start, due to behavioral issues. I was devastated at the judgment, especially since another child only a couple weeks older would be starting. I decided to go talk to Samuel.

✳✿✳

He listened as I tearfully tried to express myself—I always became emotional when trying to communicate something I was struggling about. Now I realize this probably made me look desperate and pitiful, like a child pouting about not getting their own way.

He sighed as I finished, rubbed his hand over his bushy beard, and took a leisurely sip of his maté. He then delivered his judgment upon me.

"Sounds to me like you are just upset because you are pregnant, and you hoped to get Emmet out of your hair. That's not a reason we start a child in training—they need to be surrendered, and you need to turn your heart to your son if you want him to be able to start next year."

I was crushed, but a decision had been made in council, and I needed to submit to the wisdom of the Body. All I could do was repent for not trusting and receive the decision. It would do no good to try and convince him that his judgment was not true. I would just end up in a deeper hole.

The next milestone was bar or bat mitzvah. Children as young as twelve could express their desire to make this covenant, but it was more common for them to be around fourteen or fifteen. It was a big deal—a three-day celebration. The festivities started Friday afternoon with a gathering for the parents and child to express their hearts to one another. There would be songs sung and many tears shed. Then the child would be baptized, receiving the Holy Spirit and dedicating themselves to serving their parents for the next seven years, the age of twenty, or marriage, whichever came first. Friday Night Meal was then served, followed by a much-anticipated play. These were big productions, taking several weeks to prepare.

The next day, the Sabbath, began with the customary morning gathering, followed by breakfast and then a special Children's Celebration. This was led by the new bar or bat mitzvah and was symbolic, representing their departure from childhood. There would be games and often a treasure hunt. It was so exciting for the children, but, of course, anything "fun" had high standards imposed on it.

During one bar mitzvah, I was in charge of planning the treasure hunt with another woman. At the end, there would be gift bags of "treasure" for each of the children. Another woman volunteered to go shopping for the prizes. She got colorful little rubber lizards and bouncy balls, pencils and fun erasers, pocket notebooks, tiny sewing kits, etc. Community kids don't normally get gifts (we did not celebrate birthdays), so they were all ecstatic and it was fun to watch them open their bags with pure delight.

About a week later we were rebuked in the Social Meeting for including "toys" in the gift bags, and the woman who bought them had to repent.

Saturday evening was the usual gathering followed by the child's first Breaking of Bread with their parents. Sunday began with a morning teaching and breakfast, then a big, special meal early in the afternoon so those who came from far away could head home. That concluded the weekend.

The next milestone after this is the year in training; hence the young Alef teachers. All the youth were supposed to get experience teaching, although it was mainly the young girls who were enlisted. After this, the only milestone left was the "par par" celebration. Par par is Hebrew for butterfly. When a youth reached twenty years old, the parents were supposed to release them as adults, who were no longer under their authority, to begin their service to the Body. This often meant them moving to a different community, although many youth were sent to live elsewhere long before this. And since some youth get married before they are twenty, they obviously come out from under their parent's authority at that point.

Chapter 17

A Time to Suffer

round the time I was seven or eight weeks pregnant with my third child, morning sickness hit. I didn't throw up all the time but always felt horrible, like I had motion sickness or a bad hangover. With my two small children to care for all day, as well as a full cooking schedule, I needed any "grace" that was possible. I thought back to Hyannis and how there had been compassion and special foods to help with my morning sickness. I remembered the steak and how it helped me feel so much better.

I went to one of the women on my birth team who I felt comfortable with and explained to her what I was going through, and I asked if she thought it was possible that I could get a little red meat. I explained how much it helped with my last pregnancy and what Milkah in Hyannis said about the B vitamins. She seemed sympathetic and said she would look into it for me. I felt good about the conversation and patiently waited and trusted.

A few days later, before André left for the soap shop, he let me know that we were getting together with the midwives later in the afternoon. I thought we were going to start going over everything I would need to start being faithful with: brisk walks, red raspberry tea, and so on. I was looking forward to the meeting, and then it was our Family Night afterwards.

The meeting was in our library bedroom, and we pulled in a few chairs from the dining room. Atarah and two other women soon were welcomed in, and after a couple minutes of polite small talk, Atarah got right to the point.

"Well, Tamara, I was made aware of your request, and I have never heard of anyone so selfish as to demand red meat when they are pregnant. Imagine if we had to get red meat for all the pregnant women!"

I was in complete shock. I looked pleadingly at the woman I had asked about the meat. I didn't feel like I had "demanded" anything but had respectfully submitted my request. She said nothing to defend me.

Atarah went on, "In the world, pregnant women are spoiled and pampered, giving in to all their cravings. But here in the Body, pregnancy is a time to suffer and overcome."

I then had to listen to story after story of women who had it far worse than me, who were so sick they were on bedrest and could only keep down oat broth. I should be thankful for how "easy" my pregnancy was in comparison.

I didn't say a word the whole time, feeling like such an asshole. André didn't know how to respond except to outwardly support the authority of the midwives. After they left our room, I burst into tears, and he took me out for a hamburger.

I cried on and off for the next two days. I felt like I'd been ganged up on, misrepresented, and not shown a shred of understanding or kindness by women who'd each had at least five children! But in the TT, instead of mercy and compassion for the raging hormones that accompany pregnancy, we were taught, "A woman's true colors come out when she is pregnant." Women were supposed to learn to "rule over and put their emotions under their feet."

When I was around four months pregnant, I had gained twenty pounds. Atarah warned me I needed to be careful, as she was concerned that I was gaining too much. She let me know she only gained twenty pounds with each of her five pregnancies. I had gained thirty to thirty-five with my first two pregnancies and had no trouble losing it after. I felt this was a horrible thing to say to a young, pregnant woman, and her weight gain, or lack of it, had nothing to do with me. Atarah had one of those waif-like figures, and probably weighed less than a hundred pounds on a good day.

Ironically, a severe flu soon went around, and suddenly I was extremely ill, not able to hold down anything but bone broth for at least a week. I was coughing so violently my whole abdomen hurt, and I was terrified I was going to miscarry. I ended up losing ten pounds at around twenty-five weeks of pregnancy, and no one was concerned.

My third child, Darakah, was born May 12, 2005. It was another textbook birth with no complications. She was born in my in-laws' bedroom because even though we had graduated from the library and were given two rooms, they were in what is called "the servants' quarters" and were very small.

When she was around nine months old, I started having similar problems as with my older daughter—the cracked and bleeding nipples. Not wanting to relive that nightmare or have to wean my nine-month-old, I asked right away to go see a homeopathic doctor in Bennington that other women had gone to and spoke well of. I was covered and went.

She asked me extensive details about my history and diet and had me chart everything I ate for three days. I brought her my data at my next appointment.

After careful analysis and some more questions, her conclusion was that it wasn't yeast I suffered from but that I wasn't getting enough protein from animal products for a nursing woman. My body was breaking down cells faster than they could be replaced and therefore my tissues were breaking down. She told me to eat . . . red meat! Thinking back to our diet in Rutland when I suffered this way previously, it made perfect sense.

At that point, Atarah and her family had been called to another community for a short time. When I told my husband what the homeopath had said, he told me to call Atarah and "humbly" let her know what I had been told. He thought maybe she'd rethink some of her staunch views. I didn't want to, but he was insistent, so I was obedient and called.

I was nervous as I relayed the details to Atarah, trying to recall what the doctor had said as accurately as possible and trying to sound humble. As soon as I said that I had been advised to eat more red meat, Atarah started to laugh, cutting me short.

"Tamara, this woman only has worldly knowledge. She doesn't hear from our Father," was her condescending response. She completely discredited the advice I'd been given.

Chapter 18

Women's Work

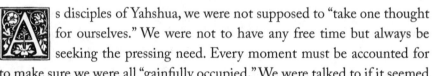s disciples of Yahshua, we were not supposed to "take one thought for ourselves." We were not to have any free time but always be seeking the pressing need. Every moment must be accounted for to make sure we were all "gainfully occupied." We were talked to if it seemed like we were spending too much time in our bedroom, even during times we weren't on the schedule to cook. If someone thought I was taking too long to lay my children down for a nap, they would come knocking on my door. This would be after I had worked in the kitchen with them for hours and was desperate for them to take a nap. I had my children woken up when they were almost asleep so many times by someone knocking, wondering if I was going to finish putting away the lunch dishes, mop the dining room, put out more utensils and napkins, or any other little task that I'd failed to accomplish before the supper crew arrived. One time, I was questioned for not pushing all the chairs back in adequately after sweeping under the tables. There was very little compassion or mercy for someone feeling overwhelmed and stressed out—it was because they weren't crying out for grace to overcome, were unwilling to suffer, or they were simply lazy and resisting Our Father's will.

Even Sabbaths weren't truly a rest from the constant work, especially for the women. We had a one-to-two-hour gathering in the morning, followed by breakfast, then lunch only a couple hours later, followed by a nap, which was standard for everyone, followed by preparation time, then the Resurrection Celebration, which was also up to two hours long, then children's supper and bedtime, all before Breaking of Bread, which was at least another two-hour gathering.

There was a weekend meal rotation, so unless we did Friday Night Meal, our team would have been up early doing breakfast, setting out and cleaning up lunch, or Breaking of Bread and children's supper. Often it was after midnight before we got to bed Saturday night. Sunday morning began with an 8:00 a.m., two-hour-long teaching, and the team that did Friday Night Meal was the breakfast team that morning. Incidentally, sleep deprivation and being constantly busy are two of the criteria used in brainwashing; the TT has those things down pat.

❈

I remember being pregnant with Darakah, making lunch three days a week, with a breakfast morning and supper night somewhere in there, and little Emmet and Meyshar always by my side. I would look forward to one of them having a bowel movement because I could sit them on the toilet and quickly go lie down in my room and close my eyes for a few precious moments while the other one looked at a book. I'd keep the door cracked open so I could hear them when they called out that they were done.

One evening, around 8:00 p.m., I had just gotten them to bed after a long day in the kitchen. André had long since headed back up to the soap shop. The next morning was my breakfast morning, and I dutifully went upstairs to check with the other woman on my breakfast team to see if there were any preps that needed to be done. She was older than me with several children, so I deferred to her.

I was exhausted, and I prayed she would only ask me to soak some millet so I could go right to bed. To my horror, she nonchalantly told me there were apples in the walk-in that needed to be sorted and used up, so she thought we could make apple crisp for breakfast. Could I please prep a five-gallon bucket of apples?

Making apple crisp for fifty-plus people was a huge endeavor. I would have to obtain cases of apples from the walk-in cooler across the property, sort out and rinse the good ones, then peel, core and slice them. Five gallons worth. It was easily over two hours of labor for one person. I didn't want to wind up in a meeting for being "unwilling," so I shoved back my rising emotions, said OK, and headed downstairs to get started.

Over an hour later, I was in the dining room where I'd set up my operation.

I wasn't even done peeling yet. I was so tired, and since it was my breakfast morning, I'd be dragging myself out of bed to head to the kitchen at 5:30 a.m.. My back was hurting, and my head was starting to ache. I was four or five months pregnant and I just wanted to go to sleep. At that point, I completely broke down. I started crying uncontrollably, by myself in the middle of the dining room, surrounded by my apple production.

A moment later, a young, single woman came walking through. She couldn't help but notice me, weeping away at my table. She came over and put her arms around me and told me how much she loved and appreciated me. I thanked her and she went on her way. I'm sure the reason she didn't offer to help me was that she was busy doing the "will" of her covering—one of the other women in the house. A single woman was never "independent" but was connected to, or covered by, a family, which pretty much gave said family nothing short of a nanny who served them however they asked.

❧

The importance of food in the TT cannot be overstated. For many, it was one of the only pleasurable aspects of life. I was even told once that the men worked long hours, and meals were one of the few things they had to look forward to, especially single men. The standards for what was considered "nice" were often ridiculous and came at the expense of the women.

One time, I was asked to cut two gallons of "matchstick" carrots for a stir-fry for Friday Night Meal. It took me over two hours, undoubtedly with countless amounts of discipline to keep my two small children focused, to accomplish this feat. I was just filling the jars with water and putting on the lids when the head woman of my weekend team walked by. "Oh no!" she said in dismay. "Those are too big. You'll need to cut them all in half again. This is for Friday night, so it needs to be nice." She opened a jar, pulled one out, and demonstrated the proper size of a matchstick carrot. I couldn't hide the anguish I felt as I told her I needed to get my children down for a nap first.

Another time I'd been asked to make cookies for a milestone celebration with both households—about eighty people. I made snickerdoodles, and with the help of my children they came out fine, just a little bigger than what I had planned on. I figured that was OK as there were enough for everyone to have one big cookie. I had just cleaned up everything and was placing the finished cookies in a container when the woman assigned as Kitchen Covering walked through and asked how they turned out. I told her they were good but a bit big, so it would be one per person.

She left the kitchen and came back a few minutes later. She had gone to confer with another woman, and they decided it would be "nicer" for everyone to have two cookies. I needed to make another batch. I nearly burst into tears. I'd already been at it for hours. "You're basically asking me to start all over?" was my stunned response.

"You have plenty of time. What else do you need to do today?" That clever question sealed my fate. I wasn't on the schedule for anything else, so any other "plans" I had, such as cleaning my room, taking my children outside, or sewing, would have been my "own will."

We didn't have the option to say no in these situations. We didn't even have the option to express dismay or any other kind of bad attitude. Absolute willingness to overcome was expected, or you'd wind up being admonished and having to repent. We were taught Ephesians 5:21—"*Submit to one another in the fear of Yahweh.*" We had to do what we were told or we were rebelling against God. In these types of situations, I couldn't help but wonder, "If Yahshua were here, would He care about the size of his carrot stick or suffer about only getting one cookie?" I wouldn't have dared say that to anyone though.

⚶

One woman in each community functioned as the Kitchen Covering. This position was tantamount to managing a busy restaurant. She was in charge of planning menus, ordering food and produce from places like Hillcrest or United Foods, shopping for items not bought in bulk, organizing the commissary, household freezers and refrigerators (of which there were several, plus a huge walk-in cooler), and planning and procuring the weekend food needs. Many people were on special needs diets such as gluten-free or nondairy, so extra provisions would be needed for them, as well as making sure each meal had an option they could eat. (Some people were excessive with their requests and secretly got dubbed as having "special greeds.") We did this on an impossibly small budget. The formula for the food budget was ten dollars per person per week. So, in a household of fifty, the Kitchen

Covering would have five hundred dollars a week.

The first time I was asked to cover the kitchen was when my eighty days were over with Darakah. It seemed daunting, but at least Emmet was on track to start training soon. I was assured there would be support, and I would get to go shopping and attend the Cooks' Meeting, which were irresistible perks. I rose to the occasion, took it on, and continued in this role for most of our remaining years in the TT.

Chapter 19

Spare Change for Underwear

ften, money was tight, and we had to get creative to meet needs. After Darakah was born, I needed new summer clothes. I had put fabric on my needs list many weeks earlier, hoping to get a few garments sewn before I had my baby, but hadn't received anything.

One Thursday night, my family had been tasked with a major basement cleanout, and I came across an old, forgotten trunk full of fabric. Most was unusable for clothing, but I was happy to find two lightweight, cotton pieces that would be enough for a couple garments. One was paisley, in various shades of pink, and the other was navy blue with tiny white dots on it. Definitely not fabric I would have picked out if I'd had a choice, but I felt good about not being picky and being thankful for what "Our Father had provided me."

I made a pair of knickers (calf-length pants) out of the paisley and a pair of culottes out of the navy. I remember one woman laughing good-naturedly about my "polka-dotted culottes," and I smiled, saying how cool they would be on hot summer days. The second time I wore them, Atarah came to me and told me I had to get rid of them and I really should be pickier about the fabrics I made clothes out of. I didn't get defensive, question, or reason but obediently changed and threw the culottes into the ragbag. I didn't get any new fabric after that, and to this day I don't really understand what was wrong with them.

A year or so later, a wedding was coming up, which always meant purse strings would get tighter, as the expenses for such an event were enormous. It also meant a huge household shuffle as we tried to accommodate the many guests who would be coming and spending the weekend. One family with two little girls offered to go stay at the "nanny's house" and open their rooms up for guests. This was a little house up behind the barn that was used for training classrooms.

The wife, Lehava, came to me on Thursday morning, while they were moving out of their rooms. I had been helping meet personal needs for the Main House, and she explained that most of her younger daughter's underwear had ripped out and needed to be thrown away, so she was down to only a couple pairs. She was worried about having enough to get through the weekend up at the nanny's house, especially because her daughter still had accidents at night, and was hoping I could get her a new package. Sounds like a simple, basic request that should have been no problem—we could get a pack from Kmart in Greenwich (ten minutes away) for five or six dollars. But I had no needs money—it had all gone toward people who needed new clothes for the wedding. Nevertheless, I told Lehava I'd see what I could do.

I asked the person who handled the community's books if I could have a few dollars to meet this specific need. I was told no and maybe someone could lend her daughter some underwear for the weekend. I resigned myself to asking other women with girls the same age if they had a pair or two to spare. But the next morning I overheard two men talking in the kitchen, and one of them mentioned he was going to Greenwich. I had an idea.

At this time on the Friday before a wedding, the household was bustling with people, as many guests from other communities had arrived early to help out with this major undertaking. I went around to different men, smiling sweetly and telling them I was trying to come up with just a few dollars to meet a pressing need. Did they perhaps have any spare change in their pockets? It only took a short time before I had enough change for the underwear. I tracked down the person I'd heard was going into town and told him of the situation, and he said he was glad to help. Yay! I put the change in a Ziploc bag and taped a piece of paper to it with the size of the underwear needed. (This man was a father himself, so I didn't feel weird asking him to get little girls' underwear.)

I was elated later when I trekked up the hill to the nanny's house, Kmart bag in hand. It was midafternoon, so Lehava had figured there would be no new underwear before the weekend. She was so appreciative you would have thought I had brought her ten thousand dollars, and the way the little girl's face lit up when she saw her new underwear nearly brought me to tears.

I loved finding ways to take care of people like this. I thought back to the person who had told me there was no money. Was there *really* no money? If one of the more prominent leader's wives had asked, would the response have been different? I didn't dwell there long, as we weren't supposed to have accusations toward people but to always "think the best."

Chapter 20

The Forgotten Tour

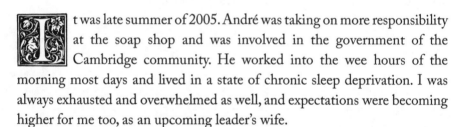t was late summer of 2005. André was taking on more responsibility at the soap shop and was involved in the government of the Cambridge community. He worked into the wee hours of the morning most days and lived in a state of chronic sleep deprivation. I was always exhausted and overwhelmed as well, and expectations were becoming higher for me too, as an upcoming leader's wife.

One day, he received a call from the Cambridge Historical Society. There was a town anniversary coming up in a few weeks, and they wanted to include our farm as part of a historical tour around the village. Of course, André said we'd love to participate and give tours of the property. That kind of thing was right up our alley and something the community would have used as an amazing evangelism opportunity. We'd serve tea and cookies, and the children would have an "offering" to sing to the guests. We'd go all out in the house, cleaning every nook and cranny, having fresh flowers in the bathrooms and a table full of our Twelve Tribes literature. There would have been a concerted effort all over the property too, planting more flowers and making sure the enormous lawn was meticulously mowed. The same effort would have been made at the soap shop, and samples would have been made available. We probably would have pulled together a hayride around the fields. It would have been a spectacular event, a highlight of the "Tour of Cambridge," if only André had remembered to tell someone.

As is often the case, as soon as he hung up the phone, something distracted him. Maybe it rang again immediately with a matter of urgency, or maybe someone came to talk to him about a "pressing need." Whatever the case, after that brief conversation he never thought of it again.

A few weeks later it was a sunny Sabbath afternoon. Emmet and Meyshar had settled down for a nap, and we had just laid down ourselves, with me nursing Darakah. André's cell phone rang, startling him as he was dozing off. It was Samuel. "Oh, no!" I heard him exclaim in horror. "I forgot all about that. I'll be right there." He literally flew off the bed in a panic.

"What's going on?" He tried to fill me in quickly as he was pulling on his shoes.

"Get the children up and get to the shop as soon as you can. We have to give tours." And then he was gone. I put my half-asleep baby in a back carrier and called the other children, who weren't at all sad to have gotten out of their nap.

We headed downstairs and passed through the kitchen so I could alert the team doing lunch cleanup to what was happening. Thankfully, it was Jonah and Talitha, who sprang into action with their children. Within moments, water was on for tea, and Talitha and her girls began cleaning the first floor at record speed. The children and I raced across the lawn and into the soap shop to find my husband speaking with a small group of five or six people. OK, this wouldn't be so bad. We would take our time showing them the soap shop and the animals at the barn, giving them more time to get ready in the house. Everyone loves babies, and within moments they were all fawning over Darakah and smiling at my other children, who were exceptionally well behaved, sensing something was amiss. Out of the corner of my eye, I saw Samuel in the office, on the phone. I assumed he was calling the other house, where he lived, to get his family to come help as well. Good, everything was going to be OK.

As my husband led the group around the shop, I glanced out the window and saw another car coming down the driveway and another after that. I got his attention and told him more people were coming. Turns out, our property was the last stop on the historical tour, which, someone in the group let us know, had a great turnout. We should expect a lot of people throughout the afternoon, they said. André and I exchanged nervous glances.

"Excuse me one moment," André said to the group. "You go greet the people just pulling in," he said to me as he quickly dialed the house and requested help at the shop ASAP.

Thankfully, there were a couple single men still doing lunch cleanup who immediately raced up to the shop, where they transformed into hospitality mode the moment they approached the next group of people. We managed to act like we had been expecting them all day, and we split the group between two of us while the other brother waited for the next vehicle already coming down the long drive. Hopefully, reinforcements from the other house would arrive soon.

As I was taking my first group up to the house after showing them the shop and barn, I saw a sight I will never forget. It was Samuel, sauntering leisurely down North Union Street toward the village. He didn't look hurried or like he was on a mission to help with this urgent situation. No, he was going back to his house for his Sabbath rest, we would find out later. I don't know who he was on the phone with earlier, but he wasn't calling for help. He had decided that André hadn't been a faithful messenger and for his great lack should feel the sting of discipline, which was to handle this situation himself.

For the next two and a half hours, André and I, with our three children and the other two men, juggled the continual trickle of cars that came down the driveway, showing them around the soap shop, letting them pet the goats at the barn, and walking them across the picturesque property up to the impressive Main House. Jonah and Talitha's families served tea all afternoon and provided support with the house part of the tour. Of course, guests were disappointed they couldn't see the upstairs because most other families were asleep in their bedrooms.

Finally, it was over, and my family showed up exhausted to the evening gathering. We felt accomplished, like we had really risen to the occasion and redeemed what could have been a huge disaster. Our children had been shining examples of good-mannered community children, and many people told us before they left that our property had been their favorite part of the tour.

Any good feelings we had were soon dashed. Instead of praising us, Samuel thought it fitting to use this situation as a case-in-point topic for the gathering, quoting the parable of the unfaithful servant and talking in depth about how the inattentive won't enter the Kingdom. I know it was humiliating for my husband, who stood after Samuel finished and repented to the entire community for his failure. There was no appreciation for any of us.

The worst thing about this situation is, had it been Samuel who had made an honest mistake, the entire community would have been expected to rally and help get his "ox out the ditch." Anyone who had not gotten out of their beds to support would have been reprimanded. He may well have repented but not because he'd been publicly admonished. And any who dared make a judgment upon his error would have been sternly rebuked for not thinking the best and having mercy.

Chapter 21

Train up a Child

hild training was supposed to be the number one priority of our lives. Raising up the next generation was key to the TT continuing toward the goal of the return of Yahshua. If our children didn't take on our hearts, we would fail just like every other movement before us. When I heard such things as a new disciple, it sounded wonderful—to be able to focus on my children in ways my own parents couldn't and provide them with such an amazing purpose for their lives. But the reality of raising children according to the TT standards was anything but wonderful.

As part of the strict upbringing, we were not allowed to be silly or "foolish" with them. That would only breed disrespect. They called it a "Bozo/Hitler complex," referring to situations where an adult was foolish with a child, and then, when the child said or did something inappropriate in response, suddenly the adult came down hard on them for their behavior. It wasn't that we had to be downright dour. In fact, we were told to smile at them often and that they should receive seven times as much encouragement as discipline. (Easier said than done.) We just had to be careful not to cross the line. Mothers were encouraged to show affection to their children but not give in to motherly instincts to "pander" or feel badly if their child was mistreated but to always support authority, no matter what.

The word "play" wasn't allowed in the customary sense. We said, "Let's work with these blocks," or "You can work with this clay." The reasoning was we didn't want our children to have a concept of play being fun and work being boring, so we didn't differentiate between the two. One time, during a child training teaching when this standard was being reinforced, a woman asked if we should say we are going to work on a game of volleyball or that the children need to practice working on their musical instruments. There wasn't a good answer, and many of us stifled a chuckle.

When we allowed our children to "work" with blocks, we were still supposed to be directing them. "Now I want you to build a tower with the green blocks," was the exact example given in a teaching to show that they shouldn't be left to themselves to have their own independent ideas but should always be under authority and expected to follow instruction. If you turned your back and they made a tower with blue blocks after you told them to use green, they should be disciplined for being disobedient.

Children, from toddlers up, were to be given a "will" at all times. They should always be doing a task that we instructed them to do. They were to be under our supervision or that of another designated adult at all times and never sent outside to play together or given free time in their room. They also were not to voice their opinion about what to do, such as asking, "Can we go for a walk?" Then it would be their will and not ours if we said yes. They were only supposed to ask, "What should I do next, Imma?" No amount of independent thought or action was allowed for children.

Not long before we left, there was a swing set outside my bedroom window, and sometimes I'd let my daughters, then twelve and nine, go out and swing together. I could hear them from my room, and of course they were instructed not to go anywhere else. Someone soon raised a concern that I wasn't out there with them or finding them a productive will in the house but just letting them "dissipate" on the swing set. Dissipation was strictly forbidden.

Children were not allowed to engage in any type of fantasy. This included any kind of make believe or pretend. An imaginary friend would never be tolerated. Two little girls couldn't play "house" together, and little boys weren't supposed to pretend their measuring cup, piece of wood, or rock was a motor vehicle by pushing them around and making engine noises. This was deemed dissipation and the inevitable result of parents not having a clear will for children. If our hearts were turned to our children, they would be at our side participating in a productive activity. They would never be left to themselves, where naturally their little minds would turn to fantasy.

Dolls weren't allowed, and little girls couldn't even "play baby" by wrapping up a pillow in a blanket and pretending to rock it. That was fantasy and was a disciplinable offense. The reasoning was there were enough real babies for girls to help with. The problem with that was not every little girl had a baby sibling, and they couldn't just walk up to someone else's baby and interact with it. That was overfamiliar and not condoned either.

I remember one of my friends from Burlington asking me questions before we moved in. "What if a child had a really creative imagination and they drew amazing creatures that weren't realistic?" I said something to the effect of, since they weren't exposed to television or books, they probably wouldn't come up with something like that. Imagination, creativity, and, quite honestly, human nature are inexcusably extinguished for children in the TT.

Even riding bicycles for fun was seen as dissipation and not allowed for children. Bicycles were only for "covered" adults who might need a quick way to get down to the café or the other house when a vehicle wasn't available.

As parents, we were never to give children incentive to obey by saying something like, "Let's get supper cleanup done quickly so we can go to the barn and see the new baby goats!" That was bribery, and if we did that, it wouldn't be clear if the children were obeying from their hearts or just because they were going to get to do something "fun" after. Only after our children did our bidding with a good attitude could we reward them in any way.

Children were never supposed to ask for food. Parents—mothers mainly—were supposed to know when the children might need a snack and be one step ahead of them. They also weren't to be given choices. One time, several leftovers were put out, buffet style, for lunch. I asked my nine-year-old daughter what she would like, because it really didn't matter to me if she chose leftover rice pilaf or quiche. Normally there were no choices at mealtimes and my children ate what was served. Someone overheard, and I was pulled aside and rebuked, told that she should be eating what I want her to eat and not what she desires. (Somehow, food and sex were connected. It says in the child training manual that if we don't control our children's appetites for food, we will not be able to control their appetites for sex.)

We never ever ended a command by saying, "OK?" We did not ask if our command was "OK" with the child. But it was said to get the child to respond. "Finish folding that laundry, OK?" They were always supposed to say "Yes, Imma" and "Yes, Abba" to any instruction, and they were to be disciplined for not listening if they failed to respond. That was a hard standard to maintain when you had several children and spent most of your time with them giving commands. We had to have a rod handy at all times.

We also were not supposed to say please or thank you to our children when it came to commanding them. The command was sufficient and didn't need a "please" in front of it. Obedience was expected and didn't require a "thank you." Of course, we could praise our children for a job well done or for being quick to obey, and we were encouraged to do so. "You did a great job making your bed!" We could even appreciate and praise them publicly at gatherings or the Victory Cup. But we didn't need to thank them.

Language was of utmost importance, and another word that took some time to eradicate from use was "kids" when referring to children. Kids are baby goats, so we never used that term when talking about children—we always said "child" or "children." We also never said "pee" or "poop." We were to use the proper terms: "urinate" and "bowel movement."

We were taught that ADHD was not an actual disorder. It would be ridiculed during child training teachings and nicknamed "DDD" (discipline deficit disorder). A child who was rambunctious or "out of line" was this way because of inconsistent discipline or because they were not given a clear will. Children in the world who were diagnosed with such disorders only needed some good, consistent spankings. TT's philosophy was, they had lazy parents who didn't care enough to discipline diligently and therefore needed an excuse for their child's bad behavior. They turned to the convenience of a diagnosis and doping them up on meds instead of bringing them under control through proper parental authority.

There were children with disabilities in the community, but many went undiagnosed because of lack of involvement in the medical system. Such children did not receive special treatment—they were disciplined as much as the next child. The only help children with ADHD get in the community is from the rod.

Three out of my four children had problems with bedwetting. It's the rare family in the community that doesn't have at least one problem bedwetter in the family. When Emmet was seven, we were asked by another couple to meet with them. That usually meant they needed to talk about something wrong in our family. They told us the reason Emmet still wet at night was that we were not disciplining him enough during the day to keep his body under control. Therefore, when he went to sleep, his body just "let loose" all night long and stayed in that place of being out of control. This was a child who got so much discipline that his bottom was usually calloused and leathery. We were even given a special balm to rub on our children's bottoms after a "good" spanking. The act of tenderly caring for the skin we had just inflicted welts on was somehow supposed to impart our love to the child.

I continually vacillated between feeling guilty about the spankings and being resolved to receive the direction that came to me so I could raise a surrendered child who would bring us honor, not shame.

Now that I look back, I realize Emmet was actually a very good and normal little boy. I cringe over how much he was spanked and feel terrible guilt. He had lots of energy, had an extremely bright and curious mind, absolutely loved people, and was always kind to other children. He was not a performer though—he'd act the same no matter who was around. That was problematic in the community, and I remember saying to him often, "Can you just be quiet when so-and-so is in the kitchen?" He got a bad rap in Cambridge for being out of line. He was impulsive and loud, often drawing attention to himself, when other children were quietly doing the same things. Then along came Meyshar, who was the complete opposite. That came with its own set of challenges.

When she was two or three years old, it was apparent she was an in-line child. Quiet, easygoing, and shy, she contentedly stayed close to me and did what I gave her to do. She sat quietly even through long gatherings. She didn't draw attention to herself.

One day, an older woman, whose teenage daughter had left the community, came to me and said I had to be creative to find ways to cross my daughter's will. Basically, I needed to do things to provoke a reaction from her so she would get used to receiving discipline. The woman told me her daughter had also been very good as a little girl and therefore hadn't been disciplined much, but it backfired when she became a youth and couldn't handle having her will crossed. I was told to wait until she was happily engaged in something, then tell her she had to stop and do something she wouldn't like to test her willingness to obey. This would bring out her rebellion, which was hiding in there and needed to be exposed before she got older.

I listened respectfully and thanked the woman for her input, but I never made it a priority to uncover this hidden rebellion. I was too busy with my household schedule and trying to rule over Emmet. Meyshar's easygoing personality was the only "grace" I had.

I had two very different children and felt like I was never doing right by either of them. I hardly enjoyed their younger years, being so consumed with all this. We could never just let our guards down, relax, and enjoy our children.

I remember talking to Michelle one time when her two boys were little. She was telling me how one night she turned off all the lights in the house to play flashlight tag with them and how much fun it was. I couldn't even comprehend doing something like that with my children and not just because logistically speaking it would have been impossible in a community household. I never "played" with my children. We never would have behaved inappropriately like that—encouraging the possibility of being "wild," their spirit getting out of control. I was secretly jealous and wondered what it would be like to engage with my children like that.

※

In the summer of 2006, we lived downtown. It was a Sunday, and a couple was moving to Ithaca. Recently, the wife and I hadn't been getting along, and I was not sad at all to see them pulling out as I smiled and waved from the porch with my children. My husband was driving them, and there was no room in the vehicle for him to take one of our children. The two other families in the household had gone away for the weekend, so I was home alone for the first time since moving to the community. I wandered freely around the house, letting my children run around and fantasizing that it was "my" house. No one was around to question my children's whereabouts or correct them for being too loud. No one was judging me for not giving them a productive will or slacking on discipline. I was in heaven.

Everyone was gathering at the Main House that night for the Minchah and dinner. It was the last thing I wanted to do. I tried so hard to always keep a good conscience, and it's not easy for me to lie, but I needed a good reason to stay down there. I couldn't just say I didn't feel like going. I waited until later than normal to lie Darakah down for a nap, then I called up to the Main House and asked to speak to one of the women who I felt wouldn't give me a hard time. "Could you let Elad know that Yeshurun is gone to Ithaca and Darakah isn't feeling well and is having a late nap, so I'm just going to stay down here with my children?" I didn't think anyone would bat an eye at that alibi, and I was right.

As soon as I knew the gathering would be in full swing, I told my children we were having ice cream for dinner! I'd never done anything so renegade and spontaneous, and their joy nearly brought me to tears. There was a Stewarts just down the road, and with Darakah in a stroller and Emmet and Meyshar skipping happily down the sidewalk, we made our way there and I let them pick out a half gallon of ice cream. When we got home, I grabbed some bowls, spoons, and a blanket, and we went out to the lawn for a picnic supper of ice cream—as much as they could eat. I felt so relaxed and savored every moment until a car pulled in a couple hours later.

❦

One evening a week we had Proverbs night, where our children would recite a proverb they learned. They would stand on a stool, loudly say their proverb, then say what they learned. Some more industrious mothers would have drawn them a picture depicting their proverb. Many children loved this and thrived on shouting their proverb out to the room and proudly sharing what lesson they gleaned. But for the shy children, it was torture. They'd get on the box, and then run back to their parents. The parents would walk them back up and command them to say their proverb, and if they didn't, they'd be taken out and spanked. Then they'd be brought back in, and the whole thing started again. I saw children taken out and spanked four or five times before they finally eked out their proverb. Then there would often be a rabble-rousing single brother who would call out from the back of the room, "Can you say that again a little louder, please?" which could cause the child to have a complete meltdown.

We were told to discipline our children "at the dawn." Literally. We were supposed to go into their rooms one time in the morning, tell them it was time to get up, and then leave. After a few minutes we were to go back in, and if they hadn't gotten up then they needed to be spanked right away. The person telling us this (a leader from Argentina) proudly told us how his five-year-old would basically be asleep standing up, practically falling over, but he knew better than to not get immediately out of bed when he was woken up. I remember sitting there and conjuring up the cringeworthy image of this sweet little boy literally tipping over but knowing if he lay back down he'd quickly be woken back up with a painful strike of the rod.

One woman said she liked to do a "gentle" awakening first, maybe sing them a little song or sit on their beds and give them a back rub for a few minutes. Then she'd leave and come back after a few minutes, and then tell them it was time to get up. She was told it was fine to do those things, but she needed to expect they would get up after being commanded.

Because we had to discipline our children immediately for the slightest infraction, I saw multiple women who wore rods on their bodies to always have one available. One woman used to put it down her back, under her bra strap, so it stuck up over her shoulder. Another would put one down the waistband of her pants. We had multiple discreet places to hide rods all over the houses—in decorative dried flower arrangements or wreaths, above the trim on bathroom doors, behind radiators in closets, behind curtains in windows. One of the biggest complaints in the household was people taking the "common" rods to bedrooms. We would label them with pieces of masking tape wrapped around the bottom. It might read "Bathroom rod. Please leave here." People also labeled their own rods. Women would sew themselves cloth rod holders that would hang on bedposts or closet doorknobs. Rods were a common part of everyday life.

Rods were actually basket-weaving materials. We bought spools of the stuff, then cut them into 18-inch sections, soaked them in water to straighten them, and rubbed them down with linseed oil to strengthen them and keep them from snapping or fraying too quickly.

We were expected to be one hundred percent consistent with disciplining on the first command, meaning we were to give a command one time, and if the child did not obey, they were disciplined. We were told if a child only got disciplined nine out of ten times for something, they would always be striving for that one time they could get away with it. It was unimaginably difficult to maintain this standard perfectly with only one child, let alone several. I went to bed most nights feeling totally condemned, remembering infractions I hadn't disciplined them for and feeling like a failure.

We were to go to one another out of "love" when we saw a parent who wasn't being diligent and consistent in their discipline. For me, it was awkward and difficult to go over to a harried woman trying to get a meal done and tell her I noticed how she told her child to stop banging his spoon on the table and he was still doing it. I usually would feel like a jerk, but this is how we were supposed to be all the time, and I was on the receiving end of such "love" more times than I could ever count. We were told if we weren't going to one another, it would give us a bad conscience, and if that child ended up falling away, part of their blood would be on our heads for not loving them enough to help their parents. Living in households of twenty to fifty people, there were always "discerning" eyes upon you and your children.

Whenever someone came to us with a concern about our children, we were expected to "receive" them. We were told that once we sided with our child against authority, we'd ruined them. We weren't supposed to ever defend our child against any accusation of wrongdoing, even if we felt the accusation was wrong. We were to thank the person and discipline the child accordingly. After the fact, when our child had seen us support authority, we could humbly talk to the person in private if we felt there had been a mistake. Ultimately, our children were "guilty until proven innocent." Even if they were proven innocent, we were told it was good for our children to learn to receive false accusations and suffer injustice because it would prepare them for the persecution they would have to face someday. Yahshua Himself was falsely accused and did not defend himself, and our goal was to become like Him. We were taught, "Defensive parents will rue their children's insolence."

One day, Meyshar, thirteen at the time, was disrespectful to me. I reprimanded her and sent her to her room. A few minutes later, the woman who lived in the room next door came knocking, asking if she could speak to me in private. We went into her room, and she told me she heard what my daughter said and was surprised I hadn't spanked her. I explained that she was on her period, and it felt awkward to expect her to pull her pants down and bend over. She told me I couldn't let that be an excuse for inconsistent discipline and that when she was a youth (this person had been in the community since age nine), she was always expected to pull her pants down or lift her skirt for discipline even when she was on her period.

We were told to discipline in this way through a child's sixteenth year, but I recall one woman bragging that she was seventeen the last time she got a spanking on the bottom.

Chapter 22

Take My Life

round the time when Darakah was a year old, I was struggling and wondering if I'd ever "get it." We'd been in the community for six years now, and I never seemed to prosper, unlike my husband who seemed to have it all together. He shared at almost every gathering, functioned in government, and was unceasingly sought after to troubleshoot the everyday community problems and give spiritual counsel to those who needed it. I was not seen in this way. I wasn't the selfless giver that he was. I knew people thought I held back and resisted serving to my full potential. I didn't feel like I complemented my husband at all in our roles in the community. I felt as if he was a shining star and I was in his shadow. Hardly a Breaking of Bread went by that he wasn't appreciated by someone. He was traveling more (he had been sent to meetings in Europe, California, and Florida) and going to important meetings regularly in nearby communities. I felt left in the dust and condemned.

As a wife, I was supposed to be one hundred percent fulfilled by building up my husband, serving quietly by his side, and meeting all his needs. He was supposed to be my "King," and my worth should come from submitting to him and raising "his" children to bring honor to him. I was to have no selfish ambition of my own. I felt hopeless that I would ever truly be that way, and I prayed about it constantly, as God would judge me for this someday.

I talked to one of the older women one day about my struggles, and her response was that I wasn't a "volunteer." I wasn't going above and beyond what was on my schedule. The reality was, I felt like I could rarely come up for a breath, and I'd collapse in exhaustion every night, especially when I had little children, was pregnant, or, much of the time, both! I didn't know how to find the time to volunteer to do more.

I never felt understood in the community, especially by women who were "powerhouses" and could easily knock out an elaborate meal with several children in tow. I was often seen as someone who resisted my portion or wasn't willing to overcome and work hard. When I pointed out that the women who were volunteering for extra chores or other responsibilities only cooked one or two meals a week, I was told those women had more children than me.

There were many popular sayings in the TT: "The most miserable disciple is one who gives ninety-nine percent;" "It wouldn't be hard if it weren't for self-regard;" and "The community is a torture chamber for the flesh." These sayings were meant to always keep us looking inward and blaming our selfish, fleshly nature anytime we were suffering about our circumstances. We were told the one who gives ninety-nine percent is the most miserable because that one percent they are holding back is not enough to satisfy their flesh, yet is keeping them from experiencing the true life that comes from giving one hundred percent.

⁂

One day, I was feeling absolutely depressed about my life and went for a walk during my children's nap. I remember asking God to just take my life if I was never going to receive the faith I needed to be the kind of wife and mother my family needed. I knew I would never leave the community on my own, but it was obvious André and I were mismatched as a couple and would never function together the way other leading couples did—traveling together, for example—and I knew André wanted that. I figured if I was out of the picture, he and the children would be devastated at first, but eventually he would marry a more suitable community wife. Then he would be happier and there would be more hope for my children's eternal destinies. I wasn't exactly suicidal—I never thought of taking my own life—but thought maybe God could orchestrate an accident.

More than once, women had talked to me about the danger of holding my husband back. I should be the one to empower him to serve in whatever way he was being called because he was doing Our Father's will. He should be able to function with confidence that I was "taking on his heart" in his absence. I should not be the kind of wife suffering about how much he was gone and pining for him to be around more to support with the children. If I ever voiced distress about this, I would get stories of women who'd had it worse than me. "When I was eight months pregnant, my husband was sent to France for three weeks and barely made it back in time for the birth." Basically, I should be thankful for the high calling given to my husband and not be a shameful, selfish wife who withheld my husband from the Body.

I began to faithfully pray this way: "If I'm never going to 'get it' and am going to end up destroying my family, please just take my life." I would honestly rather have died than go through the grueling day-to-day challenges of community life, only to have my children grow up and leave. We were told this was the greatest pain a parent could ever feel. It would be judged as my fault, and I'd have to live in shame for how I failed my husband. I didn't see how, with all my shortcomings as a wife and parent, I could ever succeed in raising wholehearted disciples.

André seemingly loved his life there and had never told me otherwise. He had attained an important status, and I thought he'd be much happier simply being able to function and not be dragged down by my neediness. He'd be free to answer any phone call, text, or knock on the door interrupting preparation time and not have to deal with my annoyance afterwards. He could work around the clock and have the kind of wife who would wait up for "intimate time," and then quietly get up early and get all the children ready for the gathering, letting him sleep a few more minutes. I was too needy and overwhelmed to be that kind of wife.

Chapter 23

Being Fruitful

ur Father did not take my life, but a new one began instead. In March 2007 I became pregnant with my fourth child. I had mixed emotions upon finding out I was pregnant. Emmet had just turned eight, Meyshar was five, and Darakah would soon be two. We were living at the downtown house, and I was busy covering the kitchen. André was working at least eighteen hours a day. The thought of another baby seemed overwhelming, and my first thought was a saying coined by my father-in-law: "You play, you pay." Women always seemed to be popping out more babies than we could handle, but each child was a gift from God, thought about and planned since the beginning of time.

I prayed diligently for a healthy baby but also faithfully prayed that this child would not wet the bed. That's where I was at. I couldn't handle more wet bedding, as the other three all regularly had accidents, and I struggled daily to keep up with washing and changing everyone's bedding. Interestingly, he was my only child who never wet the bed—not even once—after I stopped putting him in diapers.

❋

It was summer 2007, and I was four months pregnant. It was a beautiful Sabbath, and we planned to take our children fishing at a nearby river, a rare excursion. We quickly finished our cake and yogurt and headed home to gather fishing supplies. The river was about a mile and a half walk from the house. We walked through a couple small neighborhoods, past the local school, and toward the woods on the outskirts of town. We had to walk down a trail in the woods of maybe a quarter mile before we reached a steep hill that had to be meandered down cautiously, holding onto small trees all the way down for balance. At the bottom of the hill was the river, and the children happily threw rocks in the water, splashing along the edge.

We found a spot that looked good for fishing and began getting the few rods we had ready. Emmet was having a difficult time casting out, and André was trying to help him. At one point, André let the line fly, and it got caught in a tree branch that was hanging over the water a few yards away. We all followed as he and Emmet headed over to check it out. Meyshar ran to the other side of the tree, and I was following with Darakah right in front of me. The tree appeared sound, and as André waited for us to move past him, he gave a small, experimental tug on the line. To his horror, there was a loud crack as the branch broke off and fell directly onto my head. It had been about ten to twelve feet above ground, and the impact knocked me to the ground with a scream.

André helped me stand up right away, and I put my hand to my head to discover the unsettling wetness of blood. It soon began to trickle down the side of my face. Emmet panicked and started yelling and kicking André, completely at a loss as to how to handle his injured mother. Meyshar was frozen in fear. Darakah started to cry, and I almost fainted as I realized that if we had been just a few inches back, the branch would have fallen on her head.

"I'm OK, I'm OK!" I reassured them as André pulled a towel out of the backpack for me to hold on my head to try to stop the bleeding. We were in the middle of nowhere with no cell phone, a good ten-minute walk to the nearest house down a steep ravine with three panicking children, and pregnant me holding a towel on top of my head with half my face covered in blood. It was a nightmare. André picked up Darakah and as much as he could carry. He told Emmet and Meyshar they had to carry everything else, and we needed to go quickly to get help. They rose to the occasion, and we all started the climb back up to the trail.

"You OK?" André asked me every few seconds.

"Yes," I replied, unsure but not wanting to scare the children. I remembered my prior prayers for God to take my life, which I no longer asked due to being pregnant, and suddenly realized this could have been the accident I prayed for. My neck could have easily broken.

We made it out of the woods and could see the nearest house. As we approached the driveway, André told us to wait, and he would go in and ask to use the phone. I was exhausted and sat down on their lawn, still holding the towel to my head. I could see the homeowners peering out their window at the injured woman and three young children on their property. Soon my husband came out and said someone was on their way to get us. After a few minutes, an old, rusty farm truck pulled up, and we all piled in.

At this point, most people would head to urgent care for the pregnant lady with a head injury. Not us. We asked to be dropped off at the house. André called Elad, who had EMT training, to come over and check me out. He looked at my pupils, cleaned and inspected the cut on my head, and told me it didn't need stitches. I was instructed to take a couple Tylenol and lie down for the rest of the day.

The next day, I could barely move my upper body. To turn my head even a fraction of an inch was excruciating. I took more painkillers and went on with life. I don't remember anyone being concerned for my baby. I still felt movement, so it was alive. All was good.

On December 5, 2007, Arek was born. It was my longest labor, nearly twenty-four hours, and it was close to midnight when he arrived. I barely remember anything after he emerged. Annie recalls a nerve-racking night closely monitoring him, as he did not have great color at first and seemed severely congested.

I was glad to have another boy—a brother for Emmet—but I think many women, upon having a boy, have a moment of panic after the initial joy. Only forty days until you're back on the schedule. I'd once again be trying to get lunch done with a baby and a two-year-old. We were technically stay-at-home moms, and we always spoke of "working mothers" in a derogatory sense. I remember thinking I worked much longer and harder hours than any job I'd ever had in the "world;" I just had to do it with my children by my side the whole time.

Then, with a boy, came circumcision on the eighth day, done right in our bedroom with a very sharp knife and a fork. Thankfully, Arek's circumcision was perfect with no complications, but other babies were not so lucky, and I'd heard horror stories of botched jobs.

Arek was born on a Wednesday night, and after the weekend everyone went on with their normal routines. I was in our rooms (we now had two large bedrooms connected by our own bathroom) all day with baby Arek and energetic Darakah. (Meyshar had started training a few months earlier). I was fraught with postpartum emotions and, being an especially cold, snowy winter, it was hard to get outdoors much.

This may not sound so bad compared to the stress of the kitchen, but the high standard of having a will at all times, even for a two-year-old, made for long and often frustrating days. In our bedrooms, with only blocks, puzzles, or nature coloring books for entertainment, we were still expected to be commanding our children with productive tasks and disciplining them diligently. I couldn't slack up on my standards for Darakah. If she got used to doing her will during this time, being back in the kitchen with her and the baby in just a few short weeks would be a nightmare.

Reminiscent of when Emmet was a baby at our house in Burlington, I'd be counting down the hours and minutes until André walked through the door at 5:00. Sometimes Emmet was able to be with him at the soap shop after training, while other times both he and Meyshar would be home at 3:00 and I'd have the four children to manage. It just wasn't enjoyable, and I'd be wrought with guilt for being a bad mother.

One day, André came home and informed me the Government Meeting that night was starting early, right after dinner. The day had already been so long that the thought of bedtime by myself was too much, and I burst into tears.

I made it through the evening and fell into bed exhausted. Just as I was dozing off, Arek woke up and proceeded to have a two-hour fussy period. At one point, I was lying in bed with him sitting on my stomach and propped up on my knees. He was crying inconsolably, and I cried with him for a while. Then he quieted and suddenly a voice came to me, clear as day. It said, "You don't have to do this again. This can be it. You can be done." I didn't have to have any more children! I could get through this baby phase one more time and never have to do it again. I suddenly felt relief and peace wash over me. I loved my baby and knew I could overcome this one last time. I prayed for any mercy God could have for me.

Mercy came to me in the most unexpected way. When Arek was three months old, my maternal grandmother moved into the community. She was seventy-two and still in excellent shape and health. She had called me at one point and asked, "What does your community think of old people?" "We love them!" had been my enthusiastic response. We had visited her several times over the years, and she had also been to stay with us for a few days during my pregnancy. She had been one of the few relatives who had supported us when we moved into the community.

One day she called, asking, "Do you think you would have room for me there?"

"Of course!" I replied in delight. My mother and I lived with her until I was seven, and she took care of me all the time. I felt life had come full circle. She couldn't work full time and care for her own home anymore, and the community would provide her not only companionship and a secure home but family as well.

On March 11, 2008, my Nanny, Betty Ruel, moved into the Twelve Tribes. She was a godsend to me. She loved baby Arek dearly and was always more than willing to rock him to sleep or take him for a walk during my busy days. I was now covering the kitchen at the Main House again and had my active almost three-year-old to direct all day as well. I can honestly say I don't know how I would have managed without her, and she adapted to our life amazingly well, as though she had always lived that way. Of course, she still had access to her own money and car for quite a while. The TT doesn't treat all new recruits equally when it comes to expectations of what they have to give up. Another bonus was Nanny's snack tote in her closet, which we were welcome to and was always full of delectable goodies. She also had a coffee maker, and Nanny's room became a common stop for the ladies of the house who had a "headache." Life did get better having my grandmother there. She was baptized after about a year and given the name Chezikah. Thankfully she remained "Nanny" to my family.

Chapter 24

Out of Order

ince we had to be creative to earn money for personal needs, Emmet and I began making rock magnets to sell at the café. I got the idea while we were visiting Plymouth one time. There was a cute basket next to the cash register at their wholesome food market of small magnets made of flat rocks with pretty flower decals on them. They were selling for a dollar apiece.

"Do these sell well?" I asked a cashier who worked there.

"Yes, we sell out and have to make more all the time," she replied. I tucked the idea in the back of my mind.

A few months later, my family was visiting the community in Oak Hill. We were walking along the river, and I picked up a perfectly smooth, round, flat rock. Remembering the magnets, I soon had my family gathering up as many as we could hold in our pockets and tuck up in shirts. On shopping day, I found pretty decals at AC Moore and picked up some magnets. I grabbed clear nail polish to paint over the finished product. Emmet and I began testing our new industry when I got home and soon had a basket of thirty rock magnets. I of course had to get "covered" by the government to start selling them at the café and to use the proceeds for needs.

The following weekend, our community had the Friday Night Meal at our café because we were redoing the kitchen floor at the Main House. After the meal, people were sitting in the cozy booths socializing and waiting for dessert. I had just come back from taking a child to the bathroom when a man, Ezra, approached me with the dreaded question, "Can I talk to you for a minute?"

We went to a quiet corner, and he proceeded to tell me that Emmet had called his thirteen-year-old son "stupid." "OK, thank you, I'll go look into that." I dutifully replied.

Finding Emmet, I pulled him aside asking, "Why did you tell Micah he was stupid?" I didn't ask him if he *did* tell the boy he was stupid as that would have left him room to reason or lie. Our children were always guilty as charged. Anger flashed over Emmet's ten-year-old face. "He told me our rock magnets are stupid and are never going to sell, so I told him *he* was stupid!" I took a deep breath. I had to hold him accountable for his wrong reaction, which we never allowed excuses for.

"It doesn't matter what he said to you, you don't ever call someone stupid. You should have just walked away and told me or your Abba. You need to repent to him." I had to make Emmet see that I was standing on the side of authority.

We spotted Ezra and his son and strode over. I fully intended to let him know privately and "humbly" what had provoked my son to say what he did after Emmet repented for his wrong response. "I'm sorry for calling you stupid," Emmet said, looking right at Micah.

"I forgive you," he replied, a hint of a smirk on his face.

Now, I'll never know what prompted Ezra to say what he said next. He normally wasn't confrontational. But once the boys were out of earshot, he leaned closer and said to me gruffly, "Maybe you should teach your son to be more respectful to older children."

All humility left my body as I shot back, "Maybe if your *older child* wasn't going around provoking younger children, they'd respect him!" I then told him what his son had said about the rock magnets. He walked away from me in a huff.

I quickly found André and told him about the situation, barely finishing when one of the other leaders came and asked to talk to him. They went outside for several minutes. I did not expect what happened next. My husband came back in, pulled me aside, and told me I needed to go repent to Ezra for being disrespectful to him! I was infuriated and did not understand how this had come back on me. The same advice I'd given my son about his response to an older child pertained to me reacting to a man. I should have received his admonishment instead of talking back, and he had gone and reported my insubmissive behavior.

André was firm. I needed to go right then. I could see him sitting alone at a back table, looking completely dark and gloomy. "He's going to deal with what Micah said to Emmet, but you didn't need to say what you did," André said coaxingly. "Just get it over with and we'll get out of here."

Feeling complete humiliation, I obediently walked over, and not bothering to hide the emotions on my face, I robotically said, "I'm sorry for being disrespectful to you." He barely glanced up, and I caught a mumbled, "I forgive you," before I turned on my heel and went back to my family.

※❁❂

A few months later, Emmet was out on the front porch throwing a ball back and forth with a single brother in his late twenties called Harutz. I was cleaning up the kitchen when he came running in, crying and clutching his chest. "What happened?" I exclaimed. The wind was knocked out of him, and it took him a few moments. He told me through gasping breaths that Harutz had kicked him. He lifted his shirt to expose a large red area on his chest.

My maternal instincts skyrocketed. I sat him on a stool, told him to wait there, and went out to the porch. I saw Harutz leaning against the railing and nonchalantly spinning the ball in his hands. "What happened? Why did you kick Emmet?" I shot at him.

"We were tossing the ball back and forth, and instead of waiting for me to throw it, he just grabbed it out of my hands," was his explanation, spoken so calmly and slowly he almost seemed bored. I was livid.

"You are the adult not the child in this situation! You don't kick children! If my son was disrespectful, you should have come and told me!" I walked away and took Emmet to go show my husband the still prominent evidence of the immature and reprehensible actions of this man. I expected justice to occur.

Later that day André came home with that "look" on his face. He told me Harutz was going to apologize to Emmet, but there had been others out on the porch who had heard the confrontation, and I had to apologize to Harutz for my disrespectful reaction to him! Once again, I was stunned. My husband had met with a couple other leaders, and the verdict was that I should not have confronted and corrected him publicly but should have gotten a man involved immediately. Once again, I was out of order. Women did not correct men under any circumstance. I resisted as much as I dared, but he was not budging. I felt like a child as he took me to find Harutz, who I gave a half-hearted apology to just to end the ordeal.

Chapter 25

Toddler Training

ack in the early days of the community, there were groups for all ages of children, right down to baby training for babies six months and up. Women used to talk about how awful it had been to leave their nursing babies at training and then go off and work in the restaurants, teach their own training group, or cook meals for the household. The women who taught the babies described the stress of a room full of crying infants who should have been with their mothers.

As often happens in the TT, the pendulum tends to swing from one extreme to the other. A certain woman had a revelation about mothers needing to bond with their children and how baby and toddler training were inhibiting that process from happening. It went from all to nothing, and it was decided that up until age six when formal training began, children would be at their Imma's side. And what better training grounds than the kitchen? They could learn to clean, sweep, measure, chop, peel, stir, organize, do dishes, wash veggies—the possibilities were endless and could provide the children a productive will for hours. The mother could plan her meal preps around the many ways to incorporate the children, and babies too little to help could be in back carriers, still feeling close to and cared for by their mother.

I'm sure it sounded really good in theory, but the reality was far different. It was often a grueling endeavor to get lunch on the table for fifty to sixty people by noon with two or three children under the age of six, keep them all engaged in helpful tasks, and be diligent to discipline them on the first command for any disobedience. Our children were to work obediently the entire time without complaint. I've never in my life, before or since, experienced anything this stressful. We also were never to complain, as we would then be accused of resisting motherhood.

We were always told "our children are our first priority," but at 11:50 a.m., getting the meal set out on time became the priority, and the children fell to the wayside. The men coming for lunch from the soap shop did not appreciate being told lunch was going to be late, as they were on their own production schedule. Inevitably, the children sensed we were not one hundred percent focused on them and would misbehave. Then someone would pull us aside to point out the children were being wild, and we would need to go spank them, unable to ignore the men lingering around waiting for food. Add to that having a ten- to twenty-five-pound baby in a back carrier day after day for hours at a time. Even the younger mothers had bad backs and problems with varicose veins.

In summer 2009, Arek was a year and a half old, and the tide turned once again. Someone else had a revelation—not all mothers were wired the same way! Yes, some mothers could perfectly execute an elaborate meal, making it a wonderful and creative time for her children in the kitchen, leaving it spotlessly clean an hour later. And then there were women like me who were scrambling from the moment we arrived in the kitchen, battling to keep our children engaged, until the bitter end two hours after lunch was over, when I'd still be hunched over the dish sink. Ironically, it was the "super" mothers who often only cooked one or two meals a week, and the more "needy" of us cooked almost every day. That would have been seen as our salvation, the area of our life we needed to overcome.

Thankfully, the new revelation included the reinstitution of toddler training! It was recognized how hard it was for women to connect during the day with all our little children, as we were never supposed to leave them to themselves, and it often resulted in chaos to bring them to another woman's room to try and have a conversation. Inevitably, conversations were often rushed or just didn't happen. This was a problem specific to women—men always had liberty to converse with each other.

There was much rejoicing, and even a regional festival day with a humorous yet realistic skit about an overwhelmed mother in the kitchen. After the skit, a more gregarious woman stood up and yelled, "Yes, yes, yes!"

So a new era began—all our children aged one and a half and up now had a "pre-training" group they would attend for a couple hours in the mornings. It revolutionized our lives, as for the first time ever for most of us, we had a little bit of precious and guilt-free time without any children during the mornings.

Chapter 26

The Race

he TT believes there will come a point at which they will begin the forty-nine-year "race" until Yahshua's return. As the end of this time draws near, society will be so evil and degraded that God's people will have to flee to the wilderness to escape persecution. I was told there are two devastating meteors predicted decades from now, which will drastically affect the world population and create vast wilderness areas. At the same time, the TT will have produced the "Male Child." This constitutes 144,000 young men between the ages of eighteen and twenty-four who have not been "defiled by women." That is, they are pure, virgin young men. They will be sent out in the last days to give the people of the world one last chance to turn from their evil lives and become part of the Bride. But they won't be well received and will all be slaughtered. It's when the last two men have been killed that Yahshua will return to bring vengeance upon the Evil One.

After the battle, the Bride of Messiah—the TT—will be caught up in the clouds with Him for the Jubilee—the millennial reign of peace. The Evil One will be bound for a thousand years, during which the Holy, consisting of all the righteous people who have ever lived, will rule over the "nations" and will wipe the tears from their eyes for all the sufferings they endured.

The race supposedly began during Passover 2022. They had thought it was going to start in 2009 and then in 2013. 2022's supposed significance is it will put Yahshua's return around 2070, which will be about one hundred years since the TT began, and they say it took Noah one hundred years to build the ark. At one point, there was a list of things to be accomplished before the race could begin. It included priestly garments, David's Harp (instrument making), elderly care and medical facilities, Wednesday Afternoon Affairs, apprenticeship, festival grounds, apostolic centers, and so on. This list is not based on something biblical but was come up with by Meshiah. (Recent intel said this list has been revoked, but before we left it was so important it was posted in café kitchens and discussed often.)

Of all the tasks on the list, Wednesday Afternoon Affairs were the most bizarre. This was supposed to be a time for couples to have sex and was supposed to replace Family Nights. Family Nights were the equivalent of "date night" in the TT. Your children would be covered for the evening every other week, starting around 5:00 p.m. If you lived in a café community, you could go "out" to eat.

Family Nights weren't meant as a casual, fun evening. You were expected to spend preparation time reading child training teachings and talking about what was going on with each child. It was expected the couple would go to the gathering, and if you lived in a place with more than one household who gathered you could choose to go to the other house. This was normally a good way to avoid all your children swarming you only an hour after you were "free." If you went to another community, it was expected that you'd go to their minchah. We were told it would grieve the Holy Spirit if we were in a locale where a minchah was lifted up and we weren't there.

André and I got to the point where we avoided gatherings at all costs on our Family Night. For us, it was not only that our children would undoubtedly attempt to come back to us, but because of how my husband functioned. As soon as any gathering was over, there would be a beeline to him by at least one or two people who needed to mention something "quickly." I would end up loitering around for five to twenty precious, child-free minutes while he was waylaid. I'd often ask afterwards what they had needed and he'd say, "Nothing important," which infuriated me because it had been announced repeatedly not to interrupt couples on their Family Night. It was impossible for my husband to say no to people. Because of this, the easiest thing for us was to leave town.

Since André ran the soap shop, he could easily find an "errand" that needed to be run, usually involving Home Depot. We spent many a Family Night roaming the aisles of drill bits and PVC pipes as I unloaded my diatribe of never-ending household issues on him.

Life is problem-oriented in the community. Rarely did someone knock on my door for a friendly cup of tea. It was usually because there was a problem or something logistical to work out—covering children for a Family Night, how many cups of rice to soak for lunch, what we should make for Friday night dessert, and so on. Hanging out wasn't even a concept because we were to always be gainfully occupied. Our Family Night became a time for me to unload on my husband all the household problems.

One time he asked, exasperated, "Can we talk about something other than community problems?"

"Sure," I said. There was a long, awkward silence at that point. We didn't have anything else to talk about. The community was our life.

The other purpose to Family Night was, of course, sex. It was one hundred percent expected on this night, to the point that when I did the Family Night schedule, I had women ask if they could switch to the opposite week because their Family Night kept falling on their cycle.

Wednesday Afternoon Affairs were intended to be far superior to Family Nights. Half the couples and several single people would take all the children on an excursion after lunchtime. This would give the other half of the couples time to be intimate in their bedrooms for a few hours. We'd have preparation time to shower and read a teaching, then we would attend the evening gathering, get our children back, and give thanks. If a couple couldn't have sex (if a woman was on her cycle, for example), they would do the childcare. Many felt uncomfortable with this idea but couldn't voice any negativity since it was coming down from "the head." Thankfully, this never got off the ground while we were there.

Priestly garments were another item on the list. This equated to two sets of linen—minchah clothes—for every man, woman, and child. They would be made to specific measurements and styles. Everyone was supposed to change into these garments before each gathering and change out of them afterward for breakfast or supper so they didn't get dirty. This sounded like a nightmare to most of us who had several little children, and I remember really hoping that didn't happen until my children were grown. I often felt the goal was to make every aspect of our lives as stressful as possible.

After the race, when all is said and done, things will get really weird. We heard that the Holy were going to multiply exponentially and rule over other planets. There would be an infinite number of each of us out in the galaxy, ruling. We would no longer be married to our earthly spouse. Those in the nations who survived and passed from the old earth to the new were to be called Scions, and they would be able to reproduce and live normal lives again. We would be called upon to rule over all the resurrected people of the nations who had ever lived and "wipe the tears from their eyes." It was all so science fiction-like that I could hardly handle it.

Chapter 27

Hiddenite

nother requirement for the race to begin was the establishment of apostolic centers—places where leaders could gather for days at a time to hear from Our Father (basically, a fancy retreat for men). The community in Hiddenite, North Carolina, was one such locale. Meetings were scheduled every couple of weeks for anything from music to training, cafés, evangelism, cottage industry, or the rarer midwifery meeting. Each community was encouraged to send representation, so every other week the next fourteen-hour trip to Hiddenite was being coordinated throughout our region. Much money was spent on these meetings, which would begin Thursday evenings and go through Sunday. We had to send a certain stipend per person, and men from around the globe would fly over to attend. All that money on plane tickets and gas when most communities were dirt poor was hard for the "naturally minded" among us to justify, but we couldn't sow such discord. No price was too high to hear from Our Father.

Hiddenite was set up like a fully staffed resort, complete with a four-star hotel. It was the full-time job of those who lived there to prepare for and host these meetings. When the travel-weary men arrived, they were shown to their rooms, and then given a lavish welcome. For the next four days, they were served delicious meals, their rooms were cleaned and sheets changed, and there was, of course, laundry service. They were waited on hand and foot and treated like royalty for a long weekend. No wonder there was little resistance from those who were privileged to attend this cozy respite regularly.

In 2009, André had already been to a few meetings in Hiddenite. It was extremely challenging for me to have him gone for days, especially over a weekend with all its long gatherings.

One day, to my astonishment, André told me he had a cottage industry meeting coming up in Hiddenite and was going to ask if I could go with him. I kept my fingers crossed and prayed to be sent. I had never traveled beyond the New England and New York regions. Miraculously, we were told yes! I was ecstatic. We planned to bring Emmet and Arek and leave the girls with André's parents, but for some reason Emmet didn't want to go. Meyshar was more than willing to volunteer, so we ended up heading out at 4:30 on a chilly Thursday morning in early November with Arek and Meyshar cozied up together in the back.

André knew of a Cabela's in Pennsylvania that the children would enjoy, and we ended up being there over an hour. This was the closest thing to a museum or zoo they had ever seen, and they were spellbound over the displays. I was sad that Emmet and Darakah missed out. We arrived that evening, and after some quick greetings and being shown around the lodge, we were brought to our room, and I settled the children to bed.

The next morning at the gathering we all were welcomed with exuberant cheering, and then given a tour of the exquisite property. The grounds were immaculately maintained and beautifully landscaped. I was in awe of the decor and how fancy everything was, inside and out. There was even an in-ground pool!

From then on, we only saw André at mealtimes and gatherings. I helped with the laundry, spending the better part of my days gathering the men's dirty clothing, labeling it, and getting it washed, dried or hung, and returned to their rooms neatly folded by the end of the day. Meyshar was a big help with Arek, and I did manage to take them to a playground across the road and on a nice walk with one of the women I had lived with in Plymouth.

The men were in meetings all day and into the night. There was a constant crew at work preparing meals, snacks, and bottomless pump pots of maté, not to mention the continual serving and cleanup. The meals were not millet-laden sandwich spreads or beans and rice. Every dinner was like a Friday Night Meal; every breakfast was lavish, with pastries and plenty of delectable fruit such as strawberries and melons.

One afternoon, when the men were on a break, André brought me in to see the meeting room. It was huge and must have accommodated at least forty people comfortably. On a table sat a display of natural cleaners a brother had developed. They were called things like Simply Clean (instead of Simple Green). What a worthwhile endeavor! It would be awesome to be able to order these products for our households and support our brothers at the same time.

I looked at a huge dry-erase board at the front of the room that was full of writing. It looked like it had started out as a list of new ideas for community-run businesses. What it ended with was completely ridiculous things like "booger bowls" and other unsavory bathroom paraphernalia. I'm sure in long meetings some comic relief is needed. I laughed at them along with André and didn't think about that again for some time.

We left early Monday morning. Only a few weeks later André was sent to Hiddenite for another meeting. I thought back to the cottage industry meeting and asked him about the natural cleaning products. Would they be available soon? What other ideas from that meeting were being pursued? Surely thirty men gathered for three days came up with some tangible ideas that would soon come to fruition. He said he hadn't heard anything. And we never heard of those products again. We didn't hear of any new cottage industries starting up anywhere as a result of that meeting. It made me wonder about all the time and resources we were sacrificing to send entourages continually to North Carolina. I thought of all the women left behind to care for the children while the husband went for a luxurious three-day respite. I'm sure there were pertinent and productive meetings, but I became convinced they were really just R & R for the leaders.

Chapter 28

Shopping Day

n the monotony and chaos of our life, shopping day was many women's dream—a day we lived for that got us through the rest of the week. It was an entire day away from the pressure of community life and the demands of all our children. Only nursing babies came along. It was several precious, uninterrupted hours to be with another woman, just the two of us. Guards came down. Coffee was often obtained. Sometimes we went out for lunch. We relaxed. We laughed and got to know each other better. An ex-TT friend of mine once said, "I felt like a normal person for a few hours."

But we had to play it cool lest we be labeled with a "shopping spirit" and not allowed to go. Admitting that we loved getting out of the house and having a "break" for a day would not have gone over well. When you've been there long enough, you know if you desire to do something, your chances of success are greater if it seems like it's a hardship you are trying to overcome. So, if you desired to support with shopping, you might say something like, "I'd like to know what Our Father's will is as far as me helping out with household shopping. It would be hard to leave my children all day, but I want to overcome and serve our household." Voila—the perfect shopping candidate: someone who would rather stay home. Striving for something was a surefire way of not doing it because surely you were seeking your own will. Adversity is what gave us confidence we were in Our Father's will and not our own, acting out of selfish ambition.

Shopping was done in pairs, not just for the company, but to help each other resist temptation and counsel about purchases. We were supposed to keep each other from stumbling off the narrow way while surrounded by the many defiling spirits of the world.

I learned over the years that most people had two personalities: their "real" personality and their "community" personality. We rarely knew who someone really was because the spectrum of acceptable conversations and activities was so narrow. Being a woman who regularly went shopping, I frequently witnessed this change of personality. Funny thing about getting away from the community: even the most strict, principled woman would often transform, and you'd see a completely different side to her. They could be a funny, laid-back person once we were out shopping for the day. I would visibly see people relax.

Before leaving, we would pray for Our Father's protection and that we could be a "light" to any lost sheep we might encounter throughout the day. We were equipped with many lists of food, household items, personal needs, and, of course, free papers.

Personal needs shopping was the most fun, and I thoroughly enjoyed shopping for people. I loved getting home and separating everything into piles for families, then seeing children's eyes light up when they saw their new package of socks or barrettes, or their "new" thrift-store coat. Community children got so excited over simple things.

I delighted in the challenge of figuring out exactly how to meet all the needs monetarily. Except for Plymouth, we were usually poor, and there often wasn't a consistent budget for needs. We would find "free" places and take advantage of thrift store bag sales. We were sometimes scavengers and would dig through bags left at clothing drop-offs. We had to be industrious and creative to find ways to meet everyone's needs. If anyone got a monetary gift from relatives, it was expected to be turned over to the needs person to meet "the most pressing need." We'd never think to keep it for our family without getting permission. The story of Ananais and Sapphira was told regularly to drive home the evil of holding anything back for ourselves.

There came a point in Cambridge where we were doing better financially. I sold anything I could at the local consignment store, and the rock magnets sold well at the café, as well as gift baskets of Common Sense products. For the first time in years, we had needs money given from the soap shop each week, which was an amazing provision. There was even a great free place in Saratoga that supplied most of our clothing needs. We had to get vouchers every month, as it was a provision for low-income families, which we definitely qualified for. Sometimes we felt a little out of place waiting in line for our vouchers, but we always tried to be kind and strike up conversations with other mothers. A lost sheep could be found anywhere.

Saratoga is an upscale city, so we would find quality clothes, jackets, shoes and boots, baby gear, household items, and decor. You never knew what would be there from week to week. It was exciting and risk free. Having a limited budget to meet the needs of eighty-plus people meant there was a risk in spending five or six dollars on a garment at a thrift store that couldn't be returned. Whatever didn't work out from the free place, I would consign and earn more needs money. It was a beautiful cycle. My kids' eyes would light up when they saw me pull up and start unloading bags from the free place. I'd scope out the toys, games, and books for anything that was "acceptable," and sometimes even snuck something home that was on the edge, just to have a treat for my children. I always tried to grab a little something for each of them.

Just like in the normal world, there were trends that went around the community—certain styles of clothes, shoes, or bedroom decor. We all wanted our bedrooms to be nice—they were all we had autonomy over. Around this time many women wanted to get rid of their tacky plastic clothes hampers in exchange for a decorative wicker one, which were all the rage in Target at the time. They looked a bit rustic and classy at the same time. The problem was they were $49, but thanks to the free place meeting so many other needs, it was possible to start chipping away at a goal such as this.

One day in early February 2010, Rivkah and I were going shopping together. Rivkah was the wife of Malak, who was our Community Coordinator at the time. She was tall, yet graceful, and carried herself with an air of confidence that often bordered on arrogance. Yet up until this point, I enjoyed being with her, as she and her husband put significant effort into planning fun, social events for our community.

Target was our first stop, and I was happy to be getting a hamper for one of the women. We both went around the store with our lists and met at the front of the store when we were done, me with the prized hamper in my cart.

As we walked out to the van, I was talking about which ladies wanted hampers and who I wanted to get one for next. Rivkah and her family had moved to Cambridge only a few months prior. Sometime before this, Lehava was given a set of fine china from some relatives. Fine china was not something we were going to use in the community, and this woman, being a good disciple, laid her "offering" at the leaders' feet, so to speak, to decide what we should do with them. These dishes came up as a topic at a Social Meeting, and it was decided that we could sell them and use the money for needs. For whatever reason, they hadn't yet been sold.

So there we were, pushing our carts to the van with me chatting away. "Once we sell Lehava's dishes, I'll be able to get so-and-so her hamper, and then I only have two more to get."

"Wait, what do you mean?" asked Rivkah, "My husband told me just the other day that he was going to sell those and put the money toward training curriculum."

"Oh," I said matter-of-factly, "he must not realize we already decided that money could go toward personal needs, I've just been waiting for someone to sell them."

Rivkah literally gasped, making me quickly jerk my head in her direction, thinking she saw something awful in the parking lot. "What's wrong?" I asked, seeing nothing amiss.

"I can't believe you were just so disrespectful to my husband!" she exclaimed, clearly shocked. We arrived at the van in the middle of the Target parking lot. I didn't respond, just began unloading my purchases into the trunk. I returned my cart and took several deep breaths as I walked back and got in the driver's seat. Rivkah had a seven-month-old baby at the time and was buckling her into her car seat in the back.

As soon as she got in the passenger seat, I tried to explain myself. "Rivkah, I'm not meaning any disrespect. You all just moved here, and I didn't know if he was aware—"

"SHUT YOUR MOUTH, TAMARA!" she interrupted with shocking ferocity. I was literally stunned and just looked at her, noticing tears welling up in her eyes. "It's not your place to question what the men decide, and you spoke right against my husband," she said, as though I had just accused him of a heinous crime. She went on for several more minutes, passionately lecturing me about the oversight the men have and our job as women to trust and support them, never questioning their decisions. She was so emotional at the way I'd usurped her husband's authority, as though it had been my malicious intent.

I had to do something to end this horrible situation. Target was the first stop of many, so I had to spend the rest of the day with this unhinged person. When she was done rebuking me, I did the only thing I could think of that would placate her. I apologized. "OK, listen, I'm sorry that came out as being disrespectful. I honestly was just thinking out loud and making conversation. I didn't mean for it to turn into this. If the dishes are needed for other things that's fine—I'm just trying to find ways to meet needs."

We sat in awkward silence for several long minutes, Rivkah staring out her window at the parking lot, the baby starting to whimper in the back. I was envious of the other shoppers I could see in the parking lot and wished I could be one of them. I was tempted to pull out and just drive back to Cambridge, but there was shopping that had to get done before the weekend. My every instinct was to flee that van and get far away from her.

"I forgive you," she finally said. "And I'm sorry I yelled at you. Let's just forget about this and keep shopping."

"I forgive you too," came my autonomic reply.

The rest of the day I walked on eggshells, scared to say the wrong thing again. She acted like nothing out of the ordinary had happened, and by the time we got home she was joking about the whole thing. I was nervous the rest of the day, like a child who had gotten in trouble at school and was waiting for their mom to get the phone call. I thought I'd be dragged into a meeting after she told her husband about my disrespect. But nothing ever came out of it, and I have no clue what happened to those dishes. I never wanted to see them again.

Chapter 29

The Reunion

n June 2010, we were granted approval to go to my fifteenth high school reunion. I was excited to go but a bit distressed over how I would appear to people I hadn't seen in over a decade, who probably knew to some degree that I had joined some weird group. Facebook was still in its infancy, and I'd already connected to many people before word came that "disciples don't use Facebook." I didn't delete my account but rarely looked at it, especially after I saw someone comment about my "creepy family."

The first part of the reunion was taking place at a beach in the early afternoon, then we'd meet again that evening at a restaurant for dinner. The beach scene was the most concerning to me. I definitely was not going to wear my community swimsuit. I didn't want to wear a long skirt or the huge pants we wore either. It was such a ridiculous dilemma—and an unfair one because my husband could simply wear normal swim shorts and a T-shirt.

Luckily, I had time to plan, so I kept my eye out at the free place for suitable garments during the couple months prior. I found a large pair of pretty rayon pants, black with small white flowers, that I altered into knickers. I didn't make them as wide as normal. Then I found a lightweight, white button-up blouse. The bottom had a delicate lacy border. It was long sleeved, so I easily transformed it into a short-sleeved blouse. It wasn't exactly beachwear, but it was summery and the best I could pull off.

Now, the restaurant. My mother had given me a bag of clothes, most of which I consigned, but there was one shirt I stashed away. It was a simple, dark-brown, fitted, knit T-shirt that had nice beadwork along the V-neck.

I couldn't have worn it in the community, even under a tunic because of the V-neck, the short sleeves, and the sparkly beads. I just needed the perfect skirt, and the free place came through. It was a beautiful, long, crinkle rayon in tones of deep reds and oranges, and if you looked closely, the pattern around the bottom was silhouettes of people dancing. It was fun and unique, making the perfect ensemble because it was enough on the edge that I would look somewhat "normal," yet still be modest.

The day before the reunion I was in my room trying on my outfits. I put on my beach outfit, and my heart sank when I looked down at the bottom eight inches of my legs that were visible and covered in half an inch of dark hair. I hadn't shaved my legs in nearly ten years at this point. Removal of any body hair was not allowed. Women did not shave—legs or armpits. Even women who had a bad unibrow or other unattractive facial hair were made to leave it alone. It was considered vanity to care about something like that. Our Father had put that hair there, after all. I didn't even own a razor and certainly couldn't go asking around the house for one. But after all the effort I'd gone through to look somewhat ordinary, damned if I was going to ruin it all by having hairy legs. Thankfully, my husband had a beard trimmer, and by putting it on the lowest setting, I found it worked quite nicely to clean up my unruly legs.

That reunion was somewhat of a turning point for me, even though it would be another four years until we left. I remember getting to Sandbar State Park in Colchester, and one of the first people I saw was one of my best friends, Dorothea. I'll never forget the surge of emotion as I hugged her amidst the small gathering of others from our class. I had to fight back the tears. It was so hard for me to know how to be in this situation that I'm sure I was extremely awkward, not at all like I had been in high school. I'd forgotten how to simply relax and enjoy myself. I didn't know what to talk about with these people—our lives could not have been more different. I couldn't relate to their lives, nor they to mine.

That night at the restaurant, I had a glass of wine with my friends and André had a beer. It was the first time we had had drinks since joining the TT. I finally relaxed and laughed until my sides hurt. I enjoyed myself more than I had in years. I felt like the old me surfaced for a brief time, and I realized I missed "me."

I felt depressed the next day heading back to the community, wondering if I'd have to wait until my next class reunion to have a good time like that again.

Our relationships in the community were supposed to be deeper and more fulfilling than the supposed shallowness of friendships in the world. So why was I not experiencing this? I'd lived in Cambridge seven years and felt like I'd been in a work camp: I could cook a meal for fifty people and practically clean the houses blindfolded, but I felt like I had no real friends. I realized I made a clear distinction between my friends—people in the world, such as Michelle—and the women I live with—people in the community. I saw them more as work colleagues.

At one point, a newly married couple was moving to Cambridge. The woman was from France, and I'd lived with her for a short time in Rutland when she had been single. She didn't know many people in Cambridge, and I was encouraged to invite her to my room one afternoon for tea, which I gladly did. As we were catching up and chatting, I mentioned that it was the first time since I moved there that I had someone in my room for tea. She looked at me completely shocked. In France, like Rutland, that had been almost a daily norm—to have a little social tea time in the afternoon with someone. We were just too busy here, I reasoned, but still felt like it wasn't normal.

It was hard to know how to develop a "normal" friendship there because of how censored our relationships with each other were. If two women seemed to have a casual, "fun" friendship, they were deemed overfamiliar and discouraged from spending too much time together. I saw this at work when deciding which women should go shopping together. Two "less spiritual" women would not be sent out together for the day, as they would probably not be "salt" to each other, meaning they would not help each other keep their conversations pure and undefiled by worldly topics. We were told we would be judged one day for every careless word that came from our mouths. Matthew 12:36—"*But I tell you that **every careless word** that people speak, they shall give an accounting for it in the day of judgment.*"

The community used to put on a play called *The Mask*. The point of it was that in the world, everyone has to wear a mask to fit in, relationships are superficial, and we can't truly be ourselves, so we often end up giving in to peer pressure to feel accepted. But in the community, you can take off your mask, be accepted and loved, be yourself, and be the person you were created to be—fulfill the purpose God has for your life. Who doesn't want that?

The irony is that never in my life did I try as hard to be someone I wasn't than in the community. It's so backwards. You take off your "worldly" mask (who you really are) and put on your community mask. You have to conform to all the rules, beliefs, and standards or be judged rebellious and be cut off. I never felt the pressure to conform as much as I did there, and it took me a long time after leaving to get my community mask off and be myself again.

There was a free paper called, *Don't Let Your Human Voice Be Silenced.* This phrase was often displayed on large signs when we held an open-forum table at an event. I often thought about this and how, like the play *The Mask*, it was completely misleading and only pertinent when it came to agreeing with the doctrines within the community. My human voice was never more silenced than in the TT. I couldn't honestly say what I thought about most issues without being deemed disrespectful, divisive, discontented, jealous, unwilling, mistrusting, doubting, lacking faith, selfish, or a myriad of other iniquities that I would need to "cut off" so that I could have the "right mind" and prosper. The reasoning is that the TT is the ultimate truth, and once you come to the knowledge of that truth, you don't need to question anymore.

CHAPTER 30

The Getaway

t was late summer 2010, and many families had been given the chance to go camping. Every weekend I was a bit envious as I'd watch yet another family excitedly packing up a vehicle. Emmet was eleven, and our family had never done anything like that. I couldn't say anything though, because then I would have been striving and giving into complaint, jealousy, and more. Thankfully, my mother-in-law advocated for us, letting one of the leading men know that we had never been sent camping. Summer was coming to an end, so it was with great relief that I got word we were being sent.

I excitedly started packing, realizing how needy we were. Emmet had a sleeping bag, having gone on a training camping trip the summer before, and I had found one for Arek at a thrift store once. I inquired around the house, and Rivkah told me to come to her room and she would help me out.

The first thing she did was haul an enormous bag out of her closet. It was made of pretty upholstery fabric, and she told me it was her family's camping gear. It contained a six-person tent, four sleeping bags, a lantern, a couple flashlights, bug sprays, a small broom and dustpan, some plastic dishes and cutlery, and matches. She pulled a sheet of paper out of a pocket and handed it to me. It was an organized checklist of everything to bring on a camping trip. She offered to help gather up the rest of what we needed. My head was spinning. How often had their family gone camping for her to have such a convenient and well-organized cache at her disposal? It was like they could just up and camp anytime. Of course, I said nothing accusatory and appreciated her for letting us use "her" family's gear.

We headed out late in the afternoon of the next day, a Friday. André had always wanted to camp at Sunset Lake in Benson. It is a beautiful, crystal-clear lake with a small island we could camp on. With a canoe strapped to the roof of the van, we eagerly headed out. By the time we got to Benson, the children and I were all starving. I was still nursing Arek, and all we'd had to eat was fruit break. I was nearing a ravenously hungry lactating woman breakdown and couldn't fathom waiting several canoe trips back and forth to the island to eat.

We pulled over at a picnic area on the side of the road that had a grill and made up a few hot dogs. By this time, the sun was getting low; we'd be setting up in the dark.

We soon arrived at Sunset Lake, which has only a small public beach area set directly on the road. There is no parking lot; people just pull over, half on the road and half in the grass. All around that are private camps. We hadn't really thought about where we could park and leave the van for the weekend. André drove down the private road, unsuccessfully seeking a spot. It was getting later, and our children were sick of being crammed in the van. This was our long-awaited camping trip, and it seemed like it was falling apart. I wanted to cry.

André began looking up campgrounds on his cell phone. The closest one to our location was Half Moon Pond, about twenty minutes away in Hubbardton, Vermont. Being so late on a Friday in August, André called to make sure they had spots left. Thankfully, they did, and we made our way there. We paid for our spot, bought some firewood, and pulled into our lot. It was beautiful, right on the pond. Using flashlights and our campfire, we set up our tent while the children found sticks and began roasting marshmallows.

A beautiful moon was rising over the pond, and we decided to take the canoe out. All six of us donned life jackets and piled into the canoe. Emmet and André rowed, and I held Arek on my lap in the center, with the girls sitting on the floor. It was peaceful and absolutely gorgeous. We rowed around for a good hour and then headed back to the site, all of us exhausted.

The next day, we were up early making pancakes at the campfire. The children explored the shore of the pond, and we were all much more relaxed. André still wanted to go to Sunset Lake for swimming and canoeing, and he called his brother Nick, who lived nearby, to see if he wanted to meet us and hang out for the day. It turned out he and his girlfriend were going away for the night, and he offered to let us stay the night at his house. André agreed, and I was somewhat disappointed, as the purpose of our trip was to camp. As always, he had the perfect solution. We wouldn't stay inside the house but would camp in the yard. They had an in-ground pool and we could still have a fire and grill, with the luxury of toilets and a shower in the house. I agreed, rationalizing we could use the money we would save on another night at the campground for extra treats for the children.

We broke down our camp, checked out, and headed to the lake. We spent a pleasant day exploring the island, picking wild blueberries, canoeing, and even finding a rope swing hanging in a tree. We stayed until late afternoon and stopped for creemees before heading to Nick's house. The children made a beeline to the pool as soon as we got there, and André and I set the tent back up. We all crashed early that night.

We spent the next day enjoying the pool. The children were getting along, playing water games, and jumping off the diving board. It was the most relaxed day we had ever spent together, and we were in no hurry to return to the chaos of community life. I lay on a chaise lounge in the sun, fantasizing that this was our house, our pool, and just another normal day in our life. No one was around to judge us for anything. No one was pointing out that one of our children needed to be disciplined for some minor infraction that we missed. No one was judging the ice cream, potato chips, and sodas that were freely being consumed. I rolled the pant legs of my community swim shorts several inches higher than what was allowed. André and Emmet swam with no shirts on. We were living on the edge, and it felt great.

The mirage all came crashing down when André's phone rang. A situation had come up, and they needed André back for a meeting ASAP. One of the married men had been discovered having an "overfamiliar" relationship with one of the youth girls. A judgment meeting needed to happen, and they would wait until André was back to be involved. Just like that, we were ordering the children out of the pool and packing up as quickly as we could.

Years later, André would confess to me that just before he got that phone call, he was seriously considering not going back to Cambridge. He was enjoying our family for the first time he could recall and didn't want it to end. The children slept on the ride home, and André was very quiet. I assumed he was contemplating the ramifications of the circumstance he was about to be involved with. He didn't share with me any of his thoughts and feelings, and an hour later he was at the judgment meeting, having quickly judged his treasonous thoughts and resumed his role as a spiritual leader in Cambridge.

Not long after this, we were told that families shouldn't go alone on camping trips but should go with another family. If we went alone, we would undoubtedly be tempted to not follow the traditions by maybe eating chocolate, drinking coffee, or lowering our standards for child training. But if we went with another family we could "help" each other to stay on the narrow way while away from normal community life. Basically, we would spy on each other.

We only went camping one other time, a few years later, with another large family. It was just like being at the community, only without the gatherings, and in the woods.

CHAPTER 31

Three Eternal Destinies

ne of the foundational TT beliefs is the Three Eternal Destinies, as written in Revelations 22:11. It clearly describes the Holy (whom the TT believes is them) and sets apart the righteous people of the nations, who live according to their conscience, from the unjust and filthy, who will go to the Lake of Fire. This sounded spot on and got my attention when I first met the community. I never could believe in a God that would send people to Hell for believing in the "wrong" religion.

There is a snake in the grass though. If you are born in the community, having grown up your whole life with the knowledge of the "truth," and then forsake it, you do not have the chance to be righteous anymore. There are only two eternal destinies for children born there: stay and be one of the Holy or leave and go to the Lake of Fire. The same applies to anyone who gets baptized and then leaves: they will also go to the Lake of Fire. So basically, like other Christian denominations, there are only two eternal destinies once you are in the group—the third category is only for those who never denied the "truth," or never joined the TT, in other words.

For those of us who joined as adults, this created a mental conundrum. We were told we couldn't have revelation about certain things until we were baptized. Then once we got baptized—came to the knowledge of the truth—we were accountable for what we "knew" and would go to the Lake of Fire if we ever broke our covenant and denied the truth.

Every morning before regular training started, the children had their own Three Eternal Destinies teaching. Emmet told me about one class where someone had drawn a guillotine on the chalkboard. He was eight or nine years old at the time. The teacher explained what it was and told the class that by the time some of them were in their forties, they may have the privilege of dying by this method to glorify "Our Master," as the end times would be near. Emmet said it scared him out, and he thought to himself that, hopefully, he would die some other way before he was in his forties.

###

In the eternal age, we were told, we would be given a crown of glory. I'm not sure if this was a real crown like the groom placed on the bride's head at weddings or a theoretical crown. Whatever the case, back in the days of kings and queens when crowns were worn, they were heavy and uncomfortable. To cushion the head, royalty wore a diadem around their heads that the crown would sit upon.

To signify this impending honor, men began wearing simple diadems made from woven linen strips to the gatherings. Then women wore them too, and many began to crochet lacy, delicate diadems to wear over their head coverings. Then we heard children three and up should wear them. The girls enjoyed getting a pretty, crocheted diadem and sought after the lacier, more intricate designs.

Like anything in the community, the rules and standards about diadems became stricter. First, color became an issue. They couldn't be too white. This was because they were only supposed to be white after we had made ourselves completely pure, and that wouldn't happen until after the forty-nine-year race. Astoundingly, it takes about fifty years for pure linen to become white with regular washing. So, that was our direction: use pure linen, which is somewhat dark, and hand-wash our diadem every week for the next fifty years.

Then direction came that diadems should be of a certain width, because the narrow, lacy diadems all the girls liked would definitely not support their crown. So, much to their dismay, we had a "push" to make woven diadems out of linen strips like the men's. People were still getting creative in how they wove the strips, and women who had fancy embroidery sewing machines were adding a decorative stitch. Then, we heard there were only a few acceptable patterns, and each community was sent "swatches" of five different weaves on a keyring. The swatches were sent around, and each woman picked out one design. Time for another "push." They were wider, not delicate looking at all, but rather clunky, especially if someone had a smaller head. Of course, this made it a battle to get our youth girls to wear bulky, ugly diadems that they hated. Every man, woman, and child was to wear their diadem to every gathering. In the years since I've left, diadem standards have gotten even stranger, with men wearing massive three-inch-wide diadems.

CHAPTER 32

Chipmunks and Wine

n 2012, for our thirteenth anniversary, we were sent to the cabin in Oak Hill for the weekend. I had opened up to a few of the women that my husband and I had been having some difficulties, mainly in the department of physical intimacy. Simply put, I did not enjoy sex anymore. So far, I had yet to talk to anyone who could relate. Most looked at me like I'd suddenly grown another nose. So, I was still trying my best to be a dutiful wife.

When it came time for us to leave, Rivkah asked me to come to her room. On her bed, like a centerpiece, was a large basket covered with pretty fabric. She began trying to pass on vision about how important it was for my husband and I to reconnect over this weekend and how she wanted to help. In great detail, she began to tell me of times she had a certain fantasy about her husband, and each time, "Our Father" arranged circumstances perfectly so that it was able to happen. I was extremely uncomfortable, unsure how to respond, and kept glancing at the mystery basket out of the corner of my eye.

"So," she continued, "I have put together some things I thought might help make the weekend more enjoyable for you and Yeshurun." She then went over to the basket, pulled off the cover, and revealed its contents: candles, massage oils, several items of lingerie, a bottle of sparkling cider, and a CD of romantic music. She said these items helped her and her husband have a satisfying relationship and she wanted to let me "borrow" them for the weekend. I was speechless. For one, I didn't even realize people had this kind of stuff. We were not allowed to wear lingerie. Second, I was absolutely horrified by the thought of using her "sex" basket all weekend, especially with the images of her fantasies fresh in my mind.

I didn't want to crush her as she was so excited about giving me her fatted calf. She covered the basket back up and handed it to me, absolutely beaming. I thanked her, trying hard to smile and hide how appalled I was. I quickly carried it through the house to the vehicle where my husband was waiting. "What's that?" he asked as I put the basket on the backseat.

"Oh, just a few things Rivkah put together for us." He didn't ask for more details, probably assuming it was just more food. I got in and we drove off.

My mind was reeling as we headed toward Oak Hill. I was thankful for the break from our children and the hecticness of weekends, but in all honesty the thought of being alone with André for an entire weekend was sort of awkward, especially with the expectation and pressure of what the weekend was for. I glanced back at the dreadful basket, looking quaint on the backseat. Someone had made us a tray with crackers and cheese as a snack, so we pulled over at a rest area with picnic tables, only making small talk here and there.

We arrived in Oak Hill late in the afternoon and brought our things into the cabin. I carried in the basket and set it discreetly on a table in the corner. Just up the road, a normal community was in the throes of preparing for Friday night. Being sent on a "time away," we were exempt from having to participate in any of the gatherings that weekend.

So, there we were, just the two of us with zero distractions. We went into the living room and André reclined on a sofa, joking about taking a nap. Well, maybe half joking, I wouldn't have been surprised if he'd closed his eyes and fallen asleep in moments. On a good night during the week in Cambridge, André averaged about four hours of sleep, usually with an all-nighter thrown in there somewhere. He was always exhausted and understandably fell asleep anytime he "rested his eyes."

The suggestion of a nap was short-lived, as we soon heard strange noises coming from the kitchen. Something was out there, rummaging about. We froze and listened. Something was in the cabin with us. André cautiously got up from the sofa and crept toward the kitchen, where he startled a chipmunk in the kitchen window. It quickly scrambled off and out of sight. "Maybe it found a way out," said André, lying back down on the couch and closing his eyes.

I looked around the cabin, trying to envision our next forty-eight hours. We hadn't even brought a deck of cards. At least there would be dinner to make soon to pass some time. We had been sent with all the fixings for a nice spaghetti dinner one night and some chicken and potatoes for the other night, as well as waffle mix, eggs, and bread for breakfasts, deli meats and veggies for sandwiches for lunch, and plenty of fruit, muffins, cookies, crackers, and cheese. Food and sex. That's what the weekend was supposed to be about.

More rustling sounds brought my attention back to the present. "It's back," I whispered. André sat up, and we both went and peered around the corner into the kitchen. It was back in the window. "What are we going to do?" I asked.

André rubbed his bearded chin, thinking. "We've got to get it out of here. Maybe we can catch it somehow."

We spent the next half hour devising a trap consisting of a small box that we propped up with a stick over some bread and placed on the counter near the window. André found a ball of string and tied the end around the stick. We carefully unwound the string all the way back to the sofa, which we turned so we could strategically hide behind it and have a full view of the counter. André would hold the string, waiting for the chipmunk to go under the box, then yank it, pulling out the stick and trapping it under the box. I don't know what our plan was then, but we felt good about our trap.

Like two little kids, we eagerly hid behind the sofa, waiting in silence. The minutes ticked by, and I started feeling a little silly. But then we heard something and watched as the little rodent hopped up and began inspecting our trap. We held our breath and waited for it to notice the small feast. As soon as it disappeared under the box, André yanked the string. Somehow, the chipmunk was faster and did not get caught inside the box. In its disorientation though, it ended up in the sink, which gave André time to run and open the front door. "Go scare it out of the sink!" he called to me. I ran around the couch toward the kitchen, the terrified animal now frantically clawing around the sink. It got its bearings and jumped out, and I chased it right out of the open door! We were victorious!

That was as good an icebreaker as any, and we were in good spirits as we set the cabin back in order and started making dinner.

All this time, I had put thoughts of Rivkah's basket out of my mind. After dinner, André asked if they'd sent us anything good to drink. Then I remembered. With a heavy sigh, I retrieved the basket and set it on the table.

"Rivkah sent us sparkling cider . . . and all of this. . ." I pulled off the cover, revealing its contents. He reached in and pulled out one of the massage oils.

"Wow, fancy stuff," he said, reading the label. I pulled out one of the pieces of lingerie, a skimpy red satin camisole trimmed in black lace. André's eyes got big. "You plan to model that for me?" he asked with a nervous laugh.

"NO!" I retorted, "these are *Rivkah's* things!"

"Seriously?" he asked in semidisbelief. I nodded. "You don't have to wear any of that stuff, it's OK,'" he assured me.

He scanned over the half-burned candles and reached for the CD. It was labeled in black Sharpie in Rivkah's handwriting, "Anniversaries and Family Nights." There was a CD player in the kitchen, and he popped it in. The melodious tones of Nightnoise filled the cabin. He picked up the bottle of sparkling cider and headed to the kitchen for glasses. "Want some?" he asked.

"I guess so, but I don't understand why we can't have a real bottle of wine for something like this. I mean, we're in our thirties and this is our anniversary!" I responded with unplanned tenacity. He set the bottle back down.

"Want to go get some?" he asked casually.

"Seriously?"

"Why not? Let's do it!" he said, getting up, grabbing the keys, and turning off the music. I suddenly felt nervous but excited at the same time. We were about to do something "lawless." Not only were we buying alcohol for something other than the Victory Cup or Breaking of Bread, but we were "buying on the Sabbath," which was forbidden. No money was to be spent on the Sabbath. We were being seriously bad!

We hopped in the car and headed toward the main road, past the community household where Friday night was in full swing.

"We're going to have to go out of town,'" André explained as we were driving. Oak Hill was a tiny town, so any local store would surely recognize us as being from the Twelve Tribes. We stuck out in a crowd like sore thumbs.

After about twenty minutes of driving, we came upon a small general store in the middle of nowhere that had neon beer signs lighting up the windows. "This place looks good. You stay here," said André as he parked.

"How are you going to pay for this?" I asked, aware that a credit card charge from a liquor store on a Friday night in the middle of nowhere in New York would raise suspicions if some scrupulous bookkeeper in Cambridge noticed it on the monthly statement.

"Malak gave me some cash for the weekend," he said as he reached into the glove box for the ball cap he used when driving or mowing. (We weren't allowed to wear sunglasses because they were said to promote a "cool" spirit, so ball caps—plain, of course—were the only option to shade our eyes.) He got out and strode confidently into the store. I waited nervously, praying that the cashier wouldn't take one look at my bearded, pony-tailed husband and ask, "Hey, are you from the Oak Hill Kitchen?" That was the restaurant the community ran in town.

A couple minutes later, he emerged, brown paper bag in hand. Success! Community music played from a CD in the car on the way back to the cabin, and it was dark by the time we got there. We sat at the kitchen table, with two pint-size Ball mason jars and pulled our bottle out of the bag. "Darn!" André exclaimed. "I hope there's a corkscrew in the kitchen somewhere." Being out of practice with such things, it never occurred to him to get a bottle with a screw-on cap instead of a cork. We ransacked the kitchen to no avail—no one in the community would ever need one of those.

Disappointment washed over me. "Maybe we can buy one tomorrow," I suggested.

"No, I'm going to figure this out," said André, looking through every drawer and cabinet in the cabin. "Aha!" he exclaimed as he opened the kitchen closet and saw a toolbox on the top shelf. He set it on the table and rifled through it, then smiled as he pulled out a four-inch-long screw. He grabbed the bottle and began to carefully twist the screw down into the soft cork. Leaving enough of it out for a good grip, he then positioned the bottle between his legs, gripped the neck, and gently pulled, then wiggled, pulled, and wiggled some more. Slowly, the plug began to emerge. When enough of the cork was out for him to grip, he eased the rest out with a satisfying "pop."

"Piece of cake!" he exclaimed proudly and filled our jars halfway. We turned the music back on and were soon laughing and having more fun with each other than we'd had in years. Rivkah's basket remained unused throughout the weekend.

We took our time getting home on Sunday, having a nice breakfast at the Oak Hill Kitchen and taking a scenic route. I was feeling happy as we drove along listening, of course, to community music. At one point, André stopped the CD, turned on the radio, and began to scan stations. We started to talk about music we used to like, and he handed me his Blackberry phone. He told me about an app called Pandora that could be used to look up any music. For the rest of the drive home, I had a great time playing songs I used to love. I realized how much I missed music.

As we got closer to Cambridge, my mood darkened. I handed André his phone and started to mentally prepare myself for the transition from our adventurous, carefree weekend back to the community, our children, spankings, the gatherings, making lunch the following day, and so on. I realized I'd seen a side of my husband I hadn't seen in years and had forgotten he could be fun. I wondered how long it would be until we enjoyed ourselves like that again. It wasn't a given that every anniversary was celebrated. It was a "gift" from the household, not a rule.

We collected our children from their grandparents downtown and headed up to the Main House. As I was bringing some laundry downstairs, I passed one of the other women. "How was your weekend?" she asked brightly. (I knew I'd get asked this at least ten more times before the day was over.) I realized I had to be guarded. No one could know that we got wine or listened to "worldly" music. I couldn't be honest about being "normal."

"It was fun—we had to chase a chipmunk out when we got there."

"That sounds exciting,'" she responded. "We missed you all. Glad you're home," she called back to me as she continued up the stairs with her basket of laundry.

"Thanks, me too,'" I responded half-heartedly.

CHAPTER 33

A Time to Run

ometime around fall of 2012, shocking information was discovered about Sheqer. Back in the '90s, she'd had several sexual encounters with multiple single men. One of these men, now married, had left the community with his family and told the whole story to another former member. All the sordid details were put together in an email, which was sent out en masse to many community leaders. There was instant pandemonium as leaders sought to delete the emails before the allegations became widespread. At that point, they were still considered false accusations. But now enough people had read the letter, questions were being asked, and the situation could not get neatly swept under the rug.

Sheqer had been involved in judging many situations over the years where inappropriate behavior was involved, even bringing harsh discipline (forced marriages) to teenagers who'd done less than she had as a married woman. This was a volcano about to blow, and the effect could have been devastating to the entire Twelve Tribes. However, those with the most power and authority in all the tribes met to figure out how to prevent that from happening. This was supposedly Sheqer's judgment meeting.

I remember all the adults in Cambridge being called together for a Body Meeting. We all knew something serious was about to be disclosed when this happened, so it always felt kind of foreboding but a little exciting at the same time.

What we were told was that Sheqer had confessed to having inappropriate relationships with some men many years ago. She was deeply remorseful for her transgressions, and Meshiah had forgiven her. Her great discipline was the fact that the entire TT knew about her sins, and she'd have to live with that for the rest of her life. We were told not to speculate any further or cast judgment on her. That was not any of our place, Our Father had spoken, and she was forgiven. Case closed.

We all knew that had it been any other member who had fallen in this way, they would have been sent away. Many, at the judgment of Meshiah and Sheqer, had been sent away for far less in the past. I recall hearing of a man who, years before, had been sent away for seven years when it was discovered he had worked and earned money on the Sabbath. He had a family with several little children at the time.

There was a story in one of the children's readers called "The Life of the Patriarch." It was an elaboration of the story of Job. The story began with Job, who was a prominent landowner, being sued by two of his tenants for failing to fulfill his part of a contract with them. The judges who heard the couple's testimony were surprised that Job had even allowed them to press their case, as he was a very powerful man. Despite that, they ruled in favor of the tenants and passed the verdict that Job needed to honor the terms he had made with them. Job praised the judges for not acting partially, in his favor, simply because he was a rich, influential elder in the community.

The circumstances around Sheqer were in complete opposition to this story. She received unmerited mercy because of who she was, and many fell away because of this situation. To this day, she is still defended as someone who has endured much and been a great help to many in the Body.

⁂

Because of the Sheqer situation, and because I felt under the microscope more than ever, this was a challenging period for me. I began having a recurring dream that I was wearing a normal bathing suit, and I relished feeling like a "normal" person. I tried to imagine what it would be like to wear a bathing suit. I had dressed so modestly for more than ten years that I couldn't fathom how I'd once felt so confident being scantily clad. I considered my body. I wasn't overweight by any means, even after four children. I danced at gatherings, but that was the only heart-rate-increasing exercise I got. I wondered if my dreams were premonitions and if by summer I could possibly be in a place to wear a bathing suit.

It was on Christmas Day 2012 that I went out for a walk. It was a

Wednesday, a normal day of work and training. About halfway through my walk, I wondered if I'd still be able to run. I used to run for years before I had Emmet. I wanted to get back in shape and feel good about my body. I remember the exact spot I was at on the road when I decided to start running. I'm sure I looked ridiculous in my community pants and bulky winter coat, but I was beyond caring what anyone thought about me at that point. I ran until I was completely out of breath. I felt exhilarated and alive.

I decided that day I was going to run again. Three days a week, after my kids left for training, I'd head out. I plotted out a two-mile course through the village, and it only took me three weeks to attain it. Every time I went out, I'd run a little bit farther than the day before. Finally, I could run my whole circuit in about twenty minutes. Usually, no one would have even noticed I'd been gone. I'd slip up to my room, drink some water, stretch, change, and be in the kitchen to start on lunch without missing a beat. I maintained this routine for four months. I felt so much better physically and mentally. I was sleeping better and had less back pain. It all came to a screeching halt when I was asked to teach toddler training every day for the three-year-olds. I had to be ready to start my group at nine, so my window of running time was gone.

CHAPTER 34

Save Bob Dylan

vangelism was a constant endeavor in the TT. We sought any opportunity to go out as a group to hand out papers to the lost and lonely of the world. We had to make sure we had it "on our heart" to go out to accomplish our Father's will, not because of an "adventure spirit." This referred to wanting to evangelize at a concert or other event mainly for the excitement of such an outing or the break from your everyday routine. Your motivation had to be pure—you were wanting to help seek and save the lost, not looking to have a good time.

When an event was coming up, we would counsel at the Social Meeting and voice our confidence or reservations about who was being considered. Only the most upstanding disciples would be found worthy to go to an event and represent the Holy to the nations. Being chosen was a privilege.

<hr />

During the summer of 2013, the entire TT came under the persuasion that Bob Dylan was going to be saved and become a disciple of the TT. His song lyrics were deep and meaningful, so obviously that meant he was a "seeker" who desired to do God's will but unfortunately hadn't had the chance to meet His people yet. But lo and behold, he was going on tour, and we thus planned our own bus tour to follow him around. A new free paper was written with a compelling personal letter to him. Surely he would read this and be cut to the heart and want to know more about the Twelve Tribes.

A teaching came out entitled, *Why We Need to Be Praying for Bob Dylan.* We were all exhorted to believe in and pray for this endeavor, because if just one of us lacked faith he would not be saved. Since Dylan had such a big following, the news would spread like wildfire once he was saved and lead to monumental growth for the TT. The multitudes were finally going to pour in! We began excitedly speculating which community he would live in and how we would handle the flood of people that were sure to follow at his heels. And, of course, we anticipated the many things on Our Father's heart that could be accomplished if someone such as Dylan, with great wealth, surrendered it all to the Body. In addition to praying for the wealth of the nations to come in at the end of gatherings, now children were taking delight in shouting "Save Bob Dylan!"

Money was not an issue as the bus followed his tour for several weeks, armed with zealous disciples. Unbeknownst to us, we were becoming notorious and odious. Cities where he was scheduled to play next would have articles in the newspapers warning about the cult that was "stalking" Dylan. Disciples would be shouting at his tour bus trying to get his attention and personally give him a free paper. Papers were thrust upon any staff loitering around his private bus, pleading with them to get it into his hands. We basically acted like obnoxious, obsessed people.

It's inconceivable how caught up in this absurd fantasy we were. The households were continually abuzz with stories of the tour and how certain they were that Dylan was taking note of us. But, of course. Bob Dylan did not join the TT. The frenzy soon died down after the tour was over, and the continual praying ceased.

(When we first heard about Dylan, a man, not yet "in the know" about saving Bob, was visiting from another community. He heard someone pray for him at the gathering and asked me about it afterwards. I explained to him what was going on and he said, "Oh, I'm glad I asked. I didn't know if we were all going to start praying for our favorite celebrities, and I almost shouted, 'Save Weird Al too!'")

CHAPTER 35

Poisonous Books

ecause of the bubble we lived in, most of us rarely knew what was going on in "the world." It was frowned upon to listen to the news on the radio, read a newspaper, or look up news on the computer.

A short time after the election of 2008, I realized I had no idea who the president was! There was supposed to be an evening current events class for youth and interested adults, but, like many things of that nature, it would happen a few times and then peter out. And of course, we were only given information the leader of the class chose to present, with their spin on whatever the topic was.

Recreational reading of books wasn't allowed, except for rare circumstances. There was a teaching called *Books for Our Children.* The last line said, "Giving our children books to read from the world is tantamount to Jim Jones giving his followers poison Kool-Aid." Basically, the defiling, ungodly content would entice them, appealing to their flesh and eventually causing them to fall away and go to the Lake of Fire. Children could have educational nature books, but they weren't allowed books in which animals talked or that had cartoonish illustrations. Those were deemed foolish. Fictitious novels were an absolute no.

One time, a family was going to Hiddenite, and the woman found an Eric Carle book about a turtle that she thought might be suitable entertainment for her two-year-old on the long trip. She was a "good" disciple and gave the book to a leader's wife to judge if it was acceptable. The answer was no because at one point in the book the turtle was talking. Ironically, skits were common and oftentimes the children would dress up as animals and TALK! I asked several people why this was acceptable but they couldn't have a book in which animals talked. No one ever had a good answer for me.

We had to be careful of books that referenced dogs as pets. We would tear out that page or use Wite-Out. We did this often with children's books that were mostly OK but had a couple "defiling" parts. I remember looking at an old children's book from the '50s or '60s that had innocent, simple stories but the girls had short skirts, so all through the book you could see where someone had taken a marker and drawn their skirts longer.

I loved the children's book *Ox-Cart Man*. It came up in a Social Meeting that it wasn't an acceptable book because it "glamorized" a family living their own, independent life in the world (in the 1800s, no less), as though our children weren't supposed to know life existed between biblical times and the formation of the TT.

Once, a guest gave my children a factual book about the Titanic. Without me knowing, Emmet lent it to another child (they were thirteen at the time). During a "Parents Meeting," the father of the boy to whom my son lent the book brought it up. He was vague, saying, "Someone gave my son this book . . ." I'm sure he knew who the "someone" was. It's horrible being in the hot seat, not knowing if you're about to be publicly rebuked. My heart was racing and my face was on fire. Luckily, he didn't expose us, but he went on to say that if our children are given "exciting" books like that to read, they will be bored by the Bible, and that's the only book they should be excited about.

When Emmet was fifteen, he got in big trouble for reading *Tom Sawyer*, and the adult who gave him the book was "cut off." It was an ordeal of a scandalous nature—you'd have thought he'd been caught with pornography, such was the reaction of certain leaders. I couldn't believe that in 2014 my teenager wanted to read a classic and I had to think of that as "bad."

CHAPTER 36

Thou Shalt Obey All the Rules

here are countless examples of things that are not inherently wrong or even mentioned in the Bible as "sin," but once a new rule was introduced, we were taught that we would be going against our conscience if we were not obedient. It is the very definition of brainwashing according to the Freedom Center (freedomccenter.com): "the process of pressuring someone into adopting radically different beliefs by using systematic and often forcible means."

Between 2011 and 2014, so many rules were coming out that it was hard to keep abreast of every new standard. We could never express a bad attitude about any new direction, as we were told that sometimes Our Father asks us to do things that don't make sense simply to test our willingness to obey, to find out who is a faithful servant and who is in the flesh.

One of the first new rules was that everyone, including children, was to carry a cloth handkerchief, or hankie, in their pockets at all times. The reasoning behind it sounded perfectly acceptable—buying boxes and boxes of tissues was wasteful, and back in the day it was the norm for people to use hankies. The problem was it turned into an absolute rule—to the point that in some communities they were to "show their hankie" upon entrance to the morning gathering. An article came out with seventy good reasons to have a hankie. I always thought they were gross, and I cringed when I saw a man go to town blowing his nose in a hankie and then fold it up and put it back in his pocket. This was a standard I did not impose on my family. Life was stressful enough without making sure all four children had a hankie in their pockets all the time.

One day I was cleaning the entryway, and I noticed a paper lying near a basket that often contained teachings that were available to read. Picking it up, I saw it was a printed-out email addressed to several of the leading women in our tribe. It was from one of the leader's wives in California. The letter was about clothing and the standards of modesty for women. One sentence stood out to me. *We are not born with flowers covering our bodies, so why would we desire to adorn ourselves with floral fabrics?* Before I even finished reading it, Atarah came down the stairs and literally yanked it out of my hands.

"I didn't mean to leave this here. It's not for everyone to read yet. We will have a meeting soon," she informed me as she headed back upstairs with the letter.

I knew such a letter would become "new revelation," and we'd have to purge ours and our daughters' wardrobes of any floral patterned garments. Soon after, the bar was indeed raised for women's and girl's clothing. We weren't told no florals but that bright colors, large or contrasting patterns, and shiny fabrics such as crushed velvet drew attention to our garments, and, inevitably, our bodies. We were to immediately discard or turn over to be dyed any items that were judged ostentatious. A woman spent all day, fully equipped with a gas mask, dyeing our clothes either dark blue, brown, or dark purple. So many beautiful, handmade garments came out looking terrible. Then we had to be mindful that these dyed garments were always washed separately so they didn't ruin other clothes. It was ludicrous.

More "vision" was passed on that short-sleeved shirts had to go down to our elbows. This applied even to little girls, and since it's hard to find T-shirts with sleeves that long, we were burdened with the task of finding lace or other coordinating fabrics to extend all the sleeves on ours and our girls' short-sleeved shirts. Additionally, any neckline that came to a "V" had to be closed with a safety pin at our collarbone.

Dansko-style clogs (which all the girls loved, but only people who worked in the cafés and shoe stores were allowed to wear them) were banned, as we were told no shoe could have a "heel" of more than an inch and a half.

A rule was announced one winter that women and girls as young as ten were no longer allowed to wear snow pants because they were immodest. A single man in one of the other communities was overheard saying he couldn't wait for winter to see the ladies in snow pants. We were encouraged to make wool pants of the same baggy style as the regular sus pants or else wear a skirt over our snow pants.

Women looked ridiculous trudging up a hill of deep snow to sled with their children wearing full-length skirts with snow pants underneath. With all the sewing we had to do for everyday needs, the thought of also having to sew snow pants was overwhelming. The cost would have been exorbitant to get all the women and girls two to four yards of wool each. Enough people realized the idiocy of this, and by the end of winter the rule had been retracted. Even then, there were women who looked askance at those of us who readily went back to wearing snow pants.

When we first joined the community, much emphasis was placed upon men's pants being the correct length, not too long or too short. This made sense, as we didn't want their pants to be either highwaters or sloppily dragging on the ground. Hemming men's pants was a constant need, and sometimes there would be piles of them waiting for the women to attend to. Around 2013, we began hearing how men should cuff pants that were too long instead of having them hemmed because if a guest showed up who was taller and needed pants, it would be easy to accommodate them. Whew! Less work for the women! It sounded great at first.

Yet once again, it went from something reasonable to a nonsensical rule. Soon we heard, across the board, that "disciples cuff their pants," even if they weren't too long. In the middle of the gathering, men would cross the room and bend down to cuff another man's or boy's pants. The saying "show sock" took root, and pants had to be rolled high enough to see the man's socks. It was no longer a logical standard based on rational factors but just another rule to follow. Even now, when I visit or see photos from the community, every man and boy has their pants dutifully cuffed.

The funny thing was that literally every time we talked about clothing in the Cooks' Meeting and were informed of the next thing that was banned, a family would come for the weekend from Plymouth or Boston and the mother and/or daughters would be wearing the very thing we had all just purged from our closets. When I pointed this out, I was told I should be happy to be in a community that was being a good example of upholding Our Father's standards and not desire to sink to the lowest common denominator.

We were told not to compliment each other on how we looked or what we were wearing. It promoted vanity, and we didn't want any focus to be put on appearances. Not long after hearing that, I wore a new jumper on Friday night. A woman noticed and came and whispered in my ear, "I know I'm not supposed to say this, but that jumper looks really nice on you." Then she quickly walked away.

People who wore glasses were only allowed to get perfectly round bifocals. Any other shape was the flesh. Loads of money was spent when this new standard came out to replace people's perfectly good square- or oval-shaped glasses with round ones, per "Our Father's direction."

If you had a hard time about any new rule, you could go to someone and say, "I need help to have an understanding about the new glasses standard. I don't want to lack faith about it." Then the person would pass on faith to you, and if you still lacked vision they would tell you to trust and pray. Every time a group of leaders met, we believed that God was giving direction to the rest of us through them, hence we couldn't voice any "resistance" but were to pray for revelation if we lacked faith about new instruction. All questioning had to be done in a meek and humble spirit, under the impression that you wanted to "receive" Our Father's will.

If you ever spoke strongly against something, saying, "That's ridiculous! I just got a perfectly good pair of glasses, I don't see why I need to get rid of them!" you would more than likely be brought into a meeting to help judge your resistance and rebellious attitude.

> *When our Father's commands come to us, if we stop to consider the matter to see whether there is sufficient reason for us to do it, then we are still living according to the flesh. If the elders say "You need to move to . . ." and you say "What is the reason for that? I'm doing fine here," then no matter how well you may be doing in the flesh, you cannot go past that rebellion. If you cannot judge it, your sins will pile up as high as heaven, and you will receive a spirit that says you are doing all right. (Reasoning Part 1 teaching.)*

One summer, some of the teenage girls began brushing their hair straight back to wear in a higher ponytail instead of making a part down the middle and tying it lower. My own daughter began parting her hair slightly on one side. It came up in a woman's meeting that these girls were not obeying the standard. All women's and girls' hair needed to have a clear part straight down the center. One woman spoke up and said one of her girls had a cowlick that made her hair naturally want to part off-center. She was encouraged to use some hair gel to try and train the girl's hair to part down the middle. Any aspect of our life that could express the least bit of individuality was quickly curtailed.

⁂

Many played instruments, especially those who grew up there. Some were more gifted musicians than others, and often the youth enjoyed playing lively Irish and Israeli folk music together just for fun. Certain songs started to get banned because they were "complex," and so the musical "hotshots" would stand out. Melodies were to only have a certain number of beats per minute and be relatively simple to avoid this. My father-in-law would drum sometimes, and he was judged as having a "rock-n-roll spirit" because of how he drummed. Pianos were outlawed at one point—the reason given was that we were not going to be able to haul pianos out into the wilderness with us at the end times.

Board games were dubbed "bored games" and seen as unproductive and a form of dissipation and unhealthy competition. Some people still had them, hidden in closets and under beds. We heard of one community that had a "bored-game burning" and literally burned all their board games in a bonfire.

The only games that were approved were volleyball and ultimate frisbee. (I have since heard the ultimate frisbee has also been banned.) Not everyone enjoyed these games, and one Sabbath we got together a game of Wiffle Ball. Many who don't normally play the other games joined in, and everyone had a great time. We were rebuked at the next Social Meeting because Wiffle Ball was not approved, since someone might be a "hotshot" and hit a home run. Also, the batter was the center of attention, whereas in the sanctioned games, no one stood out like that.

⁂

We were continually hearing new direction about food and what we should or shouldn't be eating. One time, a family from Plymouth visited for the weekend, and they were helping in the kitchen. The wife asked if we had any black pepper. The bustling kitchen suddenly went silent as we all stopped what we were doing and looked at her, scandalized by her apostate request.

"No, of course not," someone replied, "we don't eat black pepper."

We'd been told black pepper caused prostate cancer in men and so the community was strict about never using it, or sometimes substituting with white pepper in recipes.

With a flip of her hand and an airy laugh, she said, "Oh, you all probably haven't heard yet, but we heard that black pepper is actually good for us! We've been using it in Plymouth for a few weeks now." I don't know what chain of command was contacted to verify such startling news or if we just took her word on the matter, but the next time a Frontier order was made, Cambridge was blessed with an eleven-pound shiny foil bag of black pepper for the first time in years.

Another time, we heard about the health benefits of red onions and that ideally, we all should be eating the equivalent of one onion per day. That wasn't realistic, as there were over eighty of us and we couldn't afford that many onions. It was decided that chopped red onions would be made available every morning on the tables as part of breakfast. This was not an option but a law.

Children were also expected to consume their portion of onion, and there were many principled, die-hard parents who would load their three-year-old's bowl of millet with two or three heaping spoonfuls of diced onion. Then the battle would ensue of a long spanking session forcing the child to obediently eat all their onions. If you were a lazy parent, not feeling up for the battle, and didn't give your child onions, you were sure to be approached by someone later who "happened" to notice how you weren't being faithful to take advantage of this wonderful opportunity we'd been given to help our children overcome their flesh. As parents you have extremely limited freedom to make your own decisions in regard to your children. Everything is mandated, and you are expected to take on faith and comply with whatever direction is given.

There was a pond on our property that was great for cooling off during the summer. It didn't take long for rules to crop up. We were told we shouldn't "hang out" at the pond for more than a half hour on a weekday, we shouldn't be there every day, and on Fridays we shouldn't be there at all. It wasn't promoting productivity, as life wasn't about swimming and soaking up the sun but serving. Many ladies began toting baskets of laundry to the pond to still look gainfully occupied, folding laundry while watching the children swim. Everything we did was subject to being judged.

There was also a dock with a slide attached in the middle of the pond that was one of the highlights for the children who were strong swimmers. The summer we left, the dock was nixed because sometimes only a few youth were out there, and the adults on shore couldn't hear and judge the conversations that were taking place.

CHAPTER 37

One Flesh

he TT is a patriarchal society. The proper order of the family unit is God, then husband, then wife, and last are the children. A wife would never dare attempt to usurp this order. Women are supposed to be one hundred percent submissive to their husbands- that's even part of their marriage vows. They are supposed to "win their husbands without a word"—instruction from the Bible that women were never to argue with their husbands but win them over with their "quiet and gentle spirit."

Monogamous marriage is greatly encouraged in the TT. *"Be fruitful and multiply"* is taken pretty seriously, as we were supposed to desire large families to further Our Father's Kingdom. When a man and a woman are interested in each other, they will communicate to their "coverings" a desire to go on a "waiting period." This is a sanctioned period for the couple to get to know each other in a very public manner. They don't get any unchaperoned time together but may be put on the same shifts at a café or on the same weekend team in the household. Maybe they would be sent along with some others to an event at another community, such as a wedding or bar mitzvah. Opportunities are made for them to get to know each other better in social settings.

Waiting periods can last several months, during which time they can have no physical contact until they are officially "betrothed" or engaged to be married. A "chopstick's length apart" is the standard for personal space. Once betrothed, they can publicly hold hands but still aren't allowed to be alone together. A betrothal lasts approximately seven weeks until the wedding. Their wedding day will be their first kiss.

If two youths fall into inappropriate contact before they are married, a judgment will be made on whether they need to be married. Inappropriate contact could be as minor as a kiss or touching over clothing. Forced marriages of this kind do occur, where sixteen- or seventeen-year-olds fool around and get caught. They are made to wait until they are of age, and then they either have to marry each other or leave the community. If they decide to marry, they have what is called a "brown pants" wedding. Because they didn't keep themselves pure, it is a disgraceful wedding, and they are not given the traditional wedding celebration with white clothes. They will have a private, short wedding in normal clothes.

Because of the human desires that are squenched, often for years, there are teachings on masturbation. It is acceptable for single men, as long as they don't overindulge and they shower afterwards. It is taught that men have a physical need for release. For women, however, it is not acceptable, because TT believes women do not have the same biological buildup that leads to eventual discomfort. If we caught our little girls touching themselves, we were to discourage it.

Once married and raising a family, the teachings were endless. One teaching came out called *Dominant Imma*. The gist of it was that while a wife is completely submissive to her husband, and he is the ultimate authority in the family, the Imma dominates the realm of child training. Of course, it made sense that mothers spent more time with the children than fathers, but this teaching was emphasizing the point that even when the fathers were around, the mothers wouldn't relax in any way but would continue taking charge of the children. There could be a tendency in a woman, especially if she had a long and tiring day with all the children, to anticipate the father getting home to "have a break." That was wrong. A woman should have the children under control and the bedrooms in order, so that when her husband came home at preparation time he could relax and focus on reading something aloud while the Imma continued keeping the children in order.

This also spilled over to the gatherings, and my husband was often rebuked for supporting me with disciplining the children during them. Having several children meant being in and out constantly, so we often took turns. He was told he shouldn't be leaving the gathering for discipline because he was the head, and oil came down from the head to the family. He should remain in the gathering to focus on what Our Father was saying, and if I missed most of the gathering focusing on children, then he could pass on to me later the things that were shared. From an ITN:

They (wives) serve their household well, and they serve their husbands, and *they care for their children well, and take on their husband's mind and heart when* *they raise them, because* the husbands are not with their children at home all day, but the women are. And what if a woman doesn't take on her husband's heart, if she is hard on the children all day, frustrated, and doesn't give them a will? Then the husband comes home and says, "Wife, what happened with the children today? Everything is chaotic." He wants to rule over his family, but if the wife isn't taking on his mind and heart, then she is not supporting him in what he is called to do.

Yoseph—And then read verse 11.

Ruth shel Yoseph—"A woman should learn in quietness and full submission."

Yoseph—So if you see that the wife does not quietly receive instruction with entire submissiveness, then the children are not going to be that way either. You know they are not going to be reverent. They are not going to have reverence toward their Abba or their Imma.

✢

Since this high expectation was put on women, any time there were problems with stubborn children, the relationship between the parents was quick to be scrutinized to see if an insubmissive wife was the root of the problem.

There was a permeating ideology that mothers had more "grace" to cover all their children than fathers did. If a woman's husband was away, there was no guarantee of support for her during meals and gatherings, even if she had several children. On the other hand, if a mother was shopping, sick, attending a birth, or had just had a baby herself, and the husband was covering all his children, they were sure to be divvied out so he only ended up with one or two.

One time, André wanted me to go and talk to another woman about something and said he'd watch the children. Less than five minutes into our conversation, Malak came over and interrupted us (something a woman would never dream of doing if two men were talking—it's taught that women never interrupt their husband or any man). He asked me if I was aware that my children were "running wild." I told the woman I'd be right back and found my husband across the room involved in a conversation with another man, oblivious to our children, who were indeed all over the place. But I was the "lacking" parent, not him.

I called to the children and made eye contact with André. He excused himself and came over to see what was going on. I let him know what happened and implored him to go tell Malak that I hadn't done anything wrong, that he was supposed to be covering the children while I was having a conversation he had told me to have. He did, and he and Malak laughed it off. There was always more understanding for the men.

✠

In 2013, I was given a manual entitled *Very Good*, written specifically for young girls. I was to start going over the teachings with Meyshar, then twelve, but decided to read it myself first. I raised my eyebrows at the instructions for being graceful when serving at men's meetings and suggesting that girls practice making figure eights with their hands to learn flowing and elegant movements. There were instructions on how to sit properly with knees together—the emphasis was on not drawing attention to the "less social" areas of the body.

Then I got to the chapter entitled "Submission." Reading along, I came across the sentence, "Woman is to imitate a slave." I kept rereading, hardly believing I was seeing those words in print and knowing I was never going to teach that to my daughter. The context surrounding that sentence was explaining how a good master cared for his slaves and loved them as his own family. In turn, the slaves were thankful and indebted to the master, willingly doing anything to please and serve him. This was supposed to be an analogy for the husband/wife relationship. From a teaching called *Wives*, April 30, 2002:

> *1 Pet 3:1–7: "Giving honor to their wives with value, dignity, esteem, to the highest degree, which is precious or priceless." This is man's mandate in Gen 3:16 to rule over his wife, over his slave. This is what it means to rule: to honor with dignity and esteem. He is to rule over her as a king does his domain . . . . A master will regard a slave as priceless . . . . We regard our wives*

as precious to us.

A man's mandate is to protect his wife from being less than what she could have been with a good ruler over her. He is not to rule with a lack of understanding. He needs understanding to be able to bring his woman by his side, as a master does his slave, but even if a master is harsh, a slave is still supposed to be submissive.

There are countless marriage and family teachings that give instruction to women—in fact, most marriage and family teachings are geared toward the woman, and they are very specific. From *Dysfunction Part 1*:

She should see to it that she notices him, regards him, honors him, prefers him. Venerates and esteems him, and that she defers to him, praises him, loves and admires him exceedingly.

From a 2001 teaching called *Marriage and Family—The Natural Order of Men and Women*:

"Let the woman be the learner and the husband be the teacher" (1 Timothy 2:11). Timothy gives the right instruction to the wife: she is to learn from her husband in a submissive relationship. 1 Tim 2:12 means that she should not butt in on her husband while he is speaking or teaching, as a pupil presuming to know more than the teacher, usurping his authority. She should remain silent while she is learning. Do not interrupt your husband, but learn in respect and submission to him who is your head (master). He is the one with a degree in teaching the wife; he is the one who graduated with honors from our Father to teach the wife.

This does not mean the wife cannot respond or ask questions, but only after he finishes his "lecture" (washing with the Word). "All submission" concerns the wife's attitude of an unruly manner. It does not mean just tolerating him until he shuts up, rolling your eyeballs, wagging your head, tapping your feet, or swaggering with your body.

Further instruction to the wife when being "taught":

> *So a wife who is virtuous will excel in displaying a tranquil spirit when her husband is teaching her or speaking to her, and not boil up or boil over. If she is virtuous, she should or will excel in this.*

We were encouraged to "capitulate," that is, symbolically take off our own head and come under the authority of our husbands. In return, husbands were supposed to "live with your wives in an understanding manner, regarding her as the weaker vessel" and vow to "love your wife as you do your own body."

There are teachings for the men but fairly few compared to the women. Men are commanded to bring their wives alongside them and are told their prayers will be hindered if they are not good husbands. From *Dysfunction Part 1*:

> *Let each man, without exception, love his wife as his very own body (love her, sacrifice yourself for her, listen to her concerns, take care of her, be sensitive to her needs and her hurts as you are to your own body).*

Men weren't supposed to be tyrants. Despite all these teachings, what went on behind closed doors did not always line up with how we were "supposed to be." Many women spoke many words, and many men lacked understanding. From a teaching called *Being in Salvation is Being in Order*:

> *A wife has an inborn tendency to try to usurp the headship of her husband **unless** she is ruled by her husband. Do you believe that? This is a Satanic principle to do that—wanting to be equal with or above our Father. Woman is under this satanic principle. She also has an inborn tendency to be unstable and cannot go the right course alone because she has a tendency to drift away. Although she is the helpmate of man, she has to be ruled over in order to be that helpmate.*
>
> *Man has an inborn quality to be a ruler, and woman has the inborn flaw of being able to drift out from under her covering.*

*Love brings the wife to **desire to be submissive** to her husband, and she will respect his authority **because the husband LOVES the wife**. These are the very words of the Creator. (Gen 3:16 quoted)*

There were many examples of strong, loving marriages in the community. And there were train wrecks—couples always in meetings and at odds with each other. It wasn't uncommon for a woman to not wear her head covering at the gathering because she wasn't in unity with her husband. No matter what a husband may have done wrong, there was never any leeway for a woman to express any disrespect toward him. That could be turned on her, that the reason for the husband's undesirable behavior was her insubmissiveness. Many teachings really homed in on the "fact" that Adam came first, then Eve, and she was created as the helpmate of Adam, not the other way around. And most importantly, she was the one who was deceived, and Adam followed her selflessly into death, as he could not bear to be apart from her.

There is one teaching where the following sentence was repeated three times, to really drive it home: "Man is primary, woman is secondary. Man is primary, woman is secondary . . ." I remember we were going around the room taking turns reading, and I had read ahead and seen that sentence and was fearful I would have to read that part. Thankfully, the gathering ended before we got that far. Of course, to guests, it's portrayed in a more palatable way. I remember being told that men and women are completely equal in worth, equal recipients of the Holy Spirit, just with different functions.

From a teaching called *Dysfunction Part 1*:

No interchange of roles: Male jobs are not for women. You do not really respect a woman policeman or fireman. This change of roles is demonic. It is doubtful a woman can be a lawyer, for how is she going to relate to men outside the courtroom? How is she going to relate to her husband when she goes home, since she has an exalted attitude which she has learned in order to speak in the courtroom. It is very difficult for a woman to be a lawyer."
"Women assuming professions that are only for men to have is a Satanic principle.

This means they absolutely do not agree with women becoming pastors or ministers. They don't think a woman should ever be in a place to teach a man. Women have been corrected for how they shared at gatherings if the way they were presenting themselves seemed too "teachy." 1 Timothy 2:12—*"But I suffer not a woman to teach, nor to usurp authority over the man, but to be in silence."*

Not surprisingly, feminism was seen as a form of evil, as women rising up, resisting the natural order of the family that God ordained. It was pure rebellion, and the term "feminazi" was often used in its place. One time at a teaching, the topic of voting came up and how wrong it was that women fought for their right to vote. All it accomplished was cause marriages to be divided. When only men voted, it was normal they would include their wives in making the decision, giving much thought and consideration to the wife's input. So, in casting his ballot, the man would essentially be "voting for two." There was no need for both of them to vote. Of course, this did not consider women who were unmarried or widowed. It also didn't take into accounts husbands who didn't agree with their wives and could ultimately do what they pleased.

Men were in complete control of their wives and had the prerogative to give them permission to do something or not. From a teaching called *Being in Salvation is Being in Order*:

> *The wife is commanded to submit to her husband, since women still need that ruling factor in their lives to bring them to proper submission. They need help. The husband is the head of the wife just as Yahshua is the head of the Body. The head (Messiah, the Husband) has the right to tell the Body (the Edah, the Wife) what to do, and the Body must be submissive to the head. If not, you are in disobedience, which brings death.*

For example, the Sabbath often consisted of volleyball games for the husbands, youth, and other single people. It was difficult for the wives, who had to find something to do with the younger children during that time. The Sabbath was the only day we could do something as a family, and by the time the morning gathering and breakfast were over, we only had a couple precious hours until lunch. I'd suffer when most of that time was spent waiting for volleyball to end. After lunch was nap time, which most of us desperately needed.

So, when our husbands all headed to the volleyball court, I was not the only wife to feel discouraged. But we were not supposed to complain or show any annoyance about our husbands' plans. One woman said to me, "Imagine if we told our husbands we were going to play Scrabble all morning and they had to watch all the children?" Never in a million years would such an "out of order" scenario take place. And on the off chance a few women were socializing, at the word of her husband a wife would need to go and do his bidding.

Men also unquestioningly ruled the marriage bed. Women were never supposed to deny their husbands sex, no matter the time of day or night. We were to be "always available."

One time I put pajamas on my needs list and was questioned by Rivkah before shopping day if I really meant them for myself, as if it was an odd request.

"Yes, don't you wear pajamas to bed?" I asked.

"Never!" she replied with conviction, "I want to be 'always available' to my husband."

A mother of six shared at a Bride's Supper the night before a wedding that sometimes she felt like an old worn-out sock, but even if it was two in the morning and she'd been asleep for hours, if her husband got home and wanted to "come together," she knew she had to be willing to give herself to him. This was advice being given to a young, virgin bride.

We were taught it was evil—"the ultimate rebellion"—for a woman to not desire her husband. We were always supposed to let our husbands know the day we were "clean" from our cycle, and plan to have sex that night. We were encouraged to whisper a little something in his ear earlier in the day such as, "I can't wait for tonight," to build his anticipation. Anyone who has spent hours making lunch for fifty people with young children will tell you, when you see your husband at lunch, sex is the farthest thing from your mind.

We were "unclean" after sex and were never supposed to attend a gathering without showering first. Men weren't allowed to make the loaf for Breaking of Bread if they had sex that same day. Sometimes you would see a group of men counseling together late Saturday afternoon, and they would be trying to figure out who could fill in for the man who was supposed to be making the loaf, because he was unclean.

We weren't banned from using birth control, but the teaching said, "If Our Father wants to start a new life, who are we to cut off that seed? Maybe that child would be an important part in bringing about the Male Child and the end of the age and we just prevented that from happening." So we knew it was strongly discouraged.

Obviously, the TT does not believe in divorce. From *Dysfunction Part 1*:

> *Marriage will be monogamous for a lifetime. This is the will of God. Therefore, when we talk about the gospel to people who have had multiple marriages, and they know they were at fault, they must be made aware that they have broken the second covenant, therefore they deserve the second death. But the good news is they can be forgiven. We must know exactly what to talk to people about—what to say and how to say it—to bring conviction to them, so they can see where they have sinned, where they were wrong in what they have done in the past. We must let them know that they are going to the second death, that they are not good enough to be a part of the nations.*

The fault for all divorces is placed on women. From *Dysfunction Part 1*:

> *Thousands upon thousands of divorces are caused by the mother-in-law, and the other half are caused by dysfunction—a woman trying to ascend to the role of the man, not respecting him as laid out in Gen 3:16–19—that the man is to rule over the woman, and the woman is to desire the man. This is for the world, not just for us.*

In the teaching called *Wife Takeover*, the focus is on suicide, and how twice as many married men commit suicide as women. The reason is, of course, that they have insubmissive wives whom they can't rule over and therefore feel like dogs and take their life. The statistic is true, but is, of course, one-sided. The teaching does not mention that three times as many women *attempt* suicide as men, but since women are more likely to use poison to kill themselves instead of a gun or hanging (more common to men), they are more likely to survive. And two thirds of women who do successfully kill themselves have had a previous attempt, whereas the same amount of men who die from suicide do so on their first attempt. Why are so many women attempting suicide, and why was this left out of the teaching? My guess is they would say it's from the bad conscience all these women have from trying to rule over their husbands.

Because the standard for women's behavior and the expectations put on them was unattainably high, we would inevitably fall short. And since men's behavior was in direct correlation to the wife, any faults or wrongdoing of the husband could easily be pegged on the failure of the wife in some aspect of her life. I experienced this firsthand.

CHAPTER 38

The Confession

espite my lack of faith, I did everything I was supposed to do to gain it. I made sure I prayed throughout the day and kept a good conscience. I never did lawless things like listen to the radio, read novels, buy things I wasn't covered to get, and so on. I tried so hard to be "good," hoping the saying "Obedience comes before revelation" would apply to me and God would see my heart and give me the faith I sincerely desired. I also knew if anything "bad" happened to me or my family (anything from a broken bone to a car accident to a stillbirth), there would be a judgment meeting to find out what sin God was trying to expose in my life. Over the years, countless individuals have been deeply and irreversibly hurt by judgments that were made on them after going through something horribly traumatic. Fault for the tragedy would heartlessly be placed on some area of their lives that they were not overcoming or had a bad conscience about. This very thing kept me terrified of doing anything deemed sinful for several years.

Sometime around 2009, the first Blackberry phones appeared in the community, and André was soon in possession of one. My very words when he showed it to me and what it could do was, "We are doomed." (Meaning the community). It seemed unavoidable that anyone could have the internet at the tips of their fingers and not give in to temptation. He reasoned that other leaders were getting them, and industry heads needed them as "tools" to function.

Not surprisingly, it wasn't long before he became more and more obsessed with it, constantly looking at it, even holding it under the table at mealtimes, as though I wouldn't notice. Whenever I questioned him about it, he'd get bristly and tell me he was texting Samuel or someone else of great importance. I noticed he'd roll over in bed and hours later I'd still see that glow over his shoulder.

After a few months, I told another woman how I was fighting the urge to throw his phone out the window, fully expecting a lecture on not judging my husband. But to my surprise her response was, "I don't blame you." I was getting suspicious that he was doing more than texting other leaders, but any questioning on my part only angered him and got turned back on me, like I was being unreasonable and trying to prevent him from his important duties.

One day I asked if he'd leave his phone for me to call my father, as one of the women we lived with was always tying up the household phone. He reluctantly agreed, saying he'd be back to get it shortly. I didn't know anything about smartphones and quickly started clicking on everything. I finally came across some text that wasn't familiar to me, so I found the search engine and looked up a few lines. I discovered it was a sci-fi/fantasy novel from one of his former favorite authors. He was halfway through it, so obviously he'd been reading it for some time.

Filled with righteous indignation, I went and told an older woman, Edah, who shared my shocked reaction and told me this was like a boulder that was starting to roll down a hill and gain momentum, and we needed to act quickly to stop it. She suggested I call Samuel. I went across the street to the café office to have some privacy but only got his voice mail. I was about to leave a message but suddenly hung up the phone, feeling a bit traitorous. I decided to confront André myself.

As promised, he showed up soon after to retrieve his phone. I sent the children into their room, and calmly told him what I had discovered. To my surprise he didn't try to deny it. He readily apologized and said he'd gotten "distracted" one day while he was stuck in a vehicle waiting for someone for a long time. He told me he would delete it from his phone immediately. I believed him and let it go.

Time went on, and it was better for a while, but after a couple months or so I started noticing the same behaviors in him. I point-blank asked if he was reading again. He said he wasn't and I truly wanted to believe him, but doubt got the best of me. One day his phone was in the room charging, and he went downstairs for some reason. Taking advantage of the situation, I hurriedly searched his phone and found several Tom Clancy novels that had been downloaded. I confronted him again, fuming this time because he had lied to me. He was in government, a trusted and esteemed leader. I asked how he could listen to single brothers confessing their sins and have "godly" advice for them and inspiration and faith to share at almost every gathering when he was secretly reading worldly novels and lying to me about it. It didn't seem fair—he could be "bad" and still be full of faith, while I tried so hard to be good and was always lacking! He apologized again, taking his phone off the charger and punching buttons emphatically, saying, "Look, I'm deleting them all right now!"

A couple nights later we were in our room at preparation time. I was sitting in my rocking chair flipping through the latest ITN when he came over and handed me a random cell phone. I started reading the text on the screen and recognized it was *The Clan of the Cave Bear*, the first book of my favorite series from "the world." It was a case of "if you can't beat 'em, join 'em." He realized he didn't want to stop reading books (he was also keeping up with sports, news, music, and watching the occasional movie, I later discovered), but he didn't want to keep lying and trying unsuccessfully to hide it from me, so he decided to indulge me in the same privilege. He explained to me that he wished he was one hundred percent fulfilled by everything in the community, and that was his goal. He just wasn't there yet, and reading helped him relax since he was always under so much pressure. He was sure God would have mercy on him.

I accepted this. He obviously had put thought into this, as he had procured an unused phone no one would miss and downloaded the series for me. I hadn't realized how much I missed books and began to look forward to going to bed each night to read. I struggled to keep my mind on "holy" things all day. Between the two gatherings, spiritual conversations, prayer walks, preparation time of Bible or ITN reading, spiritual stories at naptime and bedtime, and then the ITN, Bible, or free papers to read before I went to bed, I was spiritually maxed out. Now I had a glorious escape. I got even less sleep than before, but it was worth it. I felt alive again; my mind had something stimulating to think about during the day even though I had to keep it to myself.

The most beautiful thing about this was, I was covered by my "head" to be doing this, so I didn't have to feel guilty. If he could justify this, and I was simply a submissive wife, I should be protected.

Time went by, and I started to let my principled nature slide even more. I, along with another woman, of course, cleaned a local bookstore to earn money for personal needs. As I dusted the shelves, I'd be covertly checking out which title to ask André to download for me next.

Along with the books, André began regularly downloading a movie to his laptop for us to watch on Family Nights. I remember the first movie we watched, *The Princess Bride*. For some reason, André had quoted a line from the movie, and I didn't know what he was talking about. Somehow, I'd never seen that movie as a child, and he was shocked. So, we watched it in our bedroom one night. I was so mesmerized, I remember asking, "Can we watch this every night?"

It always felt surreal to me when we'd watch a newer movie. I'd think, "I wonder what I was doing when this scene was filmed. Maybe I was making lunch or was at Breaking of Bread." It struck me how "normal" life was continuing around the bubble we lived in. It seemed like a parallel universe, so far removed from where I was. Sometimes I felt like I was a part of some strange play.

André also showed me new songs he liked, and I began hurrying through my lists on shopping day so I could catch some of the *'90s on 9* radio show while I waited for the other woman to come out, quickly popping back in the CD of community music when I saw her. My kids started playing video games on André's phone or the laptop. *Brick Breaker* and *Gold Miner* were favorites. I even noticed someone playing a video game on his phone during a Social Meeting one time! I could see it reflecting in the window behind him.

We started to let the children watch certain videos, mostly community plays but also funny YouTube videos. Someone shared in a gathering about "United Breaks Guitars" and how things can "go viral" on the internet. We watched the video in our room later, and my kids became obsessed with it. They soon had every word memorized from all three "United Breaks Guitars" songs. We also downloaded the entire *Planet Earth* series.

Life went on in this vein for several months. Then, one Friday morning we had a child training teaching about what we do behind closed doors. God sees everything. If we have a guilty conscience about what goes on in our bedrooms, then our families won't prosper, our children won't take on faith, we won't be protected, we will stand before God someday and be judged unworthy of the Kingdom, and so on. It freaked me out. I glanced at André who was nodding in agreement, seemingly unfazed. At the end he stood up and spoke his conviction of said topics, and I suddenly felt anxious and distressed. I essentially had a panic attack. God saw everything we were doing. Who were we kidding? We were hypocrites living double lives and gambling with our children's safety and our eternal destinies. If any tragedy befell our family, it would surely be God punishing us for our disobedience. I was no longer comforted by the fact that the responsibility would be on André, I was terrified for us.

I waited until André and Emmet left for the soap shop, deposited Arek in my grandmother's room, told my girls to start cleaning their room, and ran to Elad's room. I knocked on the door, and as soon as he let me in and closed it behind me, I burst into tears, and said, "I think our family should leave."

He calmly encouraged me to sit, and I confessed everything we had been doing, the whole story, all the things André had brought into our lives that were taking over. I exposed it all. I couldn't live that way anymore. I wanted help; I wanted our family to prosper. I tearfully asked him, "If these are the things my family wants to be doing, why are we living here? Why don't we just leave and go to the world where we are free to do them?" He listened supportively and reassured me that I did the right thing by coming to him. He was confident we could get the help we needed and exhorted me to not lose hope.

"Leaving is *never* the answer," he said with conviction. I thanked him and went back to my children, feeling as though a huge weight had been lifted.

The weekend went on as normal, then on Sunday André and I were called to a meeting, a kahal. If one lacks faith, doesn't receive someone, or is caught in a particularly lawless behavior, they could get called into a kahal, or judgment meeting. Several elders would be present, so it could be quite intimidating. But I was relieved and looking forward to the meeting, hoping for help to come to my family. Our children were covered for the afternoon, and I entered the meeting room feeling positive. There were three other leading couples waiting for us, and they all smiled when we came in, greeting us with warm hugs.

The meeting began with everyone confirming how much our family was loved and appreciated, how needed we were, and how much they wanted to see us prosper. I relaxed, still feeling hopeful that our family would get back on the right track in God's favor. But soon the tone of the meeting changed from compassion to judgment. The focus turned directly on me—my lack of faith and how little I spoke in gatherings, my lacks as a parent and ways I wasn't ruling over my children, and, most importantly, my lacks as a wife and problems in our marriage. Even drinking coffee came up.

I had suffered with chronic constipation for years. Drinking a cup of coffee was usually a surefire cure, but coffee is not allowed. I went to Elad at one point and asked him what was more detrimental to health, a cup of coffee a day or living with chronic constipation. He confirmed the latter was worse and told me if coffee worked then I could have a cup. With Nanny living there, having a cup of coffee had been easy. I felt completely "covered" at that point.

So, when my "bad habit" of drinking coffee came up, I mentioned that conversation, saying I was under the impression Elad had covered me. He was right there, and I thought he'd back me up, but he claimed to have no recollection of saying that. How convenient for him. Now I looked like a liar too. At that point my husband tried to intervene on my behalf, and said he wondered if having a cup of coffee was any worse than drinking six to eight cups of maté a day (as many did). At that point Samuel stood up and slammed his fist down on the table, startling us all, and said harshly, "You two have your own minds about coffee. It is *bad* for you, so *no* amount of coffee is good, but you *can't* drink too much maté because it is *good* for you." This was the only time during the whole meeting that I felt in the same boat as André.

The rest of the meeting is a blur. I just remember that sense of being a child in trouble, feeling small and intimidated. I cried a lot. I was in the hot seat, feeling like I had inadvertently brought all this on myself, when I had actually exposed my husband for what *he* had allowed into our family! It was incredibly humiliating and degrading. They kept telling me it would be OK if I cut myself off and took the time I needed to sort out everything and not be under any pressure. I didn't know what I was supposed to do, and after four intense hours, I would have said yes to anything. I understand the premise of interrogation now. I finally agreed to be cut off and we left. I was shell-shocked as we walked home.

Being cut off is no light thing. It's tremendously public. There is an announcement made at the gathering that "so-and-so is not wearing their head covering or lifting their hands right now as they are going through some things." You are not allowed to drive a vehicle, handle money, teach or watch any children other than your own, attend Breaking of Bread or regular meetings, dance at gatherings, answer the household phone, or participate in any special events, and you don't wear your diadem or head covering to gatherings or raise your hands at the end to pray. It's basically adult punishment. You remain in this state of being "out of fellowship" until you publicly renounce your sin or, in certain cases, get washed or baptized. People aren't supposed to have lighthearted, casual fellowship with someone who is cut off, so they will feel the sting of the separation. Interactions with them are supposed to be based on getting to the root of their spiritual problems and bringing them back into fellowship.

I spent the next week in the state of being cut off, in meeting after meeting, being asked questions like, "Why wasn't Yahshua enough for you to not have withdrawn your affection from your husband?" I had no idea how to answer questions like this. Basically, they were blaming my lacks as a wife for driving my husband into those lawless activities. It was judged that I had withdrawn from him, therefore he was justified for the distractions and temptations he gave into. There was some truth to it all—we had drifted apart over the years, and while I did my best to offer myself for wifely duties, I had a hard time hiding the fact it was most often not something I looked forward to.

André told me they had a private meeting with him, exhorting him to give up his bad habits and lead our family in the right way. A slap on the wrist for him, but I was cut off! All the attention was on me, and to the rest of the community who didn't know all the details, André seemed like the model husband, enduring with and supporting his faulty wife through her struggles. My children were embarrassed and insecure. I just wanted to make it end.

With my tail between my legs, I approached Elad on Thursday before the evening gathering. I told him I received and accepted what they were saying and wanted to repent and be a better wife. I thought I could simply wear my head covering to the gathering that night and make a short speech to the household, repenting for my lacks and declaring my determination to take hold of the grace I know Our Father could provide to be a better wife and mother. The standard, as I understood it, was that you only needed to be washed or baptized if you had missed a Breaking of Bread due to being cut off or if you were involuntarily cut off as a discipline for something. I had not yet missed a Breaking of Bread, and, though somewhat coerced, it had essentially been my choice to be cut off.

He heard me out, then sighed as he folded his arms across his chest. "It's a pretty serious thing that you withdrew from your husband, so it's not that easy. The only way for you to really get a fresh start and be connected again is to be washed."

I once again felt that sense of panic and entrapment I'd felt in Hyannis when André told me we weren't going anywhere. I was devastated and felt betrayed. I felt like what those men were really saying was, "Why couldn't you have kept your mouth shut and covered for your husband?" Something was off. André was too necessary and important to be cut off and unable to function. He was a leader and industry head. And I had a feeling he knew about too much of the other men's dirty laundry. I walked away in despair.

I confided to my mother-in-law that weekend that I was positive all those men were doing the same things behind closed doors, so of course they could not righteously persecute my husband. "Gosh, I hope not!" I remember her exclaiming in response. I asked André point-blank about this after we left, and he said it was true—he once had witnessed one of the men looking at porn late at night at the soap shop and had found a bunch of movies downloaded on another's laptop when he had been asked to fix something on it. But I had opened a can of worms, and something needed to be done, so it was simply convenient to turn it on me.

The big night came when I was to be washed. It was Passover Monday. Everyone, including the children, would break bread together that night. It was a big deal, and I knew my family would suffer if I couldn't be there. After preparation time, as we were getting ready to leave, André held out my coat to me and cheerfully asked if I was ready. I told the children to go check on Nanny. As soon as they'd left the room, I closed the door and promptly burst into tears. I told him it wasn't fair; it should be him that was cut off and having to be washed, not me! He started all this. I was just trying to do the right thing and get our family some help, but instead I got all the blame while he got protected.

He told me I was right and said he was planning to go to the gathering and go in the water with me. He had planned to wait until we were at the gathering and surprise me.

I wasn't impressed. It was *his* own choice. And what a wonderful example he would be of the loving husband choosing to align himself to his disobedient wife—just like Adam and Eve. This selfless act of love for his wife would probably make it into the next month's ITN, inspiring couples around the world. His status would soar.

We drove up to the Main House, my dread growing as we turned down the driveway. As soon as the gathering began, I stood up to share my confession. I can't remember exactly what I said. I was on autopilot at that point and just wanted the ordeal over. As I made my public repentance, vowing to overcome and be the wife and mother my family needed, I also vowed to myself that I'd never tell on my husband again.

After I sat down, André promptly stood up and repented for not being a good ruler and example to his family. He appreciated me and did his best to lay the blame for problems in our family on himself. He then expressed his desire to be washed with me. This was of course met with an exuberant chorus of "Amens," clapping, and cheering. I felt sick, and again I had the surreal sense that I was just playing a part and had to get through this next scene.

The entire community headed down to the pond. It was mid-March, and a couple men first had to break away enough ice for us to stand and submerge ourselves in the frigid water. André and I stood at the water's edge, facing the crowd. Someone spoke for a couple minutes about the covenant of marriage and the importance of unity of husbands and wives. A couple supporting Bible verses were probably read. Then all eyes were on us.

We turned around and walked waist-deep into the water, pushing chunks of ice out of the way. Facing the crowd again, we took turns crying out our appeal for mercy and salvation, then dunked under holding hands.

Being submerged in ice water takes your breath away and causes every nerve to feel like it's on fire. We bolted to the shore into the awaiting blankets being held out. Everyone "laid hands" on us and prayed, then we went up to the soap shop to shower and change as it was closer than going back to the house.

With only a single shower stall, he suggested we jump in together to save time. I don't think we'd showered together since college and we were all alone in the huge building, so he was naturally trying to be touchy-feely and affectionate with me. He was probably also hopeful, testing out my proclamation of being a better wife. But I felt repulsed and claustrophobic in the tiny stall and wished I could have showered alone. I feigned an urgency to get back to the children and got out after a quick rinse in the blissfully hot water.

On the way back to the gathering he reached for my hand and coaxingly said, "That wasn't so bad, was it?"

Yanking my hand away, I stopped dead in my tracks, looked him clear in the eyes, and spat out, "That was absolutely horrible, and I will never, ever go through anything like that again the rest of my life." He had nothing to say in response to that, and we walked the rest of the way in silence, my hands in my coat pockets.

As we walked into the gathering room, everyone stood and erupted in clapping and cheering, celebrating our great "victory" as a family. I forced myself to smile and appear like I was rejoicing in the fact that I had been forgiven and received the Holy Spirit and a fresh new start to my life. In reality, I was more dead on the inside than before, I lost all respect for the other leaders, and I definitely did not have any desire to draw closer to my husband. If anything, the situation pushed me further from him in my heart. I knew he was untouchable, as were the other men. I saw the corruption and was powerless to do anything besides be a submissive wife and focus on raising my children. I had to move on to the next scene.

CHAPTER 39

Let Us Reason Together

ne night I had a dream that we were told the men could have multiple wives. We were about to witness the first polygamous marriage, and I turned to Rivkah and said, "I can't believe we are actually doing this."

She was crying but took me by the shoulders and shook me a little and said, "Tamara, we just have to trust and receive this." I woke up thinking if we ever went that far, I'd be out of there for sure.

Later that day I was cleaning the kitchen with another woman, and I told her the dream, fully expecting she would have the same reaction I had. She didn't. She paused from scrubbing dishes in her elbow-length rubber gloves, thought for a moment, and responded, "Wow, we'd have to be given some serious revelation in order for that to happen. Like, maybe it would be the only way to bring about the Male Child or something."

I was stunned. I realized any hair-brained idea could come down the pipeline through the anointing and there would be obedient people willing to do it. If we heard we should put a tiny pebble in our shoe, so when we stepped on it through the day and felt discomfort, we would be reminded of the suffering Yahshuah went through and stay focused on our purpose, there would be people out in the driveway looking for their pebble. We had to remember how Our Father gives us direction that makes no sense to test our willingness to obey. Then once he sees our hearts, he may not expect that of us anymore. (Like the example of Abraham and Isaac.)

We were not to reason with authority or be an "oppositional thinker." That was someone who heard direction and immediately had a questioning, doubtful response—"But what about . . ."—instead of simply receiving and obeying, through which Our Father would bless us with revelation. There was the saying, "Obedience comes before revelation." We didn't need to understand to obey. We simply had to trust. That was especially true for children, who were never to ask why when given a command. As parents, we weren't even supposed to include a reason as part of our direction. We would not say, "Pick up your shoes so no one trips over them." This would teach them to judge our commands and promote reasoning instead of simply saying "Yes, Imma," and quickly obeying. We were to give the clear command, and after the child obeyed, if we then felt it was necessary, we could explain the why to them. Our children never needed a reason to obey. From *Reasoning Part 1* teaching:

> It is possible for children to be raised to reason, to see whether what they are told fits in with their thinking. They can be raised up to reason or they can be raised up to obey. One way is death, and one way is life.
>
> A child's rebellion against authority is manifested (as ours is also) in words, thoughts, or reasons. Rebellion against authority or the Word of God comes out of his mouth. If he does not know authority, he will speak slanderous words which come out of his reasoning. This child who has learned to reason has been raised up by an overprotective, defensive parent. He has been excessively shielded by an anxious, insecure mother. The child raised by an overprotective parent who puts reason into him instead of obedience is always judging whether his discipline was right or wrong. Instead of the recognition of authority, the child takes on the attitude of the parent. The parent does not have the eyes of his reasoning put out, so the child grows up to cling to his own arguments and reasons. But the child brought up by parents who have put out their eyes of reason would be an example of rising above this ungodly reason, of living by faith, not by sight. If we live by sight, we see only what we reason. But we live by faith, not by reason. We learned reasoning from childhood through adulthood. In schools they taught us to question authority. If we did not have parents who guarded us from this, it went right into us. We need to guard

> *our children from reasoning. To cease from reasoning asks for the very life of our flesh. Our flesh is tied to Satan. Satan is the father of reason. So if we cut off our flesh, reason is cut off.*

There were many sayings to constantly remind us of these teachings, such as, "Wisdom yields to less than wisdom," "When you're strong, you're wrong," "Better to be wrong together than right alone." Any hardships and sufferings in our lives were attributed to being a vital part of our salvation. This was crafty, as it leaves absolutely no justification for anyone to ever leave or even suffer over any aspect of our life in the TT. You are simply in the flesh, and resisting Our Father's hand in your life if you aren't content and thankful for your circumstances. You are rebelling against God if you ever leave. This also leaves the community with zero accountability for the mistreatment of people, because everything that happens to us is God's will and He would never give us more than we can handle. Disciples have to be tested and purified by fire. We were clay in the Potter's hands, and of course it was uncomfortable when we were squashed down, but it was necessary to form us into the useful vessel He wanted us to be. We were always supposed to look inwardly in difficult circumstances and ask ourselves, "What is our Father wanting to show me through this?"

Ironically, we were encouraged to be open and honest, even to "stand on the table" if we thought something wasn't right, but so often that backfired. Any hard time you were having with any person or circumstance could quickly be turned back on you. You could be told you were only suffering because you were being selfish, envious, having an accusation, or not receiving your portion. Someone once told me what they'd experienced through their life was essentially, "Oh, that's wonderful how you were able to step out of line and be honest . . . but now get back in line." Or if you were emotional or came off strong in your attempt to communicate (especially if you were a woman), you could be completely dismissed on the grounds that you were just "reacting."

Another saying was, "Our Father opposes the proud and gives grace to the humble." That conveniently turned any suffering or "opposition" you were experiencing back on you—you must have pride working in you that was keeping you from receiving grace. From *Reasoning Part 1* teaching:

> *A person must live either by our Father's authority or by*

reason. You cannot drink from two cups at once. If you are not drinking from the cup of salvation, you are drinking out of the cup of evil spirits. Our Father hands us the cup of obedience. We have to walk in His way. Our Master submitted Himself to His Father's authority; He never questioned, only obeyed.

Obedience is the act or fact of obeying, the quality of state of being obedient, compliant with that which is required by authority, subjection to rightful restraint, submission to restraint, control or command of authority, being tractable...

To live by reason is so complicated. Consider the birds and flowers, how simply they live. The more we subject ourselves to authority, the simpler our lives become, and the more our offspring will be full of grace. The flowers and birds do not have reasoning. We have to live like them—as if our flesh was crucified. Our Master says, "If you obey Me, you will never die; you will never be separated from Me; you will always be near to me" (John 8:51).

Our children will reason less than the stem, and their children will reason less than them, and the third generation will not reason at all. They will be the ones who will bind the Evil One. "These are the ones who follow the Lamb wherever he goes" (Revelations 14:4). Matthew 16:24–25 had no reasoning in it at all.

One time when I was struggling with my faith, André encouraged me to bring my questions to Elad, as he did not have the answers. I asked Elad if it was true that man didn't have a conscience before the fall, since we were taught that God gave man the covenant of conscience after the fall. He affirmed that was true. I then asked how they could possibly have been held responsible for disobeying, given the fact they had no idea of right and wrong. Nothing in their existence led them to believe anything bad could happen, so they didn't know to be on guard against evil. We often called them our Father's children, and I said it would be like putting a crawling infant in imminent danger. Why would a loving God do that? Especially since He knew the suffering that would come upon humanity as a result of the fall. It didn't seem fair or as if it represented a compassionate God who truly cared about His creation.

The only wisdom Elad had for this question was that Eve could have simply obeyed, and he was quick to end the conversation by telling me that I was "treading on dangerous ground" with my questioning.

As much as we were encouraged to seek each other out and be honest with our sufferings, when someone came to us, we were not supposed to enter into any kind of mutual complaint. We were to have a "salty," spiritual response. If a woman was upset about a certain way her husband was being (harsh, not paying her enough attention, etc.), we shouldn't say, "I completely understand, my husband can be that way too." Instead, we were to remind them of our purpose as wives and how we are to win our husbands without a word and be submissive, and blah, blah, blah . . . We were never to justify someone's bad attitude or complaint or join them in it.

Likewise, when we were suffering, we were to go to the person we knew would give us the most spiritual advice, not someone who tended to suffer in similar ways and would probably have a natural response. It really started to weigh on me how every aspect of our life was controlled in some way, right down to who we talked to.

One time a woman came to me in tears, needing to talk. I went to her room with her, and she poured her heart out to me about how she'd been in the community nearly seventeen years but felt stuck in a rut. She said if you weren't born and raised there or part of certain families, you never got the same opportunities. She had never been asked to be involved in midwifery or taught to sew and felt she'd be teaching toddler training forever. I could relate, and I sympathized with her, telling her positive things about herself. The next day she came back and repented for complaining and not being content with her portion. I looked in her eyes and told her I did not forgive her and hated the fact that we had to repent for honesty. And theoretically, if I'd been "full of the spirit," I would have called her out and led her back on track instead of affirming anything she'd said. I didn't repent though.

CHAPTER 40

Controversial Teachings

ome of the most controversial teachings for which the TT comes under the most scrutiny have to do with slavery and homosexuality.

The TT believe Africans (Chamites) became slaves because of the curse Noah put on his grandson Canaan when Noah's own son Cham exposed Noah's nakedness to his brothers. *"When Noah awoke from his wine and found out what his youngest son had done to him, he said, 'Cursed be Canaan! The lowest of slaves will he be to his brothers.'" Gen 9:24–25.*

Since no time limit on this slavery was specified, they believe it should still be the proper order for Black people to be subservient to whites in society at large. It is only in the "Body of Messiah" that the curse can be broken and people of all races live together in harmony. Black people were treated as equals in the TT but had to embrace the essence of these teachings.

They believe Black people cannot rule themselves and need to be under whites' rulership. Examples such as their so-called "barbaric" lifestyles, continued social unrest, and corrupt governments in Africa are used to back up that view. Children at fourth-grade level are taught that the Civil War destroyed the "righteous" culture of the South, where Black folks served whites and were well cared for and prospered in this arrangement. They teach that harsh slave owners were rare and that in most cases the slaves were treated like family and life became much worse for them once slavery was abolished. They say that mainstream history books lie in their portrayal of what slavery looked like.

From the teaching *Dysfunction Part 1*:

Our Father did not make all men equal in capacity and potential.

He made some men certain ways and other men other ways so they could have servants. A servant would be well-off in the master's house. He would have a family, a good wife, children, a wonderful time. The master would be kind to them and they would work. And if they wouldn't work, the master would beat them with a rod or a whip, and that was appropriate. It was appropriate that a master would discipline his servants if they didn't do right, even though they were grown people. Servants should be respectful , not only to those who are kind and considerate, but those who are surly, overbearing, unjust, and crooked.

Any mention of the way families were ripped apart and sold to different plantations, the stripping away of basic rights such as learning to read, and the many accounts of terrible abuse, hangings, and more was brushed aside as exaggeration and mistruth. I told my husband once that I would never be able to agree that it was God's will for any man to ever have been the property of another, no matter how well they were treated. He only had a vague response, about how some things were just too hard to understand now but someday would all make sense.

❧

The evils of homosexuality are an unwavering part of TT doctrine. They believe homosexuality is an abomination, and "sodomites'" are destined for the Lake of Fire. The only way a gay person could be a part of the TT would be to repent and renounce that evil spirit. Someone raised there who came out as gay would be sent away. They believe homosexuals should receive the death penalty and say anyone who has AIDS could never even be saved.

In one of their ITNs, the entry from France highlighted a gathering at which a homosexual was present. A brother who was sharing pointed to him and said, "It's really sad that he is going to go to the Lake of Fire!" He was praised for bringing this "polished arrow" of truth to the condemned man. It was seen as a lifeline of God's forgiveness that this man could now grab a hold of and be saved from his wickedness.

They say for a woman to have a homosexual relationship is the same as presenting herself to an animal.

There was a marriage teaching that stated, "If a wife desires her husband, their children will not grow up to be homosexual." Homosexuality is blamed on women and whether or not they desire sex with their husbands.

It was taught that overweight people would not be able to enter the Kingdom. It was a sign of having no self-control and giving in to your appetite. If you were overweight, you were supposed to learn to love the feeling of hunger, because that meant you were denying yourself and overcoming the urge to eat too much. If you were still hungry, you hadn't overeaten. Samuel spoke of the E.L.F. diet—eat less food.

We were supposed to go to overweight people out of "love" and let them know it was because of their appetite that they were overweight and exhort them to deny themselves and lose the weight.

The Holocaust is another area where the TT have controversial beliefs. This didn't come up often, but I remember Samuel giving a teaching once and saying that he wasn't condoning Hitler killing all those Jewish people, but at the time the Jews were being odious to the nations around them, and something needed to be done to put them in their place. Hearing this was eye-opening to me and caused me to seriously reevaluate what we were a part of.

CHAPTER 41

Come Let Us Gather

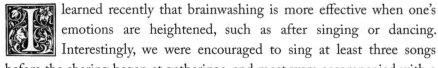 learned recently that brainwashing is more effective when one's emotions are heightened, such as after singing or dancing. Interestingly, we were encouraged to sing at least three songs before the sharing began at gatherings, and most were accompanied with a vigorous dance.

Additionally, our conversations at meals and during the day were to be centered around what was being talked about in the gatherings. Our Father would hardly be able to speak through us if we had been joking around and laughing all day. We were also to talk to our children about their purpose *"when they awoke and went to sleep and as we walked along the way,"* basically, all the time. This was always a challenge for me, as I just couldn't talk about and focus on spiritual matters all the time, but it still wasn't occurring to me to consider it brainwashing, indoctrination, or mind control.

Since we had two gatherings a day, morning and evening, that were at least a half hour long, it was understandably hard for little children to stand peacefully, hands folded, paying attention to adults rambling on. Sometimes, to have a little compassion and even show a little kindness and affection, we would hold their hands as they stood in front of us or rub their shoulders or heads a bit. Direction came to us one child training teaching that we were to stop touching the children in the gathering—it took away their dignity of being able to stand independently. Of course, instruction like this always came from an older couple who no longer had several children in the gathering, and I'm sure no three-year-old on earth is concerned over their dignity.

When babies were fussy, it was often convenient for the mother to sit off to the side and nurse them. We were discouraged from doing this, as it was training them to rely on a comfort to be peaceful, instead of developing internal control. I saw crying infants as young as four months being restrained outside the gathering room. Restraining meant holding the child on your lap, one arm holding down their arms and the other arm covering their mouths. We were to do this until the child "surrendered," that is, stopped crying and was quiet. Sometimes a child literally passed out, and we were told they needed to be awakened to continue the restraint session. If we didn't do this, when they woke up the rebellion would not be removed from their hearts. Surrender had to be willing and not from simply falling asleep.

One time, at a gathering where Meshiah was teaching, he noticed a ten-year-old girl quietly looking at the maps in her Bible. He abruptly stopped speaking and called on the girl, asking her what she was doing. In front of about fifty people, he admonished her for not paying attention. Her parents took her out and disciplined her, and then she had to repent to the entire gathering for being a "distraction." If this wasn't enough, since it was a teaching Meshiah was giving, there were scribes writing down what was spoken and shared. The example of this poor girl made its way into the monthly ITN, for the entire Twelve Tribes to read about. An example for the rest of our children to hear and fear.

When we first joined, only the men lifted their hands to pray at the end of the gathering. The reasoning was that women needed to attend the children. Around 2012, vision changed to everyone lifting their hands, including children ages three and up. The prayers lasted at least two full minutes, which doesn't sound too bad until you are trying to do this with a three-year-old. Never would a minute seem so long. Training little children to do this without being a distraction was especially tough and inevitably involved lots of spanking.

One couple had three-year-old twins and were suffering greatly dealing with this twice a day. Around this time, Parent Meetings were becoming a bimonthly occurrence. They were different from child training teachings, in that we wouldn't be "taught," but it would simply be a forum for parents to communicate about anything "on our hearts."

At first, this sounded great—an opportunity for complete openness and honesty about the issues affecting us as parents. We'd be free to express all our concerns. It soon became apparent that if we didn't express the "right" things, we were shut down.

The father of the twins expressed his frustration about hand raising. He said in the previous community he lived in, there had been more understanding for parents, and it wasn't so strictly enforced. At the next meeting he was admonished in front of everyone for bringing a "divisive" spirit to the meeting and told he simply needed to take on faith to train his children and not look for an easier way.

Another woman brought up how nervous she'd been when a certain high-ranking leader from Brazil had been sent to our community. He had passed along some new child training standards that were difficult to swallow. She confessed how fearful she'd been of his judgments about our families and how faithful our community was being in the realm of child training. She was rebuked for voicing disrespect and told she needed to be careful how she spoke of leaders. There was no such thing as freedom of speech.

❖

Every Tuesday morning was Complaint Morning. This was a chance to bring up any household concerns. It began with reading the list from the previous week to see if there was any increase in those areas. The most common complaints revolved around slamming doors, dishes, and bathrooms. Children were often blamed, although adults were just as guilty most of the time. The kitchen covering would often bring up ingredients being used "lawlessly." It could get quite tedious, after years of hearing the same things week after week. A friend who left said she felt such relief at not having to sit through Complaint Morning for the rest of her life!

Our life was a never-ending routine—gatherings, meals, preparation time, teachings, meetings, the weekend rotation. I remember one day realizing I might be doing the weekend rotation for the rest of my life, and it filled me with dread.

I recently talked to a friend who left before we did but had lived there longer than us. She spoke of how you "lose time" and how there are years she can barely recall because the way of life is a constant, endless routine, and the days turn to weeks, and the weeks to years before you know it. She described it as a wheel that just keeps turning. I found it a perfect description.

CHAPTER 42

Honor the Traditions

s the years went on, more revelation was divulged about the traditional Israeli festivals as spoken of in the Old Testament. Passover, Yom Kippur, Sukkot, Yom Teruah are a few examples of festivals we started to observe.

The one we looked forward to most was Sukkot. Otherwise known as the Feast of Booths, it represented several important events. It happens at the first full moon after Yom Kippur and signifies the end of the harvest season. It is also a time to remember the Israelites' forty years of wandering in the desert and living in temporary shelters.

The first day of this festival was called a "High Sabbath." This was a Sabbath day that was observed on a day other than the traditional Saturday. The entire community would go out and collect branches and leaves to construct our sukkah (temporary shelter). We had a designated Sukkot village on our property that centered around a large campfire. All our meals were taken outdoors during this often particularly chilly time of year. I remember one year coming out of my sukkah to find a dusting of snow on the ground!

The children absolutely loved this festival and looked forward to it all year. It was always a pleasant day gathering materials and fashioning the dwelling we would camp in for the next seven days. We would make it festive and cozy, using whatever colorful foliage was still available. People got creative—two-story structures, tree houses, A-frames, lean-tos, tepee-like structures, even, once, a cardboard box structure! We would put tarps over them to make them waterproof, and then hide the ugly tarp under layers of pine boughs or pretty, colorful sumac branches. We told stories around the campfire and had a snack every night.

One of the most loved traditions was making Australian damper (pronounced "dam-puh"). It was simply a sweet bread dough that we rolled between our fingers to make a long snake, and then wound around a stick that would be held over the campfire. It took some trial and error to cook the perfect damper so it wasn't burned on the outside but was raw on the inside. Once it was done, it would be removed from the stick, and the inside could then be filled with butter, brown sugar, and whipped cream. They were such rare and delectable treats.

Yom Kippur, the Day of Atonement, was a somber "festival" and took place before Sukkot. It was meant to be a time of "inflicting our souls" to search out our wrong and hurtful ways and cut them off. We believed if we could cut off our iniquities, they would not go into our children. Yom Kippur was ten days of this soul-searching. Every morning and evening there would be a teaching, followed by much tearful sharing, as everyone publicly exposed the things our Father revealed to them that hadn't borne fruit in their lives that year. There were many meetings for people during this time. Everyone was expected to have a heartfelt confession during the ten days.

The actual day of Yom Kippur was a day to pray and fast. No food was prepared, save a bowl of hard-boiled eggs in the refrigerator for those who could not fast for approved reasons, such as pregnant women or those with blood sugar issues. Even though the children would initially suffer about not eating all day, it always turned into a contest, and you would hear children encouraging each other throughout the day, feeling proud of themselves that they hadn't eaten yet. We would make them milky teas to help take the edge off.

Breaking of Bread that night was a joyous celebration—we were all "clean" and had a new start to overcome all the things that had been holding us back the previous year. Everyone would have fresh zeal and a positive attitude, especially during Sukkot, but as the weeks went by afterwards, everything (and everyone) would go back to normal.

❊

Passover, also called the Feast of Unleavened Bread, brought in the new year according to the Hebrew calendar. This was a time to judge the "leaven" in our lives—the things that separated us from one another. We not only had to judge this spiritual leaven, but we took it literally in the form of removing bread and any other food item or ingredient (baking powder and soda) that contained leaven. These items were boxed up and stored in chest freezers at the café building. We all had to purge any crackers or other such items from our bedrooms as well.

Then we set to cleaning—a thorough scrubbing of all the hidden places that accumulated filth over the past year. Refrigerators were pulled out, ovens pulled apart, cupboards emptied and scoured, radiators painstakingly dusted, curtains pulled down and washed, and windows meticulously scrubbed. We were encouraged to go to one another through the week and deal with any situations that had arisen over the past year that still felt unresolved or had been swept under the rug.

"What happens when trash gets swept under the rug?" we would be asked during the many teachings that week.

"It festers, rots, and starts to stink." The correlation was made with our relationships with each other when we let accusations or other difficulties build up during the year.

Passover celebrated the time when the death angel passed over Israel, killing any firstborn male (human or animal), but families who painted lamb's blood over the doors of their homes were spared. The death angel would "pass over" their home. The story told excruciating details of families huddled in their homes, clutching their firstborns, and hearing echoes of the screams of those whose sons were suddenly dead. The story was supposed to inspire gratitude in our children that they were born into the Body and protected from the evils of the world that lead to death.

The Breaking of Bread during Passover was unique, as all the children came into the room with their parents. For many, it was exciting. Others, like Emmet, wanted nothing to do with it. After experiencing it the first year we did it, he refused to enter the room the following year and helped out at a guest meal instead. He said the whole thing made him "uncomfortable." I, of course, could totally relate.

Shavuot, also called the Feast of Shouting, happens forty-nine days after Passover and celebrates the first fruits of the harvest. There is a parade to show off the beautiful produce. Communities will have a Rock of Proclamation and a festive day of games for the children. This was an actual rock or other raised platform for families to come up to one by one and give thanks for the increases they saw in their lives that year. Maybe a baby had been added to the family or a child had begun training or had a Bar or Bat Mitzvah. Any new disciples were recognized as "fruit" from that year. It was a much-looked-forward-to and pleasant day for our families.

CHAPTER 43

The Raid

t some point during the summer of 2012 or 2013, an anonymous person called social services and reported children being abused at the Common Sense Farm. A visit was scheduled for them to come and inspect our home, and all parents and children were to be present. It was a bit nerve-wracking, but we prepared for it like any other evangelistic opportunity—the house was immaculately cleaned, tea and cookies were prepared, a welcome banner was hung, and the children were prepared with an offering to sing. We littered the gathering room floor with dozens of puzzles, paper, crayons, and acceptable books. We made it clear to the children that they were to quietly "work" on the floor and be on their best behavior, while the parents sat in a circle around them, answering the questions of the social workers.

There were three women who came to investigate the alleged abuse. They began by asking basic questions about how we lived and taught our children. Then they got down to the nitty-gritty—how we disciplined them. They asked to see the object we spanked them with. Rivkah pulled out a short and flimsy rod and handed it over to the women. We watched as they passed the harmless-looking little stick among themselves, not seeming too alarmed by it. We never would have used such a lame rod for a spanking.

They began to ask questions along the lines of, "What age do you begin spanking?" "How many times a day are the children spanked?" and "On which parts of the body do you spank?"

The brave members who spoke gave vague answers that were enough to satisfy the women, such as, "We never spank until they are old enough to understand what they have done wrong." They left out that the teachings suggest starting at six months old to teach them not to wriggle during a diaper change.

Rivkah spoke up of course, and said the children only get light spankings, and sometimes her daughter would barely be paying attention, chatting or laughing during her spanking. She didn't mention the teaching that said, *"Spank your children hard enough so they will never want to do it again,"* or the one that says, *"Spanking too lightly strengthens their rebellion—it has to hurt enough to get the desired result."* We were completely downplaying and glossing over our teachings. Practically lying through our teeth. The older children knew it, of course, but knew better than to open their mouths.

Finally, after about an hour, we'd answered all their questions. The children were quickly assembled to sing, which had a positive effect on the women. Excitedly, a few children offered to take the social workers to see their classrooms and have a tour of the farm, with their parents, of course. Once they were out of the house, the rest of us breathed a collective sigh of relief. We didn't want to be found guilty of child abuse, and the only way that was possible was to be a bit dishonest.

The unimaginable did happen in September 2013. In the wee hours of the morning, authorities descended upon the community in Germany and took all children into custody following allegations of abuse. An undercover reporter, posing as a guest, set up hidden cameras in the basement and got hours of footage of children being brought down and disciplined.

This began a nightmare for the families over there, and fear set in at all TT households around the world. What if that happened to us? Would we leave if we lost our children? We were even told it was a precursor to the same thing happening in other places and that we all needed to have our faith tested. I, for one, knew that if there was even a threat of someone coming and taking my children, I'd be packing my bags.

We prayed morning and evening for the return of the children to their families. Some families left in an attempt to retrieve their children. Some of the older children escaped the foster care they were put into and miraculously made their way back to their parents, with the youngest, and scariest situation, being an eleven-year-old girl who fled alone at night. Of course the children wanted to go home—parents in the TT do love their children.

There had been one other raid, in Island Pond, Vermont, back in 1984 after allegations of child abuse reached local law enforcement. Authorities arrived at the property early in the morning and all children were taken into custody, but a few hours later a judge ruled it unconstitutional, and the children were returned home by the end of the day. The TT always saw this day as a great day of deliverance from Our Father, proof that they are His people.

It is now ten years since the raid in Germany, and many parents who have stood firm in their belief in the TT still haven't had their children returned. Most have had to flee to other countries, especially the ones who have had more children. It is a heartbreaking situation from every angle.

CHAPTER 44

Getting Real

nce you have joined the community and made a covenant through baptism, you are called a "fall away" if you ever leave. If asked at an open forum or a guest meal, TT members will nonchalantly say that no one is forced to stay, the doors are always open, and anyone can leave whenever they want. In theory this is true, but I know firsthand that it is not as easy as it sounds. There is a reason many flee in the middle of the night. If a family began packing their bags in broad daylight, they would have to deal with multiple people pleading with them not to go. They would be implored to wait until they could have a meeting with so-and-so or be offered a trip to spend time with anyone who might help them see straight. Given time, most people can be talked down from leaving.

Leaving is downright terrifying. You are scared you will be in a car wreck and your whole family killed as a result of your "rebellion." Or worse, you would be the sole survivor and have to live with the knowledge that it was all your fault. Members have been taught for months, years, or sometimes their whole lives that they are only in God's protection in the community, and the world is the Evil One's domain. Traitors become part of the category of the "cowardly and unbelieving," and the Lake of Fire awaits anyone who becomes a "Judas." This weighs heavily on many people, keeping them from daring to consider leaving.

We were told the relief people feel upon leaving is a result of them no longer being a threat to the Evil One; they are no longer opposed by him like true disciples are. Once you leave, you are treated like a leper of old: contagious and deadly. Someone described it as being treated as "subhuman." It's discouraged to interact with fall aways, as they could affect you with their deceptive spirit. It's a disconcerting place to be in. If you have family there, they will be warned about their interactions with you or even prohibited from visits.

Living inside the bubble of the community and having limited interactions with the outside world, it's easy to become convinced of the absolute degradation and evil of society. Public school, higher education, working a nine to five are all touted as heinous institutions. We were only told of certain current events, those that upheld these beliefs about the utter chaos and hopelessness outside the TT. Our children were raised with images of terror about going to school, and we were constantly giving thanks to have been saved from the pointlessness of living for ourselves and the surefire mess our lives would be if not for the Body. Years and years of this can and does put people in a state of fear about even toying with the idea of leaving. It took many years for my husband to come to a place of facing that possibility.

A year and a half before we left, there was a brief period when André's guard came down and we talked about leaving. One day, having been left with his laptop, I looked up the word "cult" online. I came across a list of red flags to look for in deciding if a group was a cult or not. I could have said yes for nearly everything on the list.

We often talked about the word "cult" because of the assumptions outsiders had of us. It was a common question. "Are you guys a cult?" We would answer along the lines of, "The word 'cult' gets its roots from the word '**cult**ure,' which simply means a distinct lifestyle and set of beliefs." Technically we could be called a cult, but felt it didn't necessarily denote something sinister, as society believes.

I started seriously pondering these things, especially as my choice of reading had recently been stories of people escaping from the FLDS group (Fundamentalist Church of Latter Day Saints). Some of the parallels between that group and ours were impossible to ignore.

One night my husband opened up to me in a way he never had, expressing dissatisfaction about various situations going on in Cambridge. I told him about the things I'd looked up and how alarmed I was by what I'd read. We ended up discussing what our options would be if we left, even talking about homeschooling the children, which André was adamant about at the time. I remember feeling hope and excitement I'd never felt before.

But we got up the next day and went on with life as normal, as though the conversation never happened.

⁕⁕⁕

Around 2012, our family was living at the Caretaker's House along with my in-laws. One day, Annie and I went for a walk and had a long talk. I missed the relationship I used to have with her before joining the community. I began pouring out the struggles I was having, including problems with André, which she could understand and provided insight, since she raised him! She also suffered with what had become of her relationship with André since joining. Similarly, they had always been open and close, but now he functioned more like her elder than her son. When she would go to him suffering, his responses were harsh and judging—less compassionate—as I experienced as well.

It was nice to have someone who understood this plight, since to everyone else in the community, "Yeshurun" was an amazing and wonderful disciple, and I was beyond lucky to be married to him. I was tired of the shocked, disbelieving responses I got from other women when I would open up to them about a struggle with André. It was as though I was complaining about Yahshua Himself. I missed who my husband had been before the community. I realized I made a distinction between Yeshurun and André, like they were two different people.

I finally talked to Edah about this because it was causing me such inner turmoil. After I told her I felt that I liked André better, she looked at me in astonishment and said, "But André didn't have the Holy Spirit!" As though that was going to cause me to come to my senses! It actually depressed me more.

After a period of spending more time with Annie, a concern was raised about the "overfamiliar" relationship we were having, especially when it came to issues in my marriage. In an unguarded moment, Annie probably mentioned something I had told her to one of the other women she was close with. You learn after a while that no conversation is ever really private. Since parents were not to be involved at all in their children's marriages, Atarah came to talk to me and told me I should be seeking counsel from women besides my mother-in-law. Feeling deflated, I received the counsel and withdrew again from Annie.

A few months later, I was still struggling, feeling depressed, and "lacking zeal." I was tempted to seek out Annie and get some things off my chest. But I was obedient and sought out another woman, K'shevah. We'd lived together in Rutland, and I always really liked her.

We sat out on the front porch and talked for a long time, and I felt much better after. I even confided to her that I'd been tempted to pursue Annie, but I was glad I resisted and talked to her instead. She said she felt honored I had sought her out, and we ended the conversation on a positive note.

Unbeknownst to me, she was actually alarmed by what I'd confided in her and told Atarah about our conversation. Next thing I knew, I was being called to a meeting with the two of them, Rivkah, and another leader's wife. It was intense, as I was grilled on the seriousness of saying I was lacking zeal, especially because of how my husband functioned and because we now had two youths I needed to pour faith into, as they were coming of age for bar and bat mitzvah. Prior household situations were brought up, questioning whether I'd received certain direction or was disrespectful to specific people. My weaknesses as a mother were laid out in detail for each of my four children. I was blindsided. Was someone keeping a log of all my faults and inadequacies, just waiting for the perfect opportunity to inundate me with them?

I just sat there, staring at my shoe, and to this day can remember the exact pattern of the tread on said footwear. I don't think I said a word the entire time and left that meeting feeling completely betrayed and discouraged. I would never seek out K'shevah again.

The next day Rivkah came knocking on my door to see how I was doing. She said she'd felt bad for me during the meeting and was surprised how I'd held it all together against the torrent of corrections I'd been assaulted by. I felt a rare surge of affection for her. I honestly told her I felt much of what was said about me was unfair, as I had asked for help during some of those situations and no one had stepped up to the plate at the time. She listened, and after she left, I noticed her and Atarah talking outside. "Great," I thought, "I'm going to get in more trouble now for not being completely 'humble.'" To my surprise, I never heard any more about that meeting from anyone.

❦

One day in the spring of 2014, André and I got called into a meeting with Malak and Rivkah. They were very somber, and I had that sick feeling in the pit of my stomach, wondering, "What now?"

After the initial couple minutes of small talk, Rivkah took a deep breath and said, "We wanted to get together with you all because we found out something we think you need to be aware of."

My heart was racing, and I started to sweat a little. What could it be? Had Emmet been stealing the wine for Breaking of Bread or been caught in some deviant sexual behavior? They both looked so serious. Rivkah leaned forward, and in a hushed voice said, "We found out that Emmet has been listening to country music." Relief washed over us, and we exchanged a glance.

"We know, he told us already," I informed them. They were surprised and wanted confirmation that we were taking this "defiling, worldly behavior" seriously and were going to nip it in the bud.

"Yes, we are dealing with him," André stated confidently. I inwardly rolled my eyes, as I knew he was doing no such thing. Since our "washing," I had noticed the same things gradually creeping back in, but I'd learned my lesson and I kept my mouth shut.

Just a few weeks prior to this meeting, a three-year-old in my toddler training group had been singing "Cruise" by FGL. He didn't know how to pronounce a single word and just belted out gibberish perfectly to the melody with an unmistakable and well-timed "FOOOOOOZE." I asked how he knew that song, and he said proudly, "My brudah!" His older brother was the same age as Emmet. I knew my family was in good company.

❦

Sometime that spring, two barn cats showed up in the garage of the Caretaker's House. Since we were battling a mouse problem, I got covered to set food out for them in hopes their presence would deter the rodents. I ended up getting attached to them, as did my children. If I was stressed, I'd go out to the garage and within minutes the cats would arrive, rubbing and purring around my legs. It was the most therapeutic thing I'd experienced in years. Having "pets" is not allowed of course, and cats are only tolerated as mousers on farms.

One morning at the child training teaching, a single brother spoke up about how he noticed "overfamiliarity" with some of the cats and had even seen them being picked up. I knew he was talking about my family. When he said this, I heard Rivkah gasp, "Disgusting!" as though he had said he saw someone handling roadkill. I tried from then on to be more covert when interacting with the cats.

Around this time, K'shevah found me a little cloth bag for a dollar at a thrift store. The pattern on the bag was differently colored cats, not cartoonish but realistic. I loved the bag because it was the perfect size for my Bible and children's notebooks.

The first time I used it, Rivkah approached me in the entryway after the gathering and said in a sad voice, "We'll have to find you a new bag."

Puzzled, I asked, "Why? This is a new bag K'shevah just found for me."

She leaned in close like she was divulging a great secret. "But it has cats on it," she said softly.

"So? They aren't foolish cats," I said. Sighing, like she was annoyed at having to state the obvious, she told me that it could promote having pets. I asked her what the difference was between that bag and the notebooks the training groups just got that had horses on the front.

"Horses are farm animals," was her explanation.

"So are cats," I bravely and uncharacteristically retorted back.

At that point she sternly admonished me for not "receiving" her. Saying nothing, I opened the bag, dumped all its contents on a nearby table, and took it straight to K'shevah, who I saw was still in the gathering room. I handed it over and thanked her for getting it for me, but I had just been told it was inappropriate. She quickly apologized for her lack of judgment, and I told her I didn't see anything wrong with the bag and was not happy with the situation. I thought for sure I'd be asked to a meeting for my public display of disrespect to Rivkah, but I never heard anything more about it. And I never got a new bag either.

I was becoming more disillusioned as the weeks went on. One evening, I was in Rite Aid buying some cough drops when I saw Hershey's Kisses on sale and spontaneously grabbed a bag. In college I used to bring them to exams, and when I'd start to panic on a question I was unsure of, I'd open one up and slowly dissolve it in my mouth while breathing deeply to calm down and think clearly. I couldn't recall the last time I'd eaten them.

On my way to the checkout counter, I could see part of the parking lot and suddenly had a fear of someone from the community walking in and catching me red-handed. I quickly ducked into an aisle, my heart leaping out of my chest. I cautiously peered around the corner to get a better view of the parking lot and make sure there were no community cars. Then I caught myself. I was thirty-seven years old, clutching a bag of Hershey's Kisses to my chest and hiding in an aisle of Rite Aid like a criminal. The utter ridiculousness of the situation hit me hard. I did not want to live my life like this anymore, I wasn't doing anything wrong, I wasn't going against my conscience in any way. I finally realized I had been brainwashed.

By this time, Facebook had been around for about five years. Since I hadn't been obedient to the rule that disciples don't use Facebook, I still had my account and began checking it more often on André's cell phone.

One day, I noticed a young man who had left the community in the "People you may know" section. I clicked on him out of curiosity and began looking through his friends. I was aghast at the number of former community members, most of whom had grown up there and many we lived with in our early years. I didn't even know most of them had left—it's not like those things are announced in the monthly ITN. I wrote a list of the families we had lived with over the years and estimated about two thirds of the children were now gone. It was eye-opening. I realized how likely it was that soon our family could be divided. If Emmet continued his worldly music and literature pursuits and didn't become a bar mitzvah soon, André would be sent away with him, and I'd be a single mother of three children. I knew I wouldn't last a day in that situation.

Around this time, I wrote my husband a letter. This is the original email I sent him:

> *I just want to be me again. I have lived almost 14 years trying to be a "disciple" here. You know the mental turmoil I have gone through, and sometimes I have felt supported by you and those have been the times I have felt closest to you. The times you*

were not giving me the right "community response." Talk about dementia—living a double life is Hell for me but somehow you bear it beautifully. You know I've said things like I can't be "me" here, because who I really am does not fit here. I have never been fully convicted of all our doctrines, traditions etc. and you know that. I have always been way more honest with you than I feel you have been with me. I think it's because I haven't had another "life," so to speak, to busy and distract myself with. Were it not for the children, I would never have endured here. I love them and don't regret being here if only for the reason we might not have them all had we never come here.

I told you a few weeks ago I feel the children don't even know who I really am. I have been oppressed here. I cry over feeling I missed out on so much when Emmet and Meyshar were little. I hardly have a really happy memory of those years. Do you? Honestly? I have no way to pass on faith about this life to my children because I don't have it anymore. And I have tried so hard and prayed in the right ways. There was such a big part of me last night that just wanted to say "what the Hell!" and watch that movie with Emmet. I have never had the kind of good time with him where we just laughed and enjoyed each other in a relaxed way. Except the other night when I laughed so hard I was crying about the way Emmet mockingly talked about going to the minchah. I couldn't help myself but I couldn't bring myself to rebuke him for disrespecting the gatherings.

I can't keep the focus of my day and my conversations with the children on Yahshua and our purpose and hearing it all the time is becoming sickening to me. We are part of something strange, and it's becoming stranger. Please don't play dumb. You have a way to act nonchalant over things that drive me nuts, such as shirt sleeve standards and hair parting and printed fabrics. I am scared to bring the children to the world, but I'm also scared I am going to go crazy if I continue on with life here. I can't do this anymore. Maybe you're thinking it's because I just read that book on the FLDS. Not true. I've said all these things to you before. We were both close to leaving over a year ago. The book was definitely interesting to read though from the angle of being in a different group. They are all complete wackos for sure. But one thing the woman said was very interesting. You know how I've made reference to "André" vs. "Yeshurun" and how it's almost like 2 people to me. And also how I have always been so happy no one ever changed my name. She made a statement to the effect that when you are in a cult there is your cult identity and your authentic identity. I have no qualms with that, it's true.

I want to not feel guilt about eating chocolate and drinking coffee. I am tired of hiding "normal" behaviors. I want to listen to music I like, take the children to a beach for the weekend, take a yoga class, get horseback riding lessons for Meyshar, make sure Emmet is being educated properly (which we both know he is not and we have to basically lie now to fill out those reports.) Your mom keeps telling me how we just have to fall in love again and to think back to what we first loved about each other. Well I first loved André. I am not going to fall in love with Yeshurun. Yeshurun has lied to me and been a hypocrite many times over the past several years. Again, please don't play dumb, you know exactly what I am talking about. It's one of your ways of manipulating a conversation to act confused and ask me questions that steer the conversation another way. Your other ways of doing this are to say "That's not the point" or "You are not listening to me." You tend to do this when I do have a point but you don't want to hear it.

Can we just be real to each other? Can you come out from under any community thinking and just be totally real? Can you validate me at all and not just get gruff and jabbing in your responses to me? Can you really find fault in how I have handled myself over the past 14 years, despite never really "getting it"? Remember when you said to me a few weeks ago you sometimes think you are too normal to be here? When you said that the word that came to my head was "FINALLY!!!!"

We do not do what we say we do, so we really are not who we say we are anyway. There are elitists and untouchable people here. I am sick of the theatrics. I want to enjoy our children, and our life and, yes, US!!! When I really think about it, there is little I would really miss here. But the thought of getting together with my friends in the world and doing something fun with them actually brings me close to tears. That is another big difference to us. You haven't suffered over family and friends in the world the way I have. So I just want to let you know I'd like to spend the night at my mom's house on Sunday night. I was almost afraid to mention it to you and then I thought "That is STUPID!! I am wanting to go to my own mother's house and I feel like I am wanting to do something really wrong!" She has done a lot of work on the house, especially with guest rooms now that it's just her and Gilles. She's been wanting me to come for so long and it's only 1 and a half hours from Island Pond. So I thought I'd follow them there and come home Monday late morning. Don't worry, I will come back. I don't feel I have to make some desperate escape. I want time for us to communicate as friends.

After I sent my husband this email, he worked it out for me to take my grandmother and all the children except Emmet to Island Pond to meet up with relatives, then go spend the night at my mother's house. We spent a pleasant day at the Island Pond community with a couple of my aunts and my mother and stepfather. We got to my mother's house in Highgate, Vermont, late in the afternoon, and I made a beeline to her phone to call Michelle. I told her I was at my mother's and wondered if she wanted to get together. "I'll be right there," was her response, and less than a half hour later she was pulling in the driveway.

By that time my children were taking full advantage of my mother's in-ground pool. Michelle and I sat at the picnic table and talked well into the evening. I forsook any taboo I'd ever had about honestly talking with someone from the "world" about my sufferings. I poured it all out to her, everything I was going through, how unhappy I was. She was so sympathetic and compassionate. There was no judgment or correcting me for complaining, or not being content, or resisting my salvation. It was just one hundred percent support and consolation. It was so refreshing and relieving. I felt a huge weight had been lifted. She finally had to go home, and we headed in.

My children had long since gone inside, and were all snuggled around my mom on the couch watching a nature show. I took in the scene, realizing I was seeing something for the first time that I should have seen hundreds of times by now.

One of the topics I had brought up with Michelle was the strict "no talking" rule for youth and children. An adult had to be present to "cover" all interactions.

"If two youths are left unsupervised, is it likely they will be discussing the proverbs?" Malak had asked us when this standard went into effect. It added another level of unnecessary difficulty to an already hectic household of several families.

I told Michelle about an incident when Emmet, then fifteen, got in trouble for being out on a porch playing instruments with another boy his age without an adult present. I was rebuking him and he asked me, "Didn't you have friends when you were fifteen?"

That question stopped me in my tracks. Of course I did, and I wanted him to have friends too.

I dutifully went back to Cambridge the next day. That evening after dinner, my younger children were tired, so I asked Meyshar to wash the dishes and come right over. André had long since disappeared back up to the soap shop. I went back to the Caretaker's House and began hanging some laundry outside. My daughter showed up a few minutes later, and nothing seemed amiss.

Moments later I saw Annah, a younger married woman with no children, walking over from the Main House. She approached me and said, "I just wanted to let you know Meyshar was having a conversation with Reah at the dish sink." (Ruth was fourteen years old.).

"Oh no!" I exclaimed with exaggerated, mock concern. "Were they mocking single brothers?"

"Um," she faltered, "I didn't actually hear what they were saying."

I said thank you and quickly walked away before my annoyance was too apparent. I found Meyshar and asked what she and Reah were talking about. "She asked me if we had a nice time in Island Pond and who we saw, and I told her," replied Meyshar warily. I inwardly rolled my eyes. This should have been an acceptable interaction between two older girls, but it was a zero-tolerance rule, so any uncovered conversations were to be reported. It made going over to meals and gatherings torture . . . twenty-plus children all together and they weren't allowed to talk to each other! I told her that was fine and went back to my laundry.

After we left the community, Emmet told me that because of the no talking rule, the youth had devised an entire system of places they could leave notes for each other around the enormous house, along with a code language to let each other know which location to find their next note. Where there's a will, there's a way, and the strictness only forced the youth into an "underground" to be able to communicate.

One evening a week or so later, I was spending time with some of the volunteers that we often had on our farm through the WWOOF'er program (Worldwide Opportunities on Organic Farms). They were usually from abroad, and it was amazing to get to know and work alongside people from all over the world. They would often be with us for weeks at a time, so we'd get to know them well. This time, there were several volunteers from France. I'd taken quite a bit of French in high school and college and had been trying to brush up my skills. They were also trying to improve their English, so we'd planned an evening language class, and André surprisingly offered to keep the children. It was just me and the four French folk, and I remember laughing and having a great time.

I was in good spirits upon returning to the Caretaker's House, and found the children huddled on my bed, engrossed in a David Attenborough nature show on the laptop. André was quick to pull me into the boys' bedroom to talk. He told me he had just gotten off the phone with his brother, Chris, and had asked him if any work was available at his company.

It took me a moment to realize the implication of what he was saying. I was speechless. Yes, I'd written him that letter, and I'd been emailing Michelle almost daily since our visit, but I was not expecting this! Come to find out, he'd been reading my correspondences with Michelle—perfectly within his rights as a community husband—and had been affected by something she'd written to me.

That Sabbath I sat outdoors with Annie and told her where we were at and about André's conversation with Chris. I figured it was only a matter of time before everyone knew anyway. Sure enough, during the Resurrection Celebration that evening, I noticed a woman crying out on the porch. Apparently, Annie had gone and talked to her about us, and she was distraught at the idea we were considering leaving. We didn't go to Breaking of Bread that night, with no apparent excuse such as illness, which immediately set off more warning bells. We had people showing up at our room immediately afterwards, full of concerns.

The next day all the training groups did presentations for the household on projects they'd been working on. I had serious doubts as I looked at the beautiful artwork and writing my children were proudly displaying and saw the genuine care of the teachers, most of whom truly did love my children. Did I really want to snatch them out of the only life they had ever known?

The meetings and conversations with us began in earnest over the next few days. When it became apparent that we were seriously on the verge of leaving, the community sprang into action with the typical solution of sending us somewhere far away. It was a Tuesday afternoon when I was asked to step outside with Malak and Rivkah. They told me our family was being sent to Arcadia, Florida, for three weeks and we could leave Thursday. The guise was that André needed to help with some work down there. I was asked to pack up as much of our rooms as was feasible in case they were needed for guests while we were gone. Oh, and could I still make supper that night? That would give me one full day to prepare my family of six for a three-week, three-thousand-mile journey, the likes of which we had never experienced.

CHAPTER 45

How to Leave a Cult

s was the desired result, the adventure was irresistible, and I happily made my "last supper," which was pizza. That consisted of five full sheet pans for our household, plus a six-gallon bowl of salad. That took up the rest of the day. That night I went into full-on planning mode. I was giddy with excitement. I phoned my mother to see if she wanted to help us do some fun things on the way down. There wasn't time for her to mail us a check, but she said if my grandmother could front us six hundred dollars, she would reimburse her. We booked three nights at a campground near Assateague Island, Maryland, which would be our first stop.

Wednesday was a blur of laundry, packing, and visits from people trying to pass on last-minute encouragement and faith. That night, we went to Stewarts with one of our favorite families for ice cream. I was feeling more alive than I had in a while, and it was so refreshing to see the excitement in my children.

We were ready to pull out bright and early the next morning, well before the morning gathering. Rivkah had made us egg sandwiches and maté to go. We were waved off by Annie, a couple other families, and my grandmother. As we drove down the long driveway, and turned onto North Union Street, I purposely did not look back, and I breathed a huge sigh of relief as we left the Common Sense Farm.

The nine-hour drive was long, but we had brought a laptop and allowed our children to watch *Mutual of Omaha's Wild Kingdom* and *Planet Earth* videos to pass the time. We stopped at a Target in Delaware and purchased an eight-person tent and new sleeping bags. We arrived at our campground at dusk, set up camp, started a fire, and relaxed.

We spent the next three days on the beach and seeking out the wild horses on Assateague. Our children had so much fun, and since there wasn't a chance of running into someone from the TT, we let the girls wear normal swimsuits for the first time in their lives. One evening, I called my mom on André's cell phone and walked around the campground wearing just yoga pants and a T-shirt. I felt like a normal person for the first time in so long.

We took our time making our way south, stopping at several communities on the way. The first was Hillsboro, Virginia, and then we had a pleasant visit in Asheville, North Carolina, spending time with one of the families we had lived with in Rutland. Our children played frisbee together until it got dark while Nahara and I sat and talked out on the porch of the yurt we were staying in. Word had definitely been passed along that our family was struggling, so people wanted to help us.

From there we spent a night at a campground in Rockwell, North Carolina, and took the children to their first zoo. We were able to make a quick stop for a meal at the Yellow Deli in Chattanooga, and then went to the community in Savannah, where we spent a whole day being shown around the quaint city. Then, we were Florida-bound.

We arrived in Arcadia late at night on the day of our fifteenth wedding anniversary. We were greeted warmly and shown to our two cabins on the small property. Exhausted, we all went right to sleep.

Arek was up bright and early the next morning, eager to check out our new environment. He was fascinated by all the lizards running around and was on an endless hunt for them, especially the geckos that changed color in your hands.

There were no bathrooms in our cabin, but we had an outdoor sink and shower. I grew quite fond of looking up at palm trees while taking a shower.

Even more foreign to us than the tropical environment was the size of the community—only five other people lived there. There were two older couples and one fourteen-year-old girl who had suffered hydrocephalus as a baby. She was the size of a six-year-old and whizzed around the house on a custom-made scooter. She was a delight, always happy and so excited to have other children around.

The man we were sent to help, Elazar, ran this community. He was around sixty and the only source of financial support for this tiny household. He repaired people's in-ground pools and up until now had been doing this solo in the sweltering heat. They were extremely poor, and their property was much in need of repairs. The first project André tackled on day one was fixing their well, which had been acting up.

We had been eating well in Cambridge by this point, but now, lunches were mainly cucumber and mayonnaise sandwiches. Elazar would get free produce that was mostly rotted, and we would salvage what we could. Sabbath lunch, usually the nicest lunch of the week, was a big bowl of popcorn. We were in heaven after we were able to go mango picking at the community in Fort Myers, and we ate several a day. But my children were hungry, especially my teenagers. André still had a credit card from Cambridge, and we offered to supplement their meals, for which they were grateful. I also bought tuna, deli meats, yogurts, crackers, and peanut butter for snacks for the children.

Even though it was the end of June in Florida, there was no AC in the downstairs of the Main House, including the kitchen. Our cabins had AC, as did the other couples' bedrooms. Despite this, we still made dinners that had to be baked in the oven, so the kitchen would be well over one hundred degrees, as the daily outdoor temps soared into the high nineties. We ran several ceiling and box fans to keep the air moving and kept spray bottles of water in the fridge to constantly spray ourselves down. The standards for modesty remained, so we wore our modest "swimsuits" all the time, which made it easy for quick, cold outdoor showers or frequent dips in the above-ground pool, which the children were thrilled about. We learned how to survive the heat.

We quickly settled into a routine. The girls and I had fun painting and redecorating the cabins, using money I had left from my mom to go to Goodwill and Habitat for Humanity. Savav, Zedek's wife, gave me sewing projects, and my children and I made new table centerpieces with seashells and sand we found at the beach. We were even sent to a spectacular Fourth of July fireworks display.

It was a whole different life, and I was enjoying myself, free from the constant pressure of a large community and the endless scrutiny. Every Saturday we went as a family to a different beach. We got to explore Sanibel, Siesta Key, Lover's Key, and Turtle Beach, an awesome black sand beach with amazing shells. One Sunday Elazar took us on a cool excursion into the Floridian wilderness. Our children all loaded into a Kubota with him to help harvest medicinal plants, called beautyberry.

In the evenings, when it cooled down to ninety-three or so, we took walks with Savav. One evening I looked down at the sidewalk and saw a penny. A lost coin! We thought it meaningful when we found a lost coin on the ground—someone would be "saved" soon. I picked it up, and only a few minutes later we ended up meeting a nice young woman. Of course, we extended her an invitation to come to our house, and to our surprise she showed up at our door the next afternoon. What a sign!

We invited her in for tea and started to get to know her. At one point, she told us she could see people's auras. She saw colors around people and began telling us all what color our auras were and what they meant. We were fascinated. Well, all except Savav. When it came time for the woman to leave, Savav had pulled her to the side and explained that while we were enjoying her company, if she wanted to come back, she needed to desire to hear about our life and that we weren't really into the "aura" thing. Sadly, we didn't see her again.

Arek and Darakah started training with Savav, and the other woman who lived there helped Arek with math. At first, he did not want to do it, but she capitalized on his love of lizards and brilliantly came up with "Lizard Math," which was a complete success. It seemed as though we could stay there forever.

But "salvation" found us. First, I got corrected when Savav saw a Nancy Drew book in my children's room. It was *The Hidden Staircase*, and it had been discarded in a free pile down the road. We always looked at free piles, and I let Meyshar grab it. Then, I got careless and let Darakah go into the pool in her "worldly" swimsuit and was rebuked for that. Then, who arrived for a meeting with us, but Samuel and Atarah, who, interestingly, had moved to Fort Myers for a time.

Samuel corrected us for buying little yogurts because they had sugar in them. He told us we were pandering to our children, and he relayed a story. A certain community had volunteered for a green-up day in their town. At the end of the day there was free ice cream in the park, and of course, the children couldn't wait. They worked hard all day in the hot sun, longer than many other volunteers. When they finished and went to get their well-deserved treat, only chocolate was left. Some families gave in and let their children have chocolate ice cream. But one family stood their ground and did not allow it for their children. They were praised for their obedience and the other families admonished for giving in to the flesh. This was supposed to enlighten us and strengthen our resolve to maintain the food standards with our children.

The straw that broke the camel's back for my husband was a week later, when Samuel and Atarah came for yet another meeting. Neither of us were up to another rebuking session; we'd had enough. We skipped the meeting, hiding in our cabins and feigning illness. We were over the endless correction and scrutiny and decided to leave. I used Zillow for the first time that night, looking at homes and dreaming of what it would be like to have our own again.

The next day we took our children to an enormous playground, and I called my mom. I was emotional as I told her we were planning to leave the community and asked if we could come up and stay with her until we figured out how to proceed. Of course, she said yes.

We played it cool the next day, not wanting to draw attention to the fact that we were planning to leave. That only made it harder, as we knew people would desperately try to get us to change our minds. I even made dinner that night. It all felt rather surreal—I knew my family was discreetly packing up our belongings as I put together a pan of eggplant parmesan.

After dinner was cleaned up, we went back to our cabins and spent the evening packing. I couldn't believe we were actually leaving. I wrote a letter thanking the household for their care of our family the past several weeks. Before I climbed into bed, I took one last look at my sleeping younger children and wondered if this was their last night of "innocence." We all got up at 4:00 a.m., quietly loaded up our van, and pulled out of the property just as it was getting light out. We had officially left the TT.

CHAPTER 46

Back to the World

he drive up north was harrowing, to say the least. We made emotional phone calls to André's parents and my grandmother. Multiple times I glanced over at André and saw he was crying. I was terrified we were all going to die any moment in a horrible car crash. As we neared North Carolina, I prayed to God that if we were making the wrong choice, would he please let us get a flat tire. I promised I would beg André to go back to Asheville and we would seek help from the community there. But our van cruised through the whole state and brought us safely to Vermont with not so much as a headlight out.

Our first few weeks out of the Twelve Tribes were fraught with uncertainty, fear, confusion, and doubt. These feelings were interspersed with fleeting moments of relief. I understood how people ping-pong in and out of the community—by the third week, with most of our days spent driving around looking for a place to live, our children engrossed in videos on the laptop, I actually found myself longing for Cambridge. The familiarity of routine was appealing in the face of this precarious transition. I'd wake up in the morning so glad to not have to drag my children to the minchah, but by evening I'd be in tears, wishing Emmet was mowing lawns and Meyshar was milking goats.

But we persevered, and nearly six months to the day that we drove away from Arcadia, we were moving into our own house. The help we received from family and friends to start from scratch with four children was amazing.

My experience speaks of the tremendous adaptability of humans and how even the most bizarre behaviors can become a normal part of everyday life. I never considered what my children would go through if we ever left, what adjusting to life on the outside would entail for them until we were in the moment. I still don't think we realize all the effects the TT had, and in many ways, still has on us. It takes a long time once you are out to realize and remember that there are many good people and not everything is dark and malevolent.

Regaining self-confidence is even longer in coming. I felt completely helpless to raise my children. I had no idea how to parent them by my own will. I had no confidence in myself as a mother. I told a friend I felt like a new parent.

My older children have had a hard time learning to be assertive and advocating for themselves. They were raised to be submissive and not question authority, with independent behavior being branded "rebellion." They were told their only future would be working at McDonalds if they ever left. Higher education and personal ambition were self-centered, evil pursuits—we were told "knowledge puffs you up." Essentially, it makes you arrogant and proud. But what really puffs up is power. I've never met any college-educated person who is more pompous and egotistical than some of the TT leaders.

When we first left, I wanted my children to experience using their imaginations and playing outside as I had as a child. I'd send them out, but they'd be back within a couple minutes, asking what they were supposed to do and wanting me out there with them. They were six and nine and had no clue how to entertain themselves and make their own fun. Other people who left with children have experienced this as well.

My children have all struggled with forming close friendships out here. I think it's because of how censored and controlled all their interactions were with other children. They were never given the opportunity to have a "best friend," never given an unsupervised moment to spend with peers. They didn't learn certain social etiquette that comes naturally when you go through the typical scenarios of engaging socially with others your age. They were constantly corrected for being "overfamiliar" if it seemed they were too close with a peer. It made them appear more mature, which is not always a bad thing, but really hindered them in forming friendships once we left. They can relate to adults incredibly well, which is great—Emmet has coffee sometimes with a friend who is a woman in her sixties!

We visited Cambridge from time to time to see my grandmother until she passed away in October 2019. We were always welcome to come and visit her.

It was so strange, going back into the houses I lived in for years and seeing how little has changed. Same tables and chairs in the dining room, same pictures on the walls, same marks on the floors I mopped hundreds of times. Same people living there. It felt surreal, like I had reentered that parallel universe. But my car was in the driveway, and I could go home. Nothing made me want to go back, although I missed my grandmother greatly. She lived a good life in the TT, even being sent to Florida for the winter the last several years of her life. She was respected and well cared for, and I don't think she ever regretted her decision.

My husband was under the impression that we would leave the TT and pick up right where we left off as far as our relationship was concerned. That was not to be the case, and years later we are still peeling through the complicated layers of indoctrination that resulted in hurt and distrust. We didn't know how drastically our relationship would have to change to fit into the narrow spectrum of a "Godly marriage." I didn't know my relationship with him was going to suffer instead of being strengthened. I had no idea of the humiliation and degradation I would experience at his hands. I didn't need my husband to "rule over me," I needed the dignity of an equal partnership. I didn't know how his deep, childhood fear of eternity and Hell would resurface and override even his inner turmoil about what was happening to our relationship. The grip of mind control is firm and relentless, consuming every waking moment, and all the while you are being convinced you have been set free from your former life of "slavery to self." The cognitive dissonance is real.

Since the TT is a collectivist culture, there is no emphasis on individuality or uniqueness. We had to adopt a "hive mind." I didn't realize how much of my personal identity I would lose, to the point that when I'd think of myself before we joined it was like remembering someone else entirely, and friends who knew me my entire life told me how different I'd become. Michelle told me I was "robotic in my emotions" and only now and then would she get glimpses of the old me. I didn't know I was going to be in danger of losing my ability to think critically without feeling guilty. I didn't know I wasn't going to enjoy my children's younger years. I didn't know how much I would miss simple freedoms like deciding what I want to eat or just going for a walk without having to get covered.

I lost my confidence and my ambition. I needed to engage my mind in more ways than making a menu or shopping list or memorizing Bible verses. The voice of my grandmother telling me I would grow stagnant came back to haunt me again and again. I wanted my children to have dreams and pursue them, not be repressed and admonished any time they had a desire for something "worldly."

The community would simply brush off my experience and say I just love my own life and hate God. They use John 12:25 to justify this: "*Those who love their life will lose it, but anyone who hates their life in this world will keep it for eternal life.*" I remember thinking many times over the years that I must really be on the right track for eternal life, because I sure hated my life. They discredit the experiences of those who have left. Since we chose to go live a life of selfishness in the world, we no longer have any discernment. They believe those who leave simply love the world and want to gratify their flesh.

I've thought many times that the community may simply be a big social experiment. Meshiah studied psychology, after all. He must have thought about the possible outcome of raising children without their being allowed imagination, independence, and more. He must have had some idea that religion is a great way to control people. Religious groups ultimately have nothing to persuade people with but fear, and it works beautifully. I recently read an article suggesting that the books of the Bible were selected for maximum control, and when you look at the social unrest of that time, that makes perfect sense.

I remember being at my mother's once while still in the TT, and I was looking through a *National Geographic* magazine. An article about child brides in Yemen really affected me, and I cringed as I read story after story of girls as young as eleven being married to men in their forties, many of them giving birth by the time they were fourteen. It was one of those circumstances where I told myself I should be thankful for the life I was raising my children in. Our situation could be so much worse.

Now that I look back on it, we did marry girls as young as seventeen, and most were pregnant within a few months.

I've concluded that life is hard no matter where you are. In the TT, when life was hard, we were told we were either being tested by our Father or being opposed by the Evil One, depending on how we were doing spiritually at the time. Out here, if life is hard, it's because we are in our own strength, opposed by our Father. I'd always think of tragedies that happened to people who had never heard of the TT—that couldn't be explained by any community saying.

The world is so much bigger than the tiny TT group, but the very nature of their lives causes them to be myopic and truly believe the world is revolving around them. Now I believe a higher power would never choose one small group among billions of humans. The same kinds of things happen to people in and out of the community. The difference is free will, not being judged over your every motive, not being controlled by the whims of people you are told are speaking for God.

Being in the TT did have some positive effects on my life today. I have been able to work full time, finish my degree, take care of my children and household, get regular exercise, and never feel as overwhelmed as I felt on an average lunch day in Cambridge. I even fit in time for hobbies such as fitness classes, knitting, reading, and writing. I never wake up dreading the day anymore. I don't have anyone constantly watching, scrutinizing and judging me. If I decide to sleep in one morning, it's OK. If I decide I'm not making dinner one night because my day was so busy and my kids eat cereal or grilled cheese, it's OK. I can give myself the grace I need and not feel condemned about it. I don't need to defend my every waking moment to anyone. I still relish little freedoms, like scanning the radio stations in the car, drinking a glass of wine and dancing around the kitchen to my favorite songs while I make dinner, laughing with my children over something incredibly "foolish," making plans with my friends, browsing books at the library, and so many other basic activities I didn't experience for fourteen years. It has given me a fresh vigor and thankfulness for life.

When we first left, my in-laws were still in the community. About a year and a half later, Darakah, then ten, wanted to visit them. She had lived with them her whole life until we left, and she missed them. We supported her desire and asked them if she could come for a few days during an upcoming school vacation. I even had fabric and was prepared to make her some suitable pants for the occasion. We waited weeks for a response, with her asking every day if there was an answer yet. Finally, the answer came, and it was "no." My in-laws had been brought into a meeting and were told they had never truly given up their sovereignty, and it wouldn't be good for their granddaughter to visit.

That put them over the edge, and they ended up leaving just days after that judgment. I was bothered by this situation and wrote to Elad. He told me he respected my in-laws but felt they "settled for something less eternally."

When explaining the community to people for the first time, the most common questions I get are, "What made you decide to join a group like that?" "What was it like living there?" and "Why did you leave?" I hope this book has adequately answered those questions and provided useful firsthand information to anyone who is considering joining the Twelve Tribes or any other similar group.

Family photos from 2000

Family photos from 2001-2006

Family photos from 2008-2011

Family photos from 2012-2014

Author's Note

2024 marks the tenth year since we left the Twelve Tribes. Many things have changed since then; my family has grown in some ways, and become smaller in others. We lost my grandmother on October 11, 2019. She chose to remain in the Twelve Tribes and was still living in Cambridge when she passed. She was well cared for by women I love very much, one who is still part of the group.

Emmet has become a father to two little girls, Ella and Emersyn, and runs his own construction business. He and his fiancée, Brenna, are building a home together. Meyshar is pursuing a career in dental hygiene at Vermont State University, and Dara takes classes at CCV and is looking to complete her EMT certification. Arek is in tenth grade, enjoys studying digital media, and has a passion for volleyball and baseball. Everyone has changed their minds about their future goals and probably will many more times, and it's refreshing to be able to encourage them in their varied interests, rather than locking them into a life of few choices and condemning them for having their own aspirations.

The Twelve Tribes has also changed. Their leader Meshiah passed away in early 2021. They have begun their so-called "Race." They are still out recruiting new members and opening up new cafés. More and more have left over the years, and some of their largest properties around the world have been sold, including a chalet in France, and a large inn in Australia. We keep in touch with many who have left and are often contacted for assistance by those who want to leave. We have helped my in-laws, several young adults, single men, and a large family leave and begin their lives over just like we did. We don't try to "recruit" anyone to leave—if someone is happy there, like my grandmother was, I am respectful and supportive of their choice.

I love enjoying my family in ways I missed out on for so long. I've taken my daughters to Florida. André and I took Arek to Arizona to visit my mom who moved there in 2016. We made our way down to Mexico and up to the Grand Canyon. We have made so many wonderful memories and look forward to so many more!

Acknowledgments

would like to thank my family for their continued resiliency in navigating these past few challenging years. My husband André, and our four children Emmet, Meyshar, Darakah, and Arek, have been nothing but supportive in my journey to get this book written and published. We always made decisions that we thought were in the childrens' best interests at the time, and deeply regret some of the hardships those decisions have caused in their lives.

Thank you to my mother-in-law Annie Mathieu who has been there from the beginning of this story, was present at the birth of all my children, and helped raise them in so many ways. She read my manuscript and gave unique insight, as she has her own experience of life in the Twelve Tribes.

I want to thank my lifelong friends Michelle Spaulding and Tiffany Bertrand for reading this memoir multiple times in its varying stages and giving me important feedback. And thank you both for your unwavering friendships during my years in the Twelve Tribes, and your selfless care for us when we left.

Thank you to my eighth grade English teacher, James Wyman, who read my manuscript and offered a valuable critique, and also Erin Chagnon for the same.

Thank you to Danielle Houston, Jamie Bushey and Pam Provost, my amazing co-workers who all read my manuscript and helped my confidence in going forward to publication.

Thank you to author Bill Schubart who, because of his presentation at the Swanton Library, I was introduced to Rootstock Publishing and the door opened to get my book published.

Tamara Mathieu

And of course thank you to Samantha Kolber and the Rootstock staff for accepting my book for publication and assisting me through this process!

About the Author

Tamara Mathieu works for Northwestern Counseling and Support Services in St. Albans, Vermont, as lead facilitator of a day program for adults with developmental disabilities. She resides in Swanton with her husband and children. She now also has two granddaughters, Ella and Emersyn. *All Who Believed* is her first book.

 **More Nonfiction from Rootstock Publishing:**

Learn about our Fiction, Poetry, and Children's titles at
www.rootstockpublishing.com.